Daily
Gifts of Hope

Daily
Gifts of Hope

DEVOTIONS *for* EACH
DAY OF YOUR
YEAR

THOMAS NELSON
Since 1798

NASHVILLE   DALLAS   MEXICO CITY   RIO DE JANEIRO

© 2012 by Thomas Nelson, Inc.

Published in Nashville, Tennessee, by Thomas Nelson. Thomas Nelson is a registered trademark of Thomas Nelson, Inc.

Thomas Nelson, Inc., titles may be purchased in bulk for educational, business, fund-raising, or sales promotional use. For information, please e-mail SpecialMarkets@ThomasNelson.com.

Scripture quotations are taken from THE NEW KING JAMES VERSION (NKJV). © 1982 by Thomas Nelson, Inc. Used by permission. All rights reserved. Other Scripture quotations are taken from the following sources: The KING JAMES VERSION (KJV) of the Bible. *The Message* (MSG) by Eugene H. Peterson. © 1993, 1994, 1995, 1996, 2000. Used by permission of NavPress Publishing Group. All rights reserved. New Century Version® (NCV). © 2005 by Thomas Nelson, Inc. Used by permission. All rights reserved. The Holy Bible, New International Version®, NIV®. Copyright © 1973, 1978, 1984, 2011 by Biblica, Inc.,®.Used by permission of Zondervan. All rights reserved worldwide. www.zondervan.com. The *Holy Bible*, New Living Translation (NLT). © 1996. Used by permission of Tyndale House Publishers, Inc., Wheaton, Illinois 60189. All rights reserved. NEW AMERICAN STANDARD BIBLE® (NASB), © The Lockman Foundation 1960, 1962, 1963, 1968, 1971, 1972, 1973, 1975, 1977, 1995. Used by permission. THE ENGLISH STANDARD VERSION (ESV). © 2001 by Crossway Bibles, a division of Good News Publishers. J. B. Phillips: THE NEW TESTAMENT IN MODERN ENGLISH, Revised Edition (PHILLIPS). © J. B. Phillips 1958, 1960, 1972. Used by permission of Macmillan Publishing Co., Inc.

Library of Congress Control Number: 2012939593

ISBN: 978-1-4002-0427-4

Printed in Malaysia

12 13 14 15 16 TWP 6 5 4 3 2 1

Introduction

> You must give your whole heart to [God] and hold out
> your hands to him for help. Put away the sin that is in your
> hand; let no evil remain in your tent. Then you can lift up
> your face without shame, and you can stand strong without
> fear. You will forget your trouble and remember it only
> as water gone by. Your life will be as bright as the noonday
> sun, and darkness will seem like morning. You will feel safe
> because there is hope; you will look around and rest in safety.
>
> —JOB 11:13–18 NCV

What a wonderful promise! Is there a woman alive today who would not want to lift up her face without shame, stand strong without fear, forget her troubles, have her life as bright as the noonday sun, and rest in safety? Imagine the influence such a woman would have on her family, friends, and coworkers. Imagine you as that woman!

The gifts of hope in this daily devotional will guide you to give your whole heart to God, reach out to him for help, put away sin, and refuse to entertain evil in your home. Your journey will include entries titled "Look Up," "Pray, Pray, Pray," "Deception and Vanity," "When We Trip," "Abounding in Hope," "God Breaks Chains," and "When Doubt Creeps In."

Each week you will encounter a "Day of Reflection." In today's busy world, it is easy to take in without taking time to reflect on the wonderful things God is showing you—and yes, even wonderful things can be difficult. Please use this day to reflect on the preceding week's entries. Along with a Scripture verse and the lyrics to treasured hymns of faith and hope, you will find a space for entering a poem, prayer, or thought.

Women of Faith speakers and writers welcome you as we journey together through a year that can be—no matter your circumstances—filled with hope!

Counting on the Heart of God

About midnight Paul and Silas were praying and singing
songs to God as the other prisoners listened. Suddenly,
there was a strong earthquake that shook the foundation
of the jail. Then all the doors of the jail broke open,
and all the prisoners were freed from their chains.

—ACTS 16:25–26 NCV

Prayer is the closest we get to life back in Eden. It is the place where
we can be most known, the most naked and vulnerable before God.

One of the most powerful examples of trust in God's un-
wavering love is found in the book of Acts where Paul and Silas
were beaten and thrown into a jail cell in Philippi. They set out
for a successful mission trip and within a day of being in the city
were stripped naked, beaten, and thrown into a cell with their
feet held down by blocks of wood.

What's remarkable about this story is that Paul and Silas were
at the darkest point of the night in the darkest circumstances they
had ever been in, and yet they were singing. Why? Because Paul
and Silas looked at the one thing that had not changed in their
situation—God. Everything else around them had gone wrong.
They were in pain and their lives were threatened, but they fixed
their eyes on what they knew to be true in the invisible world no
matter what seemed true in the visible. They stood on the truth
that God is good all the time and was watching over them. And
even though the angel released Paul and Silas from their chains,
they waited and were able to lead the jailer and his entire family
to faith in Christ.

We can't always predict the behavior of others, but we can
always count on the heart of God.

*Lord, thank you for being a constant in my life. Help me to remember
that I can always count on your love. Amen.*

A Clear Mind

But you should keep a clear mind in every situation.
Don't be afraid of suffering for the Lord. Work
at telling others the Good News, and fully
carry out the ministry God has given you.

—2 TIMOTHY 4:5 NLT

Sometimes our minds are terribly crowded, aren't they? When they are full of tasks and worries and joys and agendas, we forget how important focus and a clear mind can be. What kind of clear mind does the apostle Paul refer to here?

He instructs Timothy to be passionate about the ministry God has given him, to tell others about the good news of Jesus. When Timothy keeps this as his primary focus, the natural result is a clear mind.

How about you? Look back on your life and find the times when you took time and focus to pursue your ministry. How was your mind in those moments? How single-minded were you? In this era of rush and change and busyness, we forget how needed a clear mind is.

Spend some time asking God to refresh your mind, to show you his ministry that he's created for you to walk in. Then reorient your thoughts toward that goal. Choose to think clearly about the gospel in every situation. The kingdom will expand before your eyes.

Jesus, I want to have a clear mind. I want to have a focused life, pursuing the ministry you've allotted to me. Help me figure it out. Help me know my next steps. Amen.

Presuming

Through presumption comes nothing but strife,
but with those who receive counsel is wisdom.

—PROVERBS 13:10 NASB

When we think we have a situation figured out and we've detected what will happen, we are guilty of presuming. The truth is we don't know what tomorrow will bring. We have no assurance that the money will be in the bank or that the deal we're working on will be successful. We cannot predict our relationships. Nor can we act as if we know the future.

When we presume, the result is strife. When we presume a person is going to do something and then doesn't, relationship strife erupts. When God doesn't do what we think he should, spiritual strife grows.

The cure for presumption is humble dependence on God and tenderness toward the opinions of wise people in our lives. God will guide us. He already knows the future. He already sees the bend in the road.

But sometimes it's hard to discern what God is up to. In those instances, it's important we consult godly friends who know how to counsel from the outside with detached objectivity. While it's not always easy to ask for advice, if we do, we'll be less likely to be guilty of presumption.

Jesus, I don't want to run ahead of you or presume on the future. I want to make wise decisions. Would you send me some wise folks this week to help me discern what I need to do next? Amen.

Simple Love

Dear friends, let us love one another, for love
comes from God. Everyone who loves has
been born of God and knows God.

—1 JOHN 4:7 NIV

With all the talk about leadership and success and careers, we can forget the basics of life. It's not climbing the corporate ladder. It's not finagling a way to pay for our child's college. It's not embracing runaway success. It's not about looking younger than you are.

No, life is love. And love is God.

We are happiest when we measure our lives differently from the world. Not in how much we make, how cool we are, how popular we've become, but in how well we love.

Take an informal inventory of your life right now. Think about the relationships God has given you. How well do you love those people? Are you actively practicing grace and forgiveness? Do you treat them the way you like to be treated? Are you kind? Would the people in your life categorize you as a loving person? Why or why not?

Love is the ultimate measure of your growth. May it be that you love well this week, seeking times to actively show your love.

Jesus, open my eyes to my relationships this week. I want to love my family and friends better. I also want to be kind to strangers. Teach me to love, since love is your primary nature and language. Amen.

Your Heart's Treasures

> Do not store up for yourselves treasures on earth,
> where moth and rust destroy, and where thieves break
> in and steal. But store up for yourselves treasures in
> heaven, where neither moth nor rust destroys, and
> where thieves do not break in or steal; for where
> your treasure is, there your heart will be also.
>
> —MATTHEW 6:19–21

We can't take our physical treasures with us to heaven. We leave this earth with nothing, not even clothing. So why is it that we obsess over having more things? What benefit in the long run does stuff have on our souls? Jesus reminds us that even now thieves could steal our stuff or decay will eventually have its way. That outfit you're wearing today won't be around in a decade, most likely.

Jesus speaks of treasure in this passage. Those things we prize most show where our hearts are. If we're bent toward success, achieving is our hearts' treasure. If we're interested in provision, accumulating what we perceive as enough fills our hearts. But if our treasure isn't earthly, we exchange stuff for heavenly goods.

And heavenly reward cannot diminish. No one can steal it. Rust can't have its way. May it be that we live and work for eternal things instead of the temporary. May we invest deeply in people's lives, giving freely, sharing Jesus, sacrificing for others. All these endeavors last forever and reveal that our hearts are oriented toward Jesus, not ourselves.

Jesus, I want to store up treasures in heaven, not here. Help me remember the fleeting nature of stuff on earth, and keep me close to you so I can share you often with others. Help me invest in eternity through my relationships with others and my frequent worship of you. Amen.

A Woman of Excellence

My daughter, do not fear. I will do for you
whatever you ask, for all my people in the city
know that you are a woman of excellence.

—RUTH 3:11 NASB

If you were to gather folks in your town or city and poll them, would the consensus be that you are a woman of excellence? What kind of reputation do you have in your family? neighborhood? church? community? workplace?

Ruth, an honorable woman from the Old Testament, followed her mother-in-law Naomi back to Bethlehem, even though she was a Moabite, a foreigner. She chose not to abandon the mother of her dead husband and in the process caught the attention of Boaz, who ended up marrying her, saving both her life and Naomi's. And here we see her commended as a woman of excellence.

How can we be commended in the same manner? What did Ruth do that stands out?

She dedicated herself to her remaining family. She labored for the sake of another. She let go of her past in order to risk in the present. She placed herself in situations where only God could redeem her.

Look back on that list. Have you loved your family well? Have you worked for the sake of someone else? Let go of your past? Risked even when all seemed lost? Then you are a woman of excellence. And God and the community will commend you.

We live in a world of shame and dishonor, and we often forget that God is doing great, noticeable things in our lives. Rest today in knowing that you are a woman of excellence, silencing the voices in your head that say otherwise.

Jesus, thank you that you are making me a woman of excellence. I do want to sacrifice and risk. I do want to love my family well. Thank you for being the ultimate example of excellence. Amen.

Day of Reflection

Go therefore and make disciples of all the
nations, baptizing them in the name of the Father
and of the Son and of the Holy Spirit.

—MATTHEW 28:19

BE THOU MY VISION

Be thou my Vision, O Lord of my heart:
Naught be all else to me, save that thou art;
Thou my best thought, by day or by night,
Waking or sleeping, thy presence my light.

Riches I heed not, nor man's empty praise;
Thou mine inheritance, now and always;
Thou and thou only, first in my heart,
High King of heaven, my treasure thou art.

—IRISH HYMN, c. 8TH CENTURY

Your space—a poem, prayer, thoughts . . .

The Right Outfit

> Clothe yourselves with compassion, kindness,
> humility, gentleness and patience. Bear with each
> other and forgive one another . . . Forgive as the Lord
> forgave you. And over all these virtues put on love,
> which binds them all together in perfect unity.
>
> —COLOSSIANS 3:12–14 NIV

As God's dearly loved women, our response to his wild, all-encompassing love is to put on the right clothes—a wardrobe that reflects who he is and who he is causing us to become. We are to get up each day and pull on compassion, kindness, humility, gentleness, and patience.

Compassion is what's closest to our hearts—our underclothes. We are compassionate not by what we do externally but by what we believe about others. Compassion originates from the heart.

Kindness becomes gloves, as we use our hands throughout the day to touch the people God populates our lives with.

Humility is our bare feet, naked to touch the earth, reminding us that God is God and we are not.

Gentleness is a lambswool sweater, cozy and comforting. It tempers what we say and how we say it.

Patience is the glasses we wear when we choose to see the world not through our own agenda and expectations but through his.

What are you wearing today?

Jesus, help me put on compassion, kindness, humility, gentleness, and patience. Sometimes it's hard to make these fit, as I've grown too full of myself. Help me to be suitable for your clothes today, open to wearing your wardrobe picks. Amen.

Sing to Him!

*Sing to the LORD, all the earth; proclaim
his salvation day after day.*
—1 CHRONICLES 16:23 NIV

Did you know sparrows have disappeared from central London?
The mystery as to why remains unsolved. Perhaps, as in the
nursery rhyme about blackbirds, the European birds were baked
into pies? Really. A common offering in Britain even after
World War I was sparrow pies (probably tasted like chicken).
Sometimes at gala affairs, as many as a hundred songbirds would
be huddled in a pie. What a waste of good music!

Now, what about our music? Are we willing to sing in the
darkest night, the deepest pit, or on the highest peak? The songs
that bring the most comfort seem to be birthed out of a price we
would not willingly pay.

Let's not waste one note of the musical score we've been
given. There is something about singing, especially when you
don't feel like it, that mends your heart's tattered wings. It's not
a cure-all, but it's a beginning toward recovery for our souls. We
are fragile, and when our hearts are shattered, we can't work up a
song on our own. God will have to orchestrate it; then it's up to us
to sing, sing, sing. It may be a verse from Scripture, a song you've
heard before that suddenly becomes personal, or something
God's Spirit whispers into your thoughts. Music can help you
find your way home. Every note a lantern. Every phrase a path.

*Lord, please put your song in my heart. Help me sing to you, regardless of
my situation, knowing that you are in control. Amen.*

Sweet Wisdom

Know also that wisdom is like honey for
you: If you find it, there is a future hope for
you, and your hope will not be cut off.

—PROVERBS 24:14 NIV

We are called to become wise, to acquire wisdom. The more we grow, the more we should grow in wisdom. The writer here also reassures us that getting wisdom is sweet. Consider what honey does to the food we eat. It helps medicine taste better. It brings out the flavor of fruit. It seasons our meat. It sweetens our tea.

Without sweetener, we could still live, but we would miss out on flavor. Similarly, we can live reckless lives without wisdom, but we would miss out on God's highest. The end of this proverb adds more to wisdom. When we find wisdom, we find hope.

Why does wisdom bring hope? Because the longer we walk, the more we understand that things will change, that God is big, that problems will pass. The more we live, the more we understand that this life isn't all there is, that we have meaning in our lives beyond our lifespan.

When we find that kind of eternal perspective wisdom, we can live knowing that God sees everything we do and will reward us for our faithfulness—a sweet blessing indeed.

Jesus, help me to acquire wisdom even today. I want to live for your kingdom, for that which doesn't perish. I want to be sweet to those who are bitter, and kind to those who are unkind, knowing that you see me and will reward me. There's hope in that. Amen.

Lesson from an Ant: Diligence

Go to the ant, you sluggard; consider its ways and be wise!
It has no commander, no overseer or ruler, yet it stores
its provisions in summer and gathers its food at harvest.
How long will you lie there, you sluggard? When will you
get up from your sleep? A little sleep, a little slumber, a
little folding of the hands to rest—and poverty will come
on you like a bandit and scarcity like an armed man.

—PROVERBS 6:6–11 NIV

Ants have no one to tell them to prepare for the winter, yet they do. No one lords it over them, nagging them to harvest and store away. An ant simply works.

God wants us to discern the future and prepare for it in like manner, not by chasing after get-rich schemes but by working hard and being diligent. Industry is something prized, and working for the sake of your family is a great benefit not only to them but also for you.

Essentially this proverb speaks against laziness and excuses. Slothfulness is not a virtue. And making excuses about why we can't roll up our sleeves and help is lying and disobedience. Not that we should work ourselves to death or spend every waking hour busying ourselves. There must be balance. But if we'd like to be provided for, we have to do our part in the provision.

Jesus, I want to be industrious for your sake. Show me the work you have planned for me today. I want to be wise and prepared for the future. I don't want to deify my work, but I also don't want to be lazy, expecting others to carry my load. Amen.

All of Us Are Created in God's Image

So God created mankind in his own image, in the image of
God he created them; male and female he created them.

—GENESIS 1:27 NIV

Although we are not God, we resemble him, in the same way our
children are not us but they resemble us. We are God's offspring,
his children. He created us to love him, and he placed in us an
insatiable need for relationship with him.

Reading this verse, it's easy to personalize it. As women, we
relate to the fact that God made us uniquely in his image. And he
made man that way too. The beauty comes when we take it one
step further. Every single person on this earth is made in God's
image.

That makes us all image bearers of the King of kings. That
makes everybody the object of God's affection. That means each
person has intrinsic value. That's also why when we hate another
person, we walk outside God's laws. It's like slapping him in the
face when we despise someone he's made.

Next time you're in conflict with someone who drives you
crazy, remember this verse. That perplexing person is an image
bearer of God. They have a spark of him inside. And even if
they're unlovely in the moment, we can be lovelier still when we
love them well.

*Jesus, thank you that I'm made in your image. But thank you even
more that we all are. Please help me remember that when I'm pushing
up against someone. Help me take a moment to remember that they are
made in your beautiful image. Amen.*

The Complex Issue of Justice

For the LORD your God is God of gods and Lord of
lords, the great God, mighty and awesome, who shows
no partiality and accepts no bribes. He defends the cause
of the fatherless and the widow, and loves the foreigner
residing among you, giving them food and clothing.

—DEUTERONOMY 10:17–18 NIV

God created the whole world. He made every single person on this earth. And he passionately cares about every one. The problem? We have a justice issue. Some folks are oppressed. Some lack food and potable water. Others face discrimination. Some children have no parents. Some parents lack a spouse.

What is our responsibility? We can watch sad commercials on TV and be guilted into giving money, but will that really solve the justice issues behind poverty and inequality? It's a complex issue, to be sure.

Yet God calls us to be in this world, to notice the pain around us. We may not be able to solve everyone's problem, but we can offer a listening ear to a grieving friend. We can support ministries we know are truly reversing the cycle of poverty. We can bring a meal to an ailing widow. Compassion is always associated with action.

Sure we may feel overwhelmed. God's intention isn't that we solve every issue or help every person. We simply stick close to him and let him show us folks to love and help. Obedience in that small scale, if done by every single Jesus-follower, leads to massive help. Together, we make a difference.

*Jesus, help me see today who I can love, who I can encourage, who I can
listen to. Help me remember that one small act, when joined with others,
changes the landscape of poverty and injustice. Amen.*

Day of Reflection

*If these should keep silent, the stones
would immediately cry out.*

—LUKE 19:40

ALL CREATURES OF OUR GOD AND KING

*All creatures of our God and King
Lift up your voice and with us sing.
Alleluia! Alleluia!
Thou burning sun with golden beam,
Thou silver moon with softer gleam,
O praise Him! O praise Him!
Alleluia! Alleluia! Alleluia!*

—ST. FRANCIS OF ASSISI, 1225

Your space—a poem, prayer, thoughts . . .

God Doesn't Lie

God is not a man, that He should lie, nor a son of man,
that He should repent; Has He said, and will He not do
it? Or has He spoken, and will He not make it good?

—NUMBERS 23:19 NASB

The reliability of God is a fact. He does not lie. He does not make mistakes. He does not sin. He does what he says he'll do, and the truest integrity is in his nature.

But sometimes we forget that. We see only a limited perspective in life. We judge things by what we see, and our view cannot take in all the data. Only God sees it all. Only God knows the entirety of our situation.

With his nature as a true, integrity-infused God and his all-encompassing perspective, why do we worry? Why do we forget? Because life feels big, and our circumstances loom like mountains in front of us. We forget that God created the very mountains we fret about. He is bigger than any obstacle we face.

He knows it all, every detail, and he is the God of truth. Rest there. Choose to believe, by faith, that God will not lie to you. He will hold you. He will make good what needs to be made good. He will do what needs to be done. It may be in his timing and not yours, but he does see you right now and has your best interest at heart.

Jesus, I don't always see how you're working. I forget how big and true you are. Help me to think rightly about you, to entrust every situation to you. I am small, but you are big. I don't always tell the truth, but you always do. Thank you. Amen.

God: Our Rock and Father

You deserted the Rock, who fathered you;
you forgot the God who gave you birth.
—DEUTERONOMY 32:18 NIV

In many places in Scripture, we are called God's children, and he is called our Father. Whether we had an amazing, attentive earthly father or an absent one, the truth is God is the best Father we will ever have. He is amazing. He is attentive. He is loving and affectionate toward us. He created us.

But here we see a complaint that Moses wrote on God's behalf to the nation of Israel. He charged that they'd deserted their Father. In this instance, Moses called God a rock. A rock is a sure place, a place where you can stand and not be moved. But Israel had chosen to forget that place of security; instead they found security in themselves.

God has birthed us. He is our Father, our stability, our strength, our present helper. We neglect him when we forget all the things he's done for us. He not only created us but also provided a way for us to be in perfect relationship with him through the death and resurrection of Jesus. He has given us the Holy Spirit to be our companion. He never, ever leaves us.

Today consider all God has done for you. Choose to thank him, honor him, and sing praises to him. In doing so, you won't neglect him. Instead, you'll make him smile.

Jesus, I don't want to desert or neglect you. Help me to stop in this moment and count how many blessings you've given me. Not just physical blessings, but spiritual ones. Thank you for being my Rock and my ever-present Father. Oh how I hope in you! Amen.

Surefooted on the Mountains

God is my strong fortress, and he makes my way perfect.
He makes me as surefooted as a deer, enabling me to
stand on mountain heights. He trains my hands for
battle; he strengthens my arm to draw a bronze bow.

—2 Samuel 22:33–35 NLT

God is so many things to us according to this verse. He protects us as a fortress protects a city. He perfects our journeys. He gives us feet like a deer, able to scale cliffs and precipices with ease. He trains us. He teaches us how to fight.

What a blessing our God is to us! All we need in this life is found in him.

When you feel attacked, retreat to the fortress of our God. When you fail and you lament you'll never be perfect, rest in the fact that God perfects you. When you stumble, believe that God makes you surefooted. When the mountains of trials or fears loom before you, remember that God will place you firmly on those mountains with a song in your heart. When a battle rages around you, ask God to strengthen you and train you to fight.

In our own strength, we're needy, but with God's help, we can climb surefooted on the mountains in front of us.

Jesus, I want to face the mountains with grace, but I need your help, particularly when I feel attacked or imperfect. Please train me in your ways. I trust in you. I hope in you. Amen.

The Bible's Prescription for Anxiety

Cast all your anxiety on him because he cares for you.
—1 Peter 5:7 niv

What if I messed up my life by making wrong decisions? What if I didn't pray enough? What if I didn't have ears to hear or eyes to see? These conscientious questions could at times be agonizing. But listen to what the Bible says about those worries:

> I know, Lord, that our lives are not our own. We are not able to plan our own course. (Jeremiah 10:23 nlt)

> You can make many plans, but the Lord's purpose will prevail. (Proverbs 19:21 nlt)

These verses are foundational to an understanding of God's sovereign design for my purpose in life. In it all, God invites my participation in planning, evaluating, and ultimately choosing the options that appear to make sense to me. The safety net is simply that I participate, but I'm not in charge. He's in charge of everything concerning my options. So when I make a plan and the door closes on it, I'm reminded, "the Lord's purpose will prevail."

Proverbs 3:6 says, "Seek his will in all you do, and he will show you which path to take" (nlt). We can count on the fact that we can count on him. There is no need to be anxious. Trust God to know exactly how he intends to "grow you up" as well as how he will use you for his purposes.

Lord, thank you that I can cast all my cares on you. Help me to remember to not be anxious about anything but in everything give thanks. Amen.

Our Permanent Fortress

The LORD is my rock, my fortress, and my savior; my
God is my rock, in whom I find protection. He is my
shield, the power that saves me, and my place of safety.

—PSALM 18:2 NLT

A fortress is a military installation that prevents attacks and
damage from an enemy. It's often part of a town, and its sole aim
is to protect the citizens inside. It is a permanent place, unlike a
trench or a moveable base. When you remove the military impli-
cations, a fortress means a place or source of refuge or support.

Think of those definitions as you reread this verse.

God is our permanent military installation. He will not
move. He protects us from Satan's insidious attacks. He protects
not only us, but those we have community with. His protection
is permanent, immovable. And of course, we find refuge in God.
He is our safe place, our true supporter and friend.

The problem comes when we try to fashion our own for-
tresses out of our own strength. When we do this, we leave the
permanence of God's protection and stand alone in a field, a sure
target. In those places where we glory in our own strength, we
become vulnerable to attack.

What a blessing it is that the God of the universe is our
fortress!

*Jesus, thank you for being my permanent fortress—one that doesn't
change or move. Thank you for being my refuge, the place I run when I
find myself in harm's way in my own strength. I choose again to retreat to
your powerful fortress. Amen.*

Sheltered

The Lord is a shelter for the oppressed,
a refuge in times of trouble.

—Psalm 9:9 nlt

With the world the way it is, it's sometimes hard to understand that God is a shelter for the oppressed. Whenever we turn on our browser or switch channels on our TV, we see violence and oppression. We see men, women, and children subsisting on far too little. We see wars tearing families apart. We see terrorism.

And yet the Bible is full of references like Psalm 9:9, promising that God is the shelter for those who can't help themselves. What does that mean?

God doesn't always rescue people from their circumstances. Sometimes he sends us to be the justice they need. And sometimes their cries for relief go unanswered. The kind of shelter the psalmist is referring to here isn't an actual refuge with four walls and a locked, safe door.

God provides shelter in himself. No matter where we are or how much we're hurting, we can always run to him to be our shelter. Even when circumstances thunder out of control, God is the great steadfast One. Even to those who seem to have hopeless situations, God promises that he will be with them in their hearts if they cry to him.

Jesus, help me provide shelter for those who don't have any. More important, help me lead others to the perfect shelter only you can provide. Lift my eyes beyond physical shelters to your beautiful sheltering. Shelter my heart today. Amen.

Day of Reflection

God is our refuge and strength, an
ever-present help in trouble.

—PSALM 46:1 NIV

A MIGHTY FORTRESS IS OUR GOD

A mighty fortress is our God. A bulwark never failing.
Our helper He amid the flood of mortal ills prevailing.
For still our ancient foe doth seek to work us woe.
His craft and power are great,
And armed with cruel hate, on earth is not His equal.

—MARTIN LUTHER, 1529

Your space—a poem, prayer, thoughts . . .

Contentment: True Wealth

After all, we brought nothing with us when we came into the world, and we can't take anything with us when we leave it. So if we have enough food and clothing, let us be content.

—1 TIMOTHY 6:7–8 NLT

Paul instructs Timothy to be happy with enough food and clothing. If we really think about that, we'll realize that we typically have an abundance of both. And we have shelter on top of that. We have more clothes than we need, and our plates are often overflowing with bounty.

That's it. That's our need. So why is it that we so quickly become a complaining people? Why do we scratch at life, constantly wanting beyond our needs? Because we haven't learned the practice of contentment.

Paul equates contentment with wealth. Those who are wealthy in God's economy are those who have learned to be joyful no matter what they have. They realize the fleeting nature of stuff, so they place their trust not in things, but in God.

With God firmly planted in our hearts, contentment becomes a natural by-product of our daily lives. God knows our needs. We simply trust him, then thank him for all the abundance he sends our way. That's true wealth.

Jesus, forgive me when I'm not content with my clothes and food. Help me remember the difference between a need and a want. I want to be wealthy in contentment. Amen.

The Wilderness

Remember how the LORD your God led you through the
wilderness for these forty years, humbling you and testing you
to prove your character, and to find out whether or not you
would obey his commands. Yes, he humbled you by letting
you go hungry and then feeding you with manna, a food
previously unknown to you and your ancestors. He did it to
teach you that people do not live by bread alone; rather, we
live by every word that comes from the mouth of the LORD.

—DEUTERONOMY 8:2–3 NLT

God sometimes walks us through wildernesses in our lives. He
does this for a specific reason—to test us and prove our character.
In those places of wilderness when friends seem to be far away,
our circumstances don't change, money is scarce, or we deal with
relational heartache, God helps us to become people who long to
obey him.

He wants us to hunger only for him, to hang on his every
word. He uses times of desperation and hunger to teach us that he
alone can fill and sustain us. In the wilderness, where there is little
else to distract us, when things have been stripped away, we find
out what our mettle is, how much or little we rely on God.

Even in the midst of the wilderness, God is the God of hope.
When we are hungry, he feeds us. He reminds us of his provision
and hints afresh that a promised land is on the horizon. In those
times of wilderness wanderings, we simply need to stay very close
to him.

Wilderness living is a phase, but during that phase you will
experience deeper, more lasting growth than in times of abundance.

*Jesus, I don't much like the wilderness. I'm tired and hungry and needy.
Please show me your provision. I want to obey you here. I want to be faithful to you here. Keep me close to you. Amen.*

Living on the Edge

Our soul waits for the LORD; He is our help and our shield.
—PSALM 33:20 NASB

Living life on the edge means we're constantly at the point where something may begin, or not begin, depending on our choices. We're looking around for cliff edges that hover over good futures, praying that God will guide us in choosing the right edges to step off of. But sometimes we misunderstand, or we go charging ahead without seeking God's guidance. The awful truth is, we make mistakes. Sometimes terrible mistakes. After we've endured the consequences of poor choices and hard falls, we might be tempted to move back from that cliff edge, huddle in the darkness under the pier, and resume the pity party.

God wants us out there on the edge, constantly watching for new opportunities to connect with him more intimately, trust him more completely again. We need to live life with keen awareness of the opportunities around us, the other edges that might appear that have the potential to bring us closer to the divine. Watching with a mind-set that expects wonderful possibilities to appear in our lives at any moment gives us a whole new perspective on life.

Living on the edge isn't always the most comfortable existence, but it's a place where we tend to do more looking around for help—which, for Christians, means looking for God. When we're teetering over a precipice or plummeting into the unknown, we want to know he's right there with us. That's why the edge can be a good place to be.

Lord, thank you for being with me even when I'm living life on the edge. Thank you that I can always turn to you during those tough times. Amen.

Strange Voices

He calls his own sheep by name and leads them out
of the fold, and when he has driven all his own flock
outside, he goes in front of them himself, and the sheep
follow him because they know his voice. They will never
follow a stranger—indeed, they will run away from
him, for they do not recognize [*sic*] strange voices.

—JOHN 10:4–5 J. B. PHILLIPS TRANSLATION

This picture of a gentle shepherd leading his sheep by literally walking before them is a beautiful picture for us. Imagine a shepherd singing to his sheep, cooing over them, coaxing them forward with the lilt of his gentle commands. The sheep have complete trust in their shepherd because they are intimately familiar with his voice.

Now picture a different shepherd. Perhaps he is harsh. Or maybe he's just different. He doesn't have the same tenor as the original shepherd. He doesn't sing in quite the same way. What happens? The sheep, loyal to their shepherd, don't follow the newcomer. They don't trust him because they aren't familiar with his voice.

It's the same for us. We should be so in tune with Jesus' voice and the gentle way he leads that any other voice seems out of place. The more we listen to his voice, the more we'll be able to discern other voices. Not only that, but we'll know when to run away from destructive voices.

What a blessing it is that we have a shepherd who loves us so much, who sacrificed on our behalf and who sings over us.

Jesus, thank you for being the Good Shepherd who lays down his life for us. I want to know your voice more and more. I want to become familiar with it so that I won't be led astray by the voices of the world. Amen.

God Gives All

And God is able to make all grace abound toward you,
that you, always having all sufficiency in all things,
may have an abundance for every good work.
—2 Corinthians 9:8

There are days when we feel triumphant, victorious over our besetting sins and happy to be alive. There are other days when we feel our lack, and we'd rather cocoon ourselves away from others. In either case, the truth is this: God gives all. He is able.

God is the only source of grace in the universe, and he holds it in abundant supply. Not only that, he delights to give it to us when we approach him with open hands and hearts. God is fully sufficient. And he promises his grace will be just the right amount to help us over any hurdle (see 2 Corinthians 12:9–10).

Because God is able and he gives all, what prevents you from asking for his help? When things go well, we forget his sufficiency because we become our own sufficiency. When things don't go well, we feel bad that we're needy, or we may be angry at God for our negative circumstances. But the truth is, we need him just as much in both instances.

Every day, God supplies. Every day we have the opportunity to tap into his abundant supply. Choose today to receive that grace—enough grace to do every single good work he has for you.

Jesus, forgive me when I forget about you. And remind me when I'm worried or bothered that you are there to help. I want to run to you in the good times and bad. I love you and need you. Amen.

What If He Wasn't?

The LORD is my shepherd; I shall not want. He makes
me to lie down in green pastures; He leads me beside
the still waters. He restores my soul; He leads me
in paths of righteousness for His name's sake.

—PSALM 23:1–3

You've probably read or heard these verses a hundred or more times. And yet, have you considered reading them the opposite way?

What if the Lord was not your shepherd? What would your life be like without him? You would have no one outside of yourself, no one wise and kind and discerning to lead you as a shepherd leads his sheep. You'd have no one leading you to cool places of rest. Your soul would fret and there'd be only raging waters all around.

Thankfully none of that is true. Jesus is your shepherd. And he demonstrated his shepherding abilities by laying his life down for his sheep—all of us. When we are stressed out, if we choose to run to him, he offers us rest and peaceful pastures. He brings much-needed restoration when we feel overwhelmed or worn out or beaten down by life. If we hold his hand, we can walk down amazing paths.

A shepherd is a shepherd because he has sheep. And you are the little lamb he adores, protects, and guides. Even if today feels daunting and you want to pull your covers over your head, he is shepherd still. Rest there, little lamb.

Jesus, thank you that you're my shepherd. Please forgive me when I try to stray or I forget that you want to take me to places of rest. I love you. I need you. I lay my life once again in your capable shepherd hands. Amen.

Day of Reflection

The LORD is my shepherd, I lack nothing.
—PSALM 23:1 NIV

THE LORD IS MY SHEPHERD

The Lord's my shepherd, I'll not want;
He makes me down to lie in pastures green;
He leadeth me the quiet waters by.

My soul He doth restore again,
And me to walk doth make
within the paths of righteousness,
Even for His own name's sake.

—SCOTTISH PSALTER, 1650

Your space—a poem, prayer, thoughts . . .

From Curses to Blessings

Nevertheless, the LORD your God was not willing to listen
to Balaam, but the LORD your God turned the curse into
a blessing for you because the LORD your God loves you.

—DEUTERONOMY 23:5 NASB

When we face enemies who want to curse us—or actually do—
we can become defeated and scared. We begin to see the enemy
as towering, looming larger than God's capability. But God promises to take others' cursings and morph them into blessings for us.

Look back on your life. When have someone's curses, or ill
intents, blessed you? What happened in the aftermath? Consider
some of these things God can do to bring blessing out of painful
situations with others.

You learn by negative example what not to do. Often we
learn best by watching others make big mistakes.

You find more perseverance in your life. You're no longer as
easily broken as you were in the past.

You have the opportunity to be more like Jesus who loved
the entire world, including his betrayer, Judas. When you forgive,
you're most like him.

You realize that really only God's opinion of you matters as
you entrust your reputation to him.

You feel a kinship with Jesus because he also suffered at the
hands of others.

Rest there today. God takes the cursing and turns it into surprising blessing.

*Jesus, help me to see what you're up to when I'm facing an enemy. I want
to grow, to forgive, to lean into what you have for me. Give me your perspective as you turn this curse into a blessing. Amen.*

Leaving All

So Abram went, as the LORD had told him; and Lot
went with him. Abram was seventy-five years old when
he set out from Harran. He took his wife Sarai, his
nephew Lot, all the possessions they had accumulated
and the people they had acquired in Harran, and they
set out for the land of Canaan, and they arrived there.

—GENESIS 12:4–5 NIV

Before this passage, God promised blessings to Abram if he
would leave everything familiar and follow him. Remember that
Abram came from a pagan place with no orientation toward the
God of the universe. So to follow this command was even more
radical in light of that.

But Abram obeyed. He trusted in God's word to him. And he
left everything familiar for the sake of the greater reward.

Sometimes God calls us to similar sacrifices, small and large.
He calls us to leave behind what we're comfortable with, to walk
away from destructive relationships, to try a new ministry, to risk
in relationship. He woos us toward radical obedience.

There is great blessing when we choose to believe God and
leave everything in his capable hands. The rub comes when we
start looking at everything we're leaving behind instead of focus-
ing ahead to the blessings. The next time God calls you to risk,
make a choice to look forward, not back.

*Jesus, I want to be a risk-taking follower like Abram. Help me to let go
of the things in the past and trust you in the moment. I want to go where
you lead, though I'm scared. Help me to focus ahead instead of lamenting
what I'm leaving. Amen.*

The Gift of Life

Paul, a bond-servant of God and an apostle of Jesus Christ,
for the faith of those chosen of God and the knowledge
of the truth which is according to godliness, in the hope
of eternal life, which God, who cannot lie, promised long
ages ago, but at the proper time manifested, even His
word, in the proclamation with which I was entrusted
according to the commandment of God our Savior.

—TITUS 1:1–3 NASB

A bondservant was a slave who had been freed but who loved his master so much that he returned to him willingly. They marked this return by piercing the upper cartilage of the former slave's ear, an indication that he served willingly of his own free will.

Paul, formerly enslaved to sin, met Jesus on the road to Damascus in a flash of brilliant, blinding light. In that moment, he surrendered himself to Jesus, becoming his bondservant.

We, too, are bondservants. This means we willingly and joyfully do our Master's bidding. When he tells us to love our enemies, we do. When he tells us to serve our families, we humble ourselves and find joy in the serving. When he tells us to forgive that friend who wronged us, though it's hard, we do for his sake. Because a bondservant always does what her Master tells her to do.

There's an element of joy in this kind of service, though. Because we know that our Master has our best interest in mind, we can joyfully risk and choose difficult paths because we trust his guidance. We've already willingly returned to him, and now it's our job to happily obey him.

Jesus, help me understand what it means to be your bondservant. Thank you for being an amazing Master. I choose to follow you today even if it's hard or confusing. Amen.

Look Up

So if you're serious about living this new resurrection
life with Christ, act like it. Pursue the things over which
Christ presides. Don't shuffle along, eyes to the ground,
absorbed with the things right in front of you. Look up,
and be alert to what is going on around Christ—that's
where the action is. See things from his perspective.

—COLOSSIANS 3:1–2 MSG

In daily life, we tend to focus on our tasks, our relationships, and our issues. But the apostle Paul lays out a different way to live. He shifts our focus from this earth and all its problems to Christ, who is now seated in heaven.

When we think of things from his vantage point, our problems minimize, we see those who are hurting, and we long to participate in his mighty plan. When we pursue the things Christ loves, our lives will radically change.

Christ loves people. So we pursue them, even those who hurt us or mock us.

Christ forgave those who betrayed him. So we choose, even though it's hard, to forgive those who have betrayed us.

Christ healed others. So we open our eyes to the needs of the world so we can be his agent of hope and healing.

Christ defeated the works of the devil. So we pray for those who are caught in his wily schemes.

Shifting our focus from our daily lives to Christ dynamically changes everything.

Jesus, forgive me for looking at my feet, shuffling through life. I don't want to be a belly button gazer. Instead, help me to look up to you, where you're seated in heaven. I want to act like you, notice like you, and love like you. Amen.

Prayer Is Still the Answer

I will praise you as long as I live, lifting
up my hands to you in prayer.

—PSALM 63:4 NLT

The Daniel of the Bible was a prayer warrior. Although he did survive his enemies, he still was criticized, plotted against, and lied about. Prayer doesn't necessarily rescue us from all evil intentions or diabolical schemes, but instead it gives us a resource for comfort, wisdom, strength, and unexplainable joy in the midst of the ravenous lions of life. And when we lose our joy, the Spirit replaces it with endurance, that indestructible, internal insistence to keep on keeping on.

Many of our prayers are conversational ones in which we talk to the Lord and he kindly listens. Sometimes we sense his presence; other times we pray in faith, believing in what we can't see or feel. We pray for people in our lives, for some more than others. At times we shoot emergency requests like arrows, hoping to pierce the compassion of Christ. And sometimes we sit silently and wait for God's Spirit to counsel us. During those times we can gain the ability to survive the injustices and inequities of this life with more grace and holy ingenuity. The more acute our ears become in identifying the Lord's voice from the ongoing racket in our heads, the more sensitive and discriminating our "knowers" become.

It's human to wonder and wrestle. Give yourself permission to pray your doubts and despair. God isn't offended by our frailty. No one knows better than God that we are dust, yet he loves us still.

Thank you, God, that you hear my cry at all times. Teach me to take refuge in you at all times—the good and the bad. Amen.

Pray, Pray, Pray

Pray in the Spirit at all times and on every
occasion. Stay alert and be persistent in your
prayers for all believers everywhere.

—EPHESIANS 6:18 NLT

When we take a shower in the morning, we have space and quiet
to pray and ask God to be present with us throughout the day. As
the water cleanses our hair, we praise God for his great cleansing of us. And we pray for those who need to know that kind of
wild grace.

As we prepare food, we pray for those who will taste it. As we
add seasoning, we ask Jesus to please make us salt for this earth.
As we fold laundry, we ask God to fold us into himself, and we
intercede for those whose pants we fold.

As we run errands, we thank God for transportation. We
pray for the angry driver cutting us off, asking for mercy. When
we check out at the grocery store, we pray for the livelihood of the
cashier, and we ask God for divine appointments to bless people
we meet that day.

As we finish our day, we thank God for another twenty-four
hours of life, with health, with breath. We think of the whole
wide world and pray for those who struggle today, for those who
hurt, for those who need food or redemption or rescue.

We pray, pray, pray all throughout the day to remind ourselves we wholly depend on him for everything.

*Jesus, I want to pray all day long today, to have a continual dialogue with
you. Keep me aware of your presence even as I run errands, shop, fold
laundry, and cook. Keep me close to your heart so I can share your heart
with others. Amen.*

Day of Reflection

It is good for me that I have been afflicted,
that I may learn Your statutes.

—PSALM 119:71

MORE LOVE TO THEE, O CHRIST

More love to Thee, O Christ, more love to Thee!
Hear Thou the prayer I make on bended knee.
This is my earnest plea: more love, O Christ to Thee;
More love to Thee, more love to Thee!

Once earthly joy I craved, sought peace and rest.
Now Thee alone I seek; give what is best.
This all my prayer shall be: more love, O Christ to Thee;
More love to Thee, more love to Thee.

—ELIZABETH P. PRENTISS, 1856

Your space—a poem, prayer, thoughts . . .

Who You Are

"Don't be afraid," he said, "for you are deeply loved
by God. Be at peace; take heart and be strong!"
—DANIEL 10:19 NLT

You are not the person devalued by others' casual opinions.

You are not the sum of your righteous (or unrighteous) acts.
You are not a thing to be consumed or used.
You are not small and unworthy.
You are not insignificant.
You are not unlovely.
You are not deserving of deceit.
You are not the words spoken over you.

You are not what they say you are. You are who God says you are.

Beloved.
Welcomed.
Cherished.
Weakly powerful.
Beautifully rejuvenated.
Whole.

That's who you are.

You are deeply loved by God. Do you believe it today? Be at
peace. Be strong. Be encouraged. Let go of the destructive words
inside so you can hear the reality of God's tender, affectionate voice.

*Dear Jesus, help me hear your affirming whispers over me, your words of
courage and power and love and acceptance and grace. Forgive me for letting
other voices rule my mind and emotions. Help me feel your favor. Amen.*

Deception and Vanity

Charm is deceitful, and beauty is vain, but a
woman who fears the LORD is to be praised.

—PROVERBS 31:30 ESV

While this is a verse you've probably read before, it serves as an important reminder. We sometimes think of this verse in terms of other women. "Oh well, she is pretty. She's in danger of vanity." Or ,"That woman is a flirt. How deceptive!"

But when we obsess over how we look and bemoan the fact that we'll never be younger than we are today, we fall into vanity. If we fret over wrinkles or gray hair or extra weight, and those things border on compulsion with us—taking up our time, thoughts, and money—we are living in vanity.

And if we rely solely on our charms to get our way in this life, we are deceived. We are not ultimately in control. Charming or flirting to get our own way is not a straightforward way to live, nor is it truthful. To be honest is to simply ask for things, not relying on manipulation.

God reserves his praise for women who fear him first, who trust that he is making them more and more beautiful every day in the place where it truly counts: their souls. Praise is reserved for women who are straightforward and honest and entrust their lives to him.

Jesus, I want to fear you first, to not worry about how I look or find ways to get my own way through charming others. Help me be dependent on you. I want you to make my soul beautiful. Amen.

He Knows What Concerns You

The LORD will accomplish what concerns me; Your
lovingkindness, O LORD, is everlasting; Do
not forsake the works of Your hands.

—PSALM 138:8 NASB

This verse is one of those reminders we probably need to memorize. Jot it down on an index card today and place it on your mirror, in your car, or in your purse. Tuck it inside your journal or Bible.

God will take care of your concerns. The things that occupy your mind right now are of concern to him. He knows every worry, every fret, every stress. He sees it all. And he will accomplish what concerns you.

The prayer of the psalmist reminds God not to forget his works. We are his works, the works of his hands. And he loves us with an everlasting, never-ending love.

Rest there today. Take a deep breath. Let it out, and as you do, breathe out a prayer of concern to God. Pour everything that bothers you at his feet. Read this verse again as a holy declaration of God's concern. He loves you. Oh, how he loves you.

Jesus, thank you that you see what's on my mind. You know my worries. I choose today to believe you love me and will take care of my fears. Amen.

God Takes Pleasure in You

But the LORD takes pleasure in those who fear
him, in those who hope in his steadfast love.

—PSALM 147:11 ESV

It's hard to wrap our minds around God taking pleasure in us. We can easily understand that he would be indifferent. Or maybe disappointed in us when we mess up yet again. Maybe he tolerates us the way a babysitter tolerates a pesky toddler. But take pleasure?

He actively delights in us and takes pleasure in us when we choose to fear him. To fear him is to revere him as holy and big and amazing. It's to love him well and worship him in awe. It's to consider him as more important than anything or anyone in our lives. It's to choose him above everything.

That's what hoping in his steadfast love means. We may not be able to "feel" that love, and sometimes situations and circumstances make us question that love. But hoping in his love is choosing to trust him anyway. It's choosing to believe that he delights in us when we disappoint ourselves or when God doesn't seem to live up to our expectations. It's trusting in his love for us and loving him.

When we do that, the Scripture promises his beautiful pleasure.

Jesus, it's really hard for me to believe you take pleasure in me. Will you show me that this week? Help your love sink deep into my bones. And in the meanwhile, I want to worship you and trust in your steadfast, true love. Amen.

He Is Sovereign

For I know the plans I have for you, declares
the LORD, plans for welfare and not for
evil, to give you a future and a hope.

—JEREMIAH 29:11 NIV

Sometimes nothing is more liberating in our walk with the Lord than understanding and embracing the sovereignty of God. To say God is in charge frees you up to not be in charge. We don't know enough to be in charge. Though we do at times mumble about God's plan, we know his way is best for us. When we can't quite figure out what's going on, God can. That is reassuring. It is also reassuring that God invites our participation in what's going on.

Let's remind ourselves of the trustworthiness of God's sovereign love through these beautiful words from the Psalms: "Everything God does is right—the trademark on all his works is love" (145:17 MSG).

Where is God when we long for him to change things, to resolve the secret longings and deep yearnings within us? He's by our side, doing what he does for our well-being and for our growth in him. He is working "all things according to the counsel of His will" (Ephesians 1:11). We can all rest in that.

God, thank you that you are in control of my life. Help me to trust that your plan in my life is ultimately for your glory and my good. Amen.

The Compassionate One

For the LORD your God is a compassionate God;
He will not fail you nor destroy you nor forget the
covenant with your fathers which He swore to them.

—DEUTERONOMY 4:31 NASB

What does it mean that our God is compassionate? To be compassionate is not merely to feel pity for someone. Compassion has a component of action, of relieving suffering. God has active compassion for you, even right now. The Deuteronomy passage promises God won't fail you. He won't destroy. He remembers the covenant—another word for promise—he swore to his people.

In the New Testament, Jesus inaugurated a brand-new covenant by becoming the sacrifice for every person's sin. That beautiful, wrenching act was the ultimate exercise in compassion known to man. It's love with shoes on.

Because Jesus walked this earth as sinless, experienced the gamut of our suffering so he could understand us, and suffered and died in our place, we can rest. We can experience freedom. We can settle into the compassion he's already granted us.

Sometimes we feel far from God. Days and weeks of suffering cloud our perception of him. Yet the truth is he already acted on our behalf. He already laid down his life to save us from ourselves, our sin, our pain. And not only that, he gave his Holy Spirit to all his followers to continue that relationship of compassion.

Jesus, sweet Jesus, help me to stop right now and remember your supreme act of compassion on the cross. I forget how much you've already done. And when I'm lonely, help me to realize afresh that your Spirit lives within me. Amen.

Day of Reflection

"Though the mountains be shaken and the hills
be removed, yet my unfailing love for you will not
be shaken nor my covenant of peace be removed,"
says the LORD who has compassion on you.

—ISAIAH 54:10 NIV

JESUS, LOVER OF MY SOUL

Jesus, Lover of my soul,
Let me to Thy bosom fly,
While the nearer waters roll,
While the tempest still is high!

Hide me, O my Savior, hide,
Till the storm of life is past,
Safe into the haven guide.
Oh receive my soul at last!

—CHARLES WESLEY, 1740

Your space—a poem, prayer, thoughts . . .

The Land of Silence

If the LORD had not been my help, my soul
would soon have lived in the land of silence.

—PSALM 94:17 ESV

The psalmist's words here are dramatic—the land of silence. What does he mean by that, exactly? Silence means no voices, no people, no banter, no conversation. It means isolation and loneliness. The land of silence is that place where our fears multiply and we have no one to help us see beyond those fears.

And yet God is our help. He makes it so our souls don't have to live in isolation or fear. Our task on this earth is to simply reach for his available hand, be humble enough to receive his help, and let him heal the wounded parts of us.

When we live life apart from God, walking in our own strength, weighed down by sin, the result is isolation from others, whom we hurt in our selfishness, and from God, who cannot be in fellowship with someone who turns her back.

May it be that we rest in knowing God will help us. This week is a perfect testing ground for today's verse. Watch how God rescues you from the land of silence. Notice how he helps you rebuild your relationships. Listen to his still, small voice so that you don't have to feel alone. God is available. Right now.

Jesus, I don't want to live in the land of silence, not even with others.
Give me the wherewithal to reach for your hand today. Be my help, Lord.
Amen.

God, Our Rescuer

The LORD says, "I will rescue those who love me.
I will protect those who trust in my name. When
they call on me, I will answer; I will be with them in
trouble. I will rescue and honor them. I will reward
them with a long life and give them my salvation."

—PSALM 91:14–16 NLT

If you've ever witnessed a rescue or seen one on YouTube, you know the drama involved. Someone is stuck or trapped by machinery or earth. Without help, they will eventually die. The only hope for the trapped one is someone from the outside, particularly someone with excavation expertise.

It's the same with our lives. We were stuck under an impossible pile of sin rubble and we had no hope for rescue. We were pinned by the devil's schemes. But God saw our sorry state and planned the ultimate rescue. He sent Jesus, the great excavator, to rescue us. He took each piece of rubble upon his shoulders and carried it away, securing our rescue.

Just as coal miners rejoice to see the light of day after captivity, or little girls cling to their mommies after a frightening situation, we rejoice and cling to God, who is our rescuer.

And not only does he rescue us, protect us, and help us in trouble, he also gives us life so we can be part of his great plan to rescue others. What an amazing God we serve.

Jesus, you are my rescuer. I could just stop there and be done with my prayer because that's enough. But you reward me with life today, and I entrust you with my life to serve your purposes. I'm humbled and so thankful. Amen.

Perfect Love

For thy Maker is thine husband; the
LORD of hosts is his name.

—ISAIAH 54:5 KJV

If you've put your faith in Jesus Christ, you can enjoy deep contentment. We can bask and revel in the reality that we have been completely accepted and are totally loved by the Son of God. We can pick the petals off daisies and say dreamily, "He loves me" with the absolute assurance that "He loves me not" will never, ever apply to us again.

But to be content in Christ's affection isn't the same thing as being complacent. We aren't just hoping for something that may not happen. We aren't buying *Brides* magazine on the off-chance that we'll snag a man. The dress isn't going to stay in the closet sealed in plastic because we are officially engaged to the King of kings and Lord of lords. We've been bought with the most costly dowry ever paid. And though this season of betrothal is stretching longer than some of us would like, a wedding more wonderful than we can possibly imagine really is right around the corner. Therefore, may we seek to be content in the already, sighing as we admire the sparkling rock Jesus slid onto our finger, but conscious of the not yet. Satisfied with our salvation but still eagerly awaiting consummation.

Dear Jesus, I can't believe you picked me! And I can't wait to ride off in a limo with you! Please help me to rest in your love yet also look forward to the wedding party. Amen.

God, Our Helper

O our God, won't you stop them? We are powerless against
this mighty army that is about to attack us. We do not
know what to do, but we are looking to you for help.

—2 CHRONICLES 20:12 NLT

There are times in our lives when we can't move forward. The
giants seem gigantic. The circumstances loom like mountains.
Our enemies seem an insurmountable force. We can't see our
way around the situation, and we're near panic.

But notice what David does in this passage. He recognizes
the plight. He sees that he cannot succeed. He knows he is cor-
nered. So instead of despairing and surrendering to his very real
enemy, he calls on someone more powerful: God.

Only God can help us out of impossible situations. He is the
impossible God. Nothing is too hard for him. Nothing escapes
his notice. He is capable of routing even the most formidable
army because of his power and strength.

Next time you're up against something impossible, seek out
your impossible God. Look to him for help and perspective. Rest
in his ability, not yours. Watch and wait in anticipation of what
he will do in the situation, by faith. God is in the impossibility
business.

*Jesus, I'm facing a looming challenge and I can't see my way around it.
I choose like David to look to you for help. Please help me trust you
even when things seem dark. Please be my strength and joy even in the
unknown. Do your thing, Lord. Amen.*

Rock, Not Roll

Everyone then who hears these words of mine and
does them will be like a wise man who built his house
on the rock. And the rain fell, and the floods came,
and the winds blew and beat on that house, but it did
not fall, because it had been founded on the rock.

—MATTHEW 7:24–25 ESV

Many of us "hear" Jesus' words. They are recorded in Scripture, usually in red letters. And since we hear them, we assume we're fine. But Jesus says that in order to be steadfast and able to withstand life's terrible storms, we need to actually do what he says.

Those who obey him assure that they have a strong, rock-like foundation. When the storms brew fiercely, we will not roll down the slippery hillside of life. Instead, we'll stand strong. Obedience, then, is the means by which we become more capable of thriving through the storm.

What does Jesus ask of us? To love him. To love others. To meet needs. To worship. To be humble. To trust him. When we do that, we're living on the rock. When we forget him, hurt others, turn away from needs, worship ourselves, live in pride, or choose to trust in our own abilities to solve problems, we're in danger of the slippery slope.

Every day we have a choice to obey Jesus. And as we do, we experience the blessing of knowing we're rock solid.

Jesus, I want to obey you today. Open my eyes to new opportunities to follow you. Prepare me for the storms heading my way. I want my feet to stand firmly on you, not my own ways of doing things. Amen.

When We Trip

The LORD sustains all who fall, and raises
up all who are bowed down.

—PSALM 145:14 NASB

Tripping comes when an unexpected rise meets an unsuspecting foot. Sometimes life throws us unexpected rises aplenty. And we trip. Fall down. Face planted on the sidewalk of life. This kind of tripping take us by surprise and threatens to sideline us for the race God has set out before us. And yet, in this verse is a hope-filled, joyful promise.

The psalmist reveals the heartbeat of God when we walk through difficult circumstances. God sustains us when we fall. He nurtures us, helps us heal. He sustains us, supplying life-giving strength when we need it. When life pushes us down and we find ourselves needy and wanting, God raises us up, if we let him.

Have you tripped this week? Has an unexpected rise met you, careening you to the ground? If so, take heart. God is in the business of taking your injury and rejuvenating you in the aftermath.

Write this verse down on a small index card and place it in your purse. Let it serve as a reminder for the next time you stumble or find yourself bowed under painful circumstances. Let it remind you that you're never alone, that God is mindful of you—even your stumbles and tumbles.

Jesus, thank you that even when I trip, you are there to sustain me and lift me from my fall. I choose right now to reach upward for your hand, and I trust that you have good things in store for me. Amen.

Day of Reflection

The LORD Almighty is with us; the
God of Jacob is our fortress.

—PSALM 46:7 NIV

GOD IS THE REFUGE OF HIS SAINTS

God is the refuge of His saints,
When storms of sharp distress invade;
Ere we can offer our complaints,
Behold Him present with His aid.

Let mountains from their seats be hurled
Down to the deep and buried there;
Convulsions shake the solid world;
Our faith shall never yield to fear.

—ISAAC WATTS, 1719

Your space—a poem, prayer, thoughts . . .

Trusting in Horses

You said, "No, we will get our help from Egypt.
They will give us swift horses for riding into
battle." But the only swiftness you are going to see
is the swiftness of your enemies chasing you!

—ISAIAH 30:16 NLT

When life is going well, we tend to forget to grab onto God's hand. And sometimes, when life careens out of control, we turn away from God's strength because we want physical or tangible solutions to our issues. We turn back to what seemed to work in the past, forgetting that trusting in horses—the tried and true— also means turning back to Egypt, the land of slavery.

We are apt to turn to horses when we're afraid. Or because we can't see our way out of a situation and God seems terribly silent or distant to us. In those situations, we shed our confident trust in God and seek out ways to fix our problems.

We may scheme of ways to find more money to pay our bills. Or ask someone to talk to our spouse about his issues. Or give into drama to try to get our way. There are many ways we can take, but the best way is simply turning to God.

The Scripture encourages us to have a quiet confidence, not in our scheming but in God's abilities. So abandon your plans, slow down, and choose to rest in God's provision.

Jesus, sometimes I would rather run to what I know than hold your hand in trust. I'm so sorry. Help me to take everything that is bothering me right now and hand it over to you. I need quiet confidence. Amen.

Like Trees Bearing Fruit

But they delight in the law of the LORD, meditating
on it day and night. They are like trees planted along
the riverbank, bearing fruit each season. Their leaves
never wither, and they prosper in all they do.

—PSALM 1:2–3 NLT

When you notice trees whose roots reach near rivers or lakes,
you'll see stateliness, growth, and substance. Because they're
constantly near water, they thrive.

Our life with God can be just like that. How? By finding
delight in God's ways. How do we cultivate that kind of life? By
reading God's Word, obeying it, and pondering it. As we steep
ourselves in the Bible, our minds drift away from our issues and
problems and focus on God's ability and majesty. When we take a
moment to stop and reflect on verses like today's, we're reminded
afresh that every little snatch of time directed toward God bears
fruit in our lives.

Whether it's daytime or nighttime, we always have the opportunity to be near God's Word. We can read it on our cell phones,
pick up the Bibles near our bedsides, or remember verses we've
memorized. Each morsel nourishes our souls, makes our roots
reach down deep, and creates fruit that lasts.

Prosperity, according to this verse, comes from that kind of
focused, joyful attention on the words of God.

*Jesus, I want to be like the tree planted by water. I want to know you,
your words, and your ways. Help me to stop in moments throughout the
day and night to remember you and what you said. Amen.*

The Proud

Look at the proud! They trust in themselves,
and their lives are crooked. But the righteous
will live by their faithfulness to God.

—HABAKKUK 2:4 NLT

When we think of proud people, we think of haughty, stiff-necked folks who think they're better than the rest of us. We might point to puffed-up celebrities. Or sports heroes. Or politicians. Or authors. Or speakers. It's always "them."

But look closely at this verse. The proud are people who trust in themselves. Have you ever done that? Trusted in your own ability to run your life, figure out your current problem, or fix that relationship? The result of trusting in our abilities is a proud heart and a crooked life.

Oh to have a meek heart, one that readily trusts God to do what only he can do. This verse implies that when we live in dependence like that, our lives will straighten out, no longer crooked.

The prophet Habakkuk says that if we are God's righteous servants, we will live by our faithfulness to God. We will be faithful to what he asks us. We will trust in his ability to lead, not our ability to follow.

Jesus, I don't want to be a proud person trusting only in myself. I want to live by my faithfulness to you. I trust your ability to guide me, not in my ability to live my life in my own strength and by my own terms. Amen.

Open Line to God

Continue steadfastly in prayer, being
watchful in it with thanksgiving.
—COLOSSIANS 4:2 ESV

Prayer is not just something we do—it is who we are. On our knees or as we walk through each day, prayer is our birthright. Our ongoing conversation and relationship with God through the sacrifice of his Son, Jesus, defines us. All the Father has ever wanted is unbroken relationship and love between his heart and ours. Because of Christ's sacrifice, there is no one keeping a list of what we get right and what we get wrong. We are invited every moment of every day to live in his presence.

There is no greater gift that we are given on this earth, after our salvation, than the open line we have directly to the heart of God. There are moments when all we want to do is kneel. There are moments when all we can do is lie on our faces and call on the name of Jesus. There are moments when we want to stand with our faces toward the warmth of the sun and talk with our Father or battle against the driving rain as we share our hearts with him.

Share everything you love and everything that troubles you with him. Sing, cry, scream, laugh, dance, and rejoice always, knowing you are in his presence, loved and received. This doesn't mean every prayer will be answered as we might hope it would, but there is a day coming when this detour will end and we will be home free. Until that day we have our Father who loves us, our Savior who died for us, and the Holy Spirit who intercedes for us when we don't know what to say.

Lord, thank you for the open line to you where I can bring my requests
and burdens any time of the day. Help me remember to always come to
you in prayer instead of trying to figure things out on my own. Amen.

Witness

> He told them, "You don't get to know the time. Timing
> is the Father's business. What you'll get is the Holy
> Spirit. And when the Holy Spirit comes on you, you
> will be able to be my witnesses in Jerusalem, all over
> Judea and Samaria, even to the ends of the world."
>
> —ACTS 1:7–8 MSG

Luke recounts what Jesus told his disciples before he ascended into heaven. These were Jesus' last instructions. He told them not to bother with timing or worry about who should do what. Their primary aim was to be a witness—wherever that might take them.

The Greek word for witness here is *martyr*. Simply put, when the Holy Spirit comes upon us the moment we become Christ followers, God gives us the power to die for his sake. He empowers us to live in such a way that we can't help but share about him, even if that sharing means imprisonment or possible death. It's the kind of power that brings a holy boldness coupled with an immediacy to act.

It's not that we try to be a witness; it's that we are. By nature of being followers of Jesus, we are witnesses. Sure, life pelts us and we get distracted. But we must not forget that the Holy Spirit within us bursts forth in witnessing.

Say it now. I am a witness for Jesus.

Jesus, it's difficult to grasp that I have the power to be so bold for you. Forgive me for thinking about my own stuff and forgetting to spread the good news about you wherever I go. I am your witness. Amen.

Finish Your Course

I have become its servant by the commission God
gave me to present to you the word of God in its
fullness—the mystery that has been kept hidden
for ages and generations, but is now disclosed to the
Lord's people. To them God has chosen to make
known among the Gentiles the glorious riches of this
mystery, which is Christ in you, the hope of glory.

—COLOSSIANS 1:25–27 NIV

Paul's ministry was simple: tell everyone about Jesus, particularly those outside the church. Did you know that God has a you-shaped ministry, tailor-made just for you? Spend some time seeking him about what that could be.

Ask your circle of friends or a close-knit group of e-mail friends: *What is my one thing?* When they think of you, how do they see you? How has God uniquely gifted you to reach others? In a crowd of a thousand people, what skills and gifts that you have would stand out? And, yes, you *do* have some!

Of course, we are all called to love our families, pray for our enemies, share Jesus, and season our conversations with grace. But what ministry has Jesus specifically given you?

Once you determine this—and don't shortchange the process; this could take weeks and months—ask God to give you joy and strength to finish your course, to fulfill the ministry he has given you. If it's cooking for homeless people, do it with vigor. If it's serving your children in this stage of your life, love them joyfully. Whatever it is that he's calling you to, do it in the power God provides.

*Jesus, I'd love to know what I'm uniquely qualified to do on this earth.
Help me discern through my family and friends what my one thing is.
Amen.*

Day of Reflection

Trust in the LORD with all your heart, and lean
not on your own understanding; In all your ways
acknowledge Him, and He shall direct your paths.

—PROVERBS 3:5–6

TRUST AND OBEY

When we walk with the Lord, In the light of His Word,
What a glory He sheds on our way!
While we do His good will, He abides with us still,
And with all who will trust and obey.

Trust and obey, for there's no other way
To be happy in Jesus, but to trust and obey.

—JOHN H. SAMMIS, 1887

Your space—a poem, prayer, thoughts . . .

Wait for the Lord

I would have despaired unless I had believed that
I would see the goodness of the LORD in the land
of the living. Wait for the LORD; Be strong and let
your heart take courage; Yes, wait for the LORD.

—PSALM 27:13–14 NASB

The psalmist promises something sweet in these verses—that we will see God's goodness here, right now, in this moment. It's not some future promise or assurance. It's true now while we live on this earth.

While that's an important promise to cling to, the next part of the verse helps us learn how to see the goodness of God: the secret of waiting. God's timing isn't on our schedule. He doesn't always come through in the manner in which we want him to, and often he seems tardy.

Yet when we learn the art of waiting for him, of not running ahead of him in fear, we will begin to perceive his goodness. When we wait for him and wait on him, we find courage. When we realize that God is big and he sees us, our hearts strengthen.

May it be that we learn to wait for and on God this week. May we actively pursue him and anticipate his goodness right now. God wants us to live expectant lives like that, always looking for his activity in our lives.

Jesus, I don't like waiting. It's hard. And I'm impatient. But I want to know and see your goodness. I don't want to run ahead of you in fear. Teach me to wait. Amen.

Contentment

I have learned in whatever state I am, to be content.
—PHILIPPIANS 4:11

Paul was not only a witness for Christ, but he was also—and continues to be—a witness and an example of contentment. His sense of contentment is nearly unbelievable in view of where he spent much of his life.

Because of his zeal in communicating the good news of Jesus, Paul spent years in prison. Those who had an earlier loyalty and allegiance to Paul and his zeal to persecute Christians turned on him, arrested him, and ultimately executed him in Rome. And yet, while sitting in jail prior to his execution, Paul wrote these words:

> I have learned in whatever state I am, to be content: I know how to be abased, and I know how to abound. Everywhere and in all things I have learned both to be full and to be hungry, both to abound and to suffer need. I can do all things through Christ who strengthens me. (Philippians 4:11–13)

Paul's words provide a simple but profound definition of contentment. Shockingly, it has nothing to do with our circumstances. Most of us assume if we could just change our circumstances we would be content. If I were Paul, I might have said, "Just get me out of jail, and I'll be content." But he said contentment didn't depend on whether or not he was in jail, whether or not he was hungry or had just eaten a platter of pasta. He knew contentment is an inside job. His trust and faith in Christ got him through it all.

Lord, thank you for always providing for me. Help me to be content with what you've given me. Amen.

What Do You Trust?

A wise man scales the city of the mighty and brings
down the stronghold in which they trust.

—PROVERBS 21:22 ESV

What do you trust today? In this verse, you see the cunning of the wise man who knows how to dismantle mighty enemies. He takes down the very thing they place their trust in. If it's a wall surrounding a city, promising protection, then he demolishes it.

Who is the wisest? God. And he scales the city of your heart and sometimes pulls down the strongholds in which you trust. What do you trust in more than God? Is it security? Money in the bank? Favor? Everyone liking you? A stable family?

Our God is a loving God, but he is also a jealous God. He knows that for your abundant well-being, you will ultimately be dissatisfied if you place your trust in things, people, money, or fame. He knows that he alone can deeply satisfy. So from time to time, he allows some of your weak foundations to be shaken. This is a loving act on his part, though it doesn't always feel that way in the moment.

Right now you have the choice to realign your allegiance, from trusting in what you see to trusting in the God who sees. What do you trust?

Jesus, I admit that sometimes I run to things or money or people to fully satisfy me. I trust them more than I trust you. But I want to trust you most. Amen.

God, Our Confidence

Do not be afraid of sudden fear nor of the onslaught of
the wicked when it comes; For the LORD will be your
confidence and will keep your foot from being caught.

—PROVERBS 3:25–26 NASB

We fear what we don't see. We worry about what might happen.
We invent scenarios of disaster when no disaster looms. And
sometimes we turn around in a normal day, and suddenly we're
seized by fear.

But God has a solution for being a fearful woman. It's himself, pure and undecorated. Choosing to place our trust moment
by moment in God's care will silence the voices of fear in our
heads. It will stop our hearts from palpitating and will give us
courage when genuine danger approaches.

God is our confidence. We may feel weak or needy or unsure,
but if we actively turn from ourselves and our own small strength,
he will give us the confidence we need to live a victorious life.

Look back over your week. When were you weak? Terrified?
Worried? And yet, how did God care for you? How did he take
notice of you? In what ways was he your confidence? In light of
that, choose to place your confidence in him today.

*Jesus, I confess I am sometimes a fearful woman. I don't always trust you.
Sometimes I don't do things because I'm terrified. Would you please be
my confidence today? Help me to place my hope in you this week. Amen.*

Do You Grow When You're Hurt?

> But the more they afflicted them, the more they
> multiplied and the more they spread out, so that
> they were in dread of the sons of Israel.
>
> —EXODUS 1:12 NASB

Typically, we tend to shrink back when other people or life assault us. During those times of trial and stress, our tendency is to retreat, not advance. Yet the Israelites thrived under their slavery conditions. They grew and multiplied so much that Egypt grew terrified of them.

How can we come to a place where we grow under difficulties? By picturing ourselves beyond the trial. What kind of person do you want to be after your current trial? Angry? Resentful? Depleted? Bitter? Or would you rather see yourself as stronger? Resilient? Less frantic? More dependent?

Right now, in the midst of the trial, is the time to decide to lean on Jesus. He loves to come alongside you, to whisper words of encouragement and help you grow through the affliction. In your own strength, you can't. But with the strength of Jesus, you can.

Pain has the potential to stagnate us, but it needn't do that. With a new perspective and dependence on God who supplies joy in the journey, you can thrive and grow despite your circumstances.

Jesus, I choose right now to let you help me through this trial. I can't do it on my own. I don't want to become bitter and angry. Would you grow me through my hurt? Amen.

Day of Reflection

In God I trust and am not afraid.
What can man do to me?
—PSALM 56:11 NIV

'TIS SO SWEET TO TRUST IN JESUS

'Tis so sweet to trust in Jesus, just to take Him at His word;
Just to rest upon His promise;
just to know "Thus saith the Lord."
Jesus, Jesus how I trust Him!
How I've proved Him o'er and o'er!
Jesus, Jesus, precious Jesus! O for grace to trust Him more!
—LOUISA M. R. STEAD, 1882

Your space—a poem, prayer, thoughts . . .

A Set-Apart Day

God blessed the seventh day and sanctified
it, because in it He rested from all His work
which God had created and made.

—GENESIS 2:3

God sanctified the seventh day, calling it Sabbath. To sanctify something means to set it aside or apart—to make it distinctively different.

God commanded in the Ten Commandments that we are to observe this set-apart day, to take a rest from our labor every week. While we are no longer under the law, the principle of rest remains.

When we rest from work, we show God we trust him to provide our needs. We no longer see ourselves as our sole source of provision. In rest, we reveal our dependency. We also prove our worth has nothing to do with our output. We are worthy simply because God created us and loves us.

We also stop and take time to cherish the relationships God has brought into our lives when we rest. We pull away from the hurried life to truly listen to our friends and family, to take walks, to do things that rejuvenate us.

Taking a strategic break every week not only reveals our dependence on God, but it also serves to replenish us for the week ahead. We are not machines, running endlessly without stopping. We are humans with limitations. Let yourself be refreshed this week.

Jesus, there's so much to do. It's hard for me to rest. But I realize that when I work like crazy, I'm not trusting you to provide for me and my family. Help me to slow down, to contemplate, to engage with people. Amen.

Light and Truth

Send out your light and your truth; let them
guide me. Let them lead me to your holy
mountain, to the place where you live.

—PSALM 43:3 NLT

How do light and truth guide us? Light shows us a path in front
of us, particularly in the darkness. And truth? In a world crowded
with darkened opinions, truth cuts through that darkness with
clarity and freedom.

God is light. He created light as his first act at the dawn of
this earth. He cannot help but be the very thing that scatters the
darkness. Jesus said he is the light. He also said he personified
truth because he spoke the truth. He said, "I tell you the truth,"
seventy-eight times in the New Testament.

Jesus becomes the light and truth we need to find deep, abiding fellowship with God. He is the avenue to relationship with
our heavenly Father. Which also means that if we are to approach
him, we must have those twin characteristics of light and truth.

In what ways does your life scatter darkness? How do you
stand up against evil in your generation? How do you represent the irresistible light of Jesus? And what of truth? Are you a
woman of truth, deeply connected to the Bible? Do your actions
and words match up? Are you authentic? Do you share the truth
of the gospel?

As we are light and truth, we experience more of God, and
our lives overflow with abundant hope.

*Jesus, help me to be light and truth to this crazy world. I know it's dark,
and many people love lies rather than truth. Give me the courage to be
both light and truth. And thank you for leading me to you via your light
and truth. Amen.*

Elisha, Faithful Friend

Elijah said to Elisha, "Stay here please, for the
LORD has sent me as far as Bethel." But Elisha said,
"As the LORD lives and as you yourself live, I will
not leave you." So they went down to Bethel.

—2 KINGS 2:2 NASB

Have you had a friend like Elisha who stuck with you through
every mountain and valley of your life? If so, thank Jesus for that
person. It's a rare friend who walks alongside us in trials and joys
aplenty.

Take a moment today to remember some of those friends.
Send a note of thanks for being like Elisha to you, perhaps even
citing this verse. Sometimes we forget to say thank you for other
people's faithfulness and kindness.

Then spend some time looking over your relationships.
When have you been Elisha to a friend or family member? Who
is God asking you to serve and serve alongside? Who has God
placed on your heart who needs specific encouragement? Who
could benefit from your presence or an in-person prayer?

Life can be a lonely journey, and it's best traveled with
friends.

*Jesus, thank you for the example of Elisha not leaving his friend Elijah.
Thank you that he chose to inconvenience himself for the sake of his
friend. I want to be a friend like that. Show me how and give me strength.
Amen.*

Abounding in Hope

May the God of hope fill you with all joy and
peace in believing, so that by the power of the
Holy Spirit you may abound in hope.

—ROMANS 15:13 ESV

To abound means to have plenty, to overflow, to have abundance or plenty. But as we look around at the world today, seldom do we see people abounding in hope. Instead, hopelessness reigns. Apathy categorizes many. And some folks, without hope, even take their lives.

We cannot live without hope. We need it to survive. What, then, is biblical hope? Romans 15 hints at it here. God is the source of hope, and the person of the Holy Spirit, indwelling us, is the vehicle of living abundantly in a life of hope. With him inside, we can abound in hope.

Hope springs from God alone. He rescued us. He longs for relationship with us. He provided a way to make that kind of dynamic relationship possible. We hope because of what he did. And ultimately, we know that when we die, we will walk with him forever.

But hope isn't just a future thing. It's a now thing. Hope enables us to live an abundant, joy-filled life in the great right now. We may not see circumstances as hopeful, but because we are connected to the God of the universe, we can endure them with a paradoxical joy.

Jesus, I need more and more and more of your hope. Remind me, through the Holy Spirit, that I am a hope ambassador for you. I want to live in light of my future hope, but I also want to joyfully walk in hope right now. Amen.

It's All About Him

O Lord, hear; O Lord, forgive. O Lord, pay attention and
act. Delay not, for your own sake, O my God, because
your city and your people are called by your name.

—DANIEL 9:19 ESV

We might believe that God pardons us and forgives our sins for
our sake. After all, we're the ones in need of pardon, right? But
this verse says that God does things for his own sake, for his
renown in the land. Daniel appeals to God's desire to show himself great on our behalf.

Everything in this life flows from the Life Giver—God himself. He created us not for our sakes but for his. He spoke the
universe into existence by his power, for his pleasure. He acts on
behalf of his interests because he alone holds the entire cosmos
together, and he alone weaves our lives into an intricate, mind-
boggling master plan.

When we stop and realize that everything on this earth is
for God's sake, we start to live life differently. We no longer seek
our own glory or try to stand on pedestals to proclaim our fame.
No, we take a megaphone and magnify God and his works on our
behalf.

In the midst of your daily life, remember these simple truths:
God is big and his plans are big and his glory is big. Living for
those ends results in a bigger life.

*Jesus, it's all about you. Not me. Not others. You. Help me to remember
your glory, your fame, your renown. I choose today to live for you, to
amplify you. Amen.*

Puzzle Pieces

Depend on the Lord; trust him, and he will take care of you.
—PSALM 37:5 NCV

We are always going to rub up against life's confusing parts. Nothing is static. What once was, may no longer be. Try as we might to nail things down, to keep them in place, they have a way of morphing into something else—whether it's changing weather patterns, adjusting to a different location, or everyday activities that frustrate and challenge us.

You may be committed by faith to Christ, in whom you believe, but ponder with uncertainty many of the particulars. Take shelter under the marvel of his mystery. For there you don't have to know answers; you're just asked to trust. God doesn't ask you to defend his reputation or to debate with others doctrinally, but he does make it clear we're to love.

The puzzling pieces of our lives, like the misshapen glass pieces in a stained-glass masterpiece, don't seem to fit until the Creator sands, foils, and solders them into place. Then we see, and what looked hopelessly missing is pieced together in such a way that the picture appears seamless.

We are temporarily confined to this planet in a leaky earth suit. One day that will change, and then we will see what we can't imagine, and we will understand what we can't comprehend. Then, and only then, the puzzling aspects will be solved, the last pieces will slide into place.

God, you are bigger than anything I am able to comprehend. Make me in awe of your greatness and mystery. Teach me to revel in your overwhelming goodness and ability to make all the pieces work for good. Amen.

Day of Reflection

May his name endure forever; may it continue as long as the sun. Then all nations will be blessed through him, and they will call him blessed.

—PSALM 72:17 NIV

JESUS SHALL REIGN

Jesus shall reign where'er the sun
Does it successive journeys run;
His kingdom spread from shore to shore,
Til moons shall wax and wane no more.

To Him shall endless prayer be made,
And endless praises crown His head.
His name like sweet perfume shall rise
With every morning sacrifice.

—ISAAC WATTS, 1719

Your space—a poem, prayer, thoughts . . .

My God

> The LORD is my strength and my song; he has
> given me victory. This is my God, and I will praise
> him—my father's God, and I will exalt him!

—EXODUS 15:2 NLT

In this passage, Moses uses the words, "my father's God," which means that his faith was passed down to him from his father.

But Moses had to act on that. He had to make God his own God. Just because his father was a follower did not automatically mean Moses would follow hard after God. For us it's the same. If our parents knew Jesus, that doesn't necessarily mean their faith was magically imputed to us. Instead, we must decide whether or not we want to follow too.

If we have children, the same thing is at play. We can share our faith with them, but ultimately it's their decision.

But once the decision is made, our hearts can't help but burst into song for the Lord. Because once we taste his provision and strength, we must sing. God may have given victories to our parents, but when we experience our own victories, our natural response will be praise.

Jesus, I want to own my faith, to make it mine. And for those around me who don't yet know you, help me to be faithful to share you with them so they can experience the joy and victory I've experienced. I love you! Amen.

Free Flight

Our soul has escaped as a bird out of the snare of the
trapper; the snare is broken and we have escaped.

—PSALM 124:7 NASB

God's heart for us is to live uncaged, freedom-filled lives. He
wants to set us free from our sin, our past, our hurt, our anguish—
anything that might have enslaved us. He longs for us to escape
the cages we push up against.

Actually, because of Jesus, our cages have been unlocked.
His death and resurrection have made a perfect way to be free.
Yet sometimes we forget that. We prefer the comfort of the cage
because freedom is unfamiliar and scary. Our sin becomes our
way of life. The way we see ourselves as victims becomes our
comfort zone.

Our wings are not clipped. The world awaits us outside our
cages. Be brave today to fly, to be free, to trust in the saving work
of Jesus. It's time to escape what has held you back.

God's heart for you is that you would live an abundant life,
soaring on his strength. What prevents you from believing this?
God has set you free today. Live in the truth of that. You've
already escaped!

*Jesus, I want to live free. Thank you for securing my freedom. I don't
want to hang out in the cage anymore. I want to fly. Give me the strength
to risk life outside the cage. Amen.*

His Laws, My Treasure

Your laws are my treasure; they are my heart's delight.
—PSALM 119:111 NLT

God's laws sometimes get a bad rap. We often perceive the laws of God as less than grace-filled. After all, Jesus fulfilled the law.

Why did God bring the law? To give us a framework for how to live successfully on this earth. It was his intent to give us a snapshot into his heart, to see how he viewed our lives and how we would best live. But God also knew the deeper intent of the law: to reveal our inability to follow it.

So he sent Jesus not to abolish the law—oh, how it still exists—but to fulfill it. Jesus lived the law perfectly. He made God's laws his treasure. His heart's delight was to do the Father's will at all times, in every moment.

If we're to be like Jesus, then we can joyfully proclaim what the psalmist wrote above. God's laws are a treasure; we delight in them because they point us to the One who fulfilled the law and empowers us to live with victory today.

Jesus, thank you for fulfilling the law in the way you walked this earth. Teach me to delight in the law, to treasure your precepts. I know I can do what's right only in your amazing strength. Amen

Idols

You must not make for yourself an idol of any kind or
an image of anything in the heavens or on the earth
or in the sea. You must not bow down to them or
worship them, for I, the LORD your God, am a jealous
God who will not tolerate your affection for any other
gods. I lay the sins of the parents upon their children;
the entire family is affected—even children in the
third and fourth generations of those who reject me.
But I lavish unfailing love for a thousand generations
on those who love me and obey my commands.

—EXODUS 20:4–6 NLT

When we read the Ten Commandments, we often skip over these
verses thinking they have nothing to do with us. But God is very
clear. We must not have idols.

An idol is something we fashion or think about that replaces
God. It's what we go to first when a problem arises. It can be food
or drink or people or the need for approval. It may be completing
a to-do list or succeeding in business. Whatever we actively seek
to fill us is in danger of becoming an idol.

God is after our deep allegiance to him. He wants our affection and our hearts. He knows that if we seek life outside of him,
ultimately we will be dissatisfied and then look for love in all the
wrong places. He knows our addictive nature.

God promises to lavish his love on the generations beyond
us if we choose to love him above everything. That's an amazing
promise!

*Jesus, forgive me for running to other things in this life to fill me. I forget
that you are the only One who can fill up my heart. Thank you for lavish-
ing love on me when I follow you. Amen.*

The Laughter Effect

He will yet fill your mouth with laughter
and your lips with shouts of joy.

—JOB 8:21 NIV

A woman who was overloaded with packages was making her way toward the back of a plane and didn't realize her purse strap had looped around the arm of a seat as she passed by until it jerked her abruptly to a stop. The man in the seat was trying to unleash it when the woman swung around and saw him tugging on her strap. Not understanding she had done this to herself, she snapped, "What's wrong with you, mister? Let go of my purse." The man threw his arms up to indicate he didn't want her purse. That's when she saw the looped strap and realized what had happened. "Oops." She grinned sheepishly. "My fault." The sweet man smiled. "I couldn't have used it anyway; it doesn't match my shoes."

Ever notice how a good giggle renews your energy and refreshes your attitude? Maybe that's why comical folks are so popular. Humor makes everyone's life a little easier. Next time you're in a fowl mood, look for a reason to quack up. Humor can cause an enemy to become a friend. And just as this man turned the tone of a potentially unpleasant situation by retaining his humor, we, too, can redirect small calamities into giggle breaks.

Who makes you laugh?

Lord, help me to remember to giggle more and stress less, for humor makes life a little easier. Amen.

Door in the Wall

Then we can spend our time in prayer and
preaching and teaching the word.
—ACTS 6:4 NLT

Yes, it is hard to pray. It's much easier to spend our free time flopping down and turning on the television than following the example of Christ and pulling away from the noise and distractions for alone time with our Father. Every believer has experienced the difficulties of an intentional prayer life. But when we persist in seeing prayer as a challenge—as a wall between us and God—and walk away in defeat, we walk away carrying the same burdens we arrived with.

Instead, we need to imagine that there's a door in that wall, like C. S. Lewis's wonderful wardrobe that took Lucy into Narnia in *The Lion, the Witch and the Wardrobe*. Prayer is our escape from this world. It is not a chore or something we'll be tested on at the end of each week. It's our time to crawl into our Father's embrace and lay our cares upon him. Jesus told us that in this world we will have many troubles, but not to be afraid because he has overcome this world (John 16:33). It's only when we are able to quiet the noises outside and within that we remember all his amazing promises to us. Prayer is not something that belongs on our to-do list, but rather on our to-live list!

Lord, thank you for the connection of prayer that I have to you. Help me
to always find the door in the wall. Amen.

Day of Reflection

There is rejoicing in the presence of the angels
of God over one sinner who repents.

—LUKE 15:10 NIV

O HAPPY DAY, THAT FIXED MY CHOICE

O happy day that fixed my choice
on Thee my Savior and my God!
Well may this glowing heart rejoice,
And tell its raptures all abroad.
Happy day! Happy day!
When Jesus washed my sins away!
He taught me how to watch and pray,
and live rejoicing every day
Happy day! Happy day!
When Jesus washed my sins away!

—PHILIP DODDRIDGE, 1755

Your space—a poem, prayer, thoughts . . .

God Loves Us All

Surely it is you who love the people; all the holy
ones are in your hand. At your feet they all bow
down, and from you receive instruction.

—DEUTERONOMY 33:3 NIV

We say the words, "God loves everyone," but sometimes we forget he does. When we curse someone or gossip about another person, we devalue folks, showing us we've forgotten God's passion for them.

In this passage, written by Moses, we see God's concern for all mankind. He holds us all in his capable hands. Once we've chosen to bow down at God's footstool, he gives us instruction on how to live. And he gives this freely to all.

This means we're all on the same playing field. We all need to be in God's hands. We all need his instruction. Instead of viewing others as those whom God should ignore, why not pray that God would be kind to our enemies, to bless them with his provision and wisdom? When we pray for our enemies, we agree afresh that God loves every single person he created.

Similarly, we can ask God to give us his perspective on the people he created. When you're in conflict with someone, ask God to show you the person's heart, to see how much God loves her. Asking that may change the way you view both the person and the situation.

Jesus, I need your perspective on people who hurt me. Remind me again that you love them passionately. Keep that close to my heart so I can choose to pray for them and bless them. I appreciate your heart for the whole wide world. Help me to love like you. Amen.

Jesus, Fellow Sufferer

Dear friends, do not be surprised at the painful
trial you are suffering, as though something
strange were happening to you. But rejoice that you
participate in the sufferings of Christ, so that you
may be overjoyed when his glory is revealed.

—1 PETER 4:12–13 NIV

Peter tells us not to be surprised if trials come our way. We shouldn't see that as strange or out of the ordinary. On the contrary, trials are normal for the believer because we are following in Jesus' footsteps.

Notice Jesus' life. Yes, he lived a full life, and he loved the people he surrounded himself with. Yes, he experienced the joyful parts of human life—good food, good friends, good company. But he also experienced extreme rejection by the religious leaders. Folks connived to put him to death. He went hungry sometimes. He understood loneliness. And the culmination of his earthly life was crucifixion.

If we follow him, there will be trials. Peter gives us a painful reassurance: when we suffer, we participate in Jesus' sufferings. That may not sound fun at first read, but remember how it is when you suffer alongside a friend. There comes a deep camaraderie in the pain together.

That's what it's like when we suffer alongside Jesus. And the Scripture promises that the more we suffer with him, the more we'll be full of joy when we see him glorified.

Jesus, I am stuck in a trial right now, and it's painful. Help me to see that my suffering can actually be something I do alongside you. Thank you for being with me even now. Amen.

God Breaks Chains

He brought them out of darkness and the shadow
of death, and broke their chains in pieces.

—PSALM 107:14

Everyone loves a good story. And good stories have conflict and
terror and suspense and intrigue and a satisfying conclusion.
When we look at our own stories, we begin to discern the hard
places, the dark places, and the times when we felt our life ebbing
away from us.

It's in that retrospective look that we can trace the path of
the hero of our story. Jesus is the hero who pulled us out from the
darkness of our sin. He rescued us from the power of death. He
saw our slavery to sin, to ourselves, to others' abuse, to this world
system, and he broke each chain to set us free.

We, therefore, live shortchanged lives if we believe we're the
heroes in our own story. We didn't rescue ourselves. We can't
break the chains that capture us. We are helpless without Jesus.

Take a moment to think back on your epic tale. Notice the
times God rescued and broke chains. Thank him for all the
restoring he's done, all the healing he's wrought. We serve a
heroic God.

*Jesus, I don't want to be the hero of my story. I want to remember all the
times you rescued me and severed my chains. Thank you for acting on my
behalf when I couldn't. Amen.*

His Work Is Complete

The Son radiates God's own glory and expresses the
very character of God, and he sustains everything
by the mighty power of his command. When he had
cleansed us from our sins, he sat down in the place of
honor at the right hand of the majestic God in heaven.

—HEBREWS 1:3 NLT

The first part of this verse is stunning in its simplicity. Jesus radiates God's glory. He is the exact representation of God the Father's character. Not only that, he is the sustainer of everything we see. Amazing!

But let's look at the second part of this verse. Not only did he perfectly represent his Father, but he also fulfilled his mission to cleanse us completely from our sins. Even right now, we are perfectly cleansed because of his sacrifice on the cross.

When someone completes a busy day at work, the reward is rest. When we finish what we're doing for the day, often we sit at dinner and unwind after all the toil of the day. Jesus did the same thing after his completed work on the cross. He sat down at God's right hand. He finished his work.

Because his work is completed, we can rest too. We don't have to be haunted by our sins or worried about our future sins. Right in this moment we are free. The past is forgiven. Now is forgiven. The future is forgiven. All because Jesus finished his work.

Jesus, thank you for your sacrifice on the cross. I still can't believe you did that on my behalf. I love you for it. Help me to rest in the truth of your forgiveness. I don't want to be weighed down with regret. I don't want to live in the moment sad about my sin. Nor do I want to worry about the future. Thank you for setting me free. Amen.

Our Defense Attorney

My dear children, I write this to you so that you will not sin. But if anybody does sin, we have one who speaks to the Father in our defense—Jesus Christ, the Righteous One. He is the atoning sacrifice for our sins, and not only for ours but also for the sins of the whole world.

—1 JOHN 2:1–2 NIV

We all sin. That's an easy fact. How victorious we are depends on our response to sin.

If we dismiss our sin and don't think it's a big deal, we alienate ourselves from God. While he is still available to us, our sin causes a break in relationship, just like when a friend hurts us. We still love our friend, but we have a rift to deal with. If our friend doesn't acknowledge the rift and never apologizes, the relationship suffers.

If we dwell on our sin and heap condemnation and shame upon ourselves, we'll live defeated lives. We'll start thinking that we'll never amount to anything, that we'll be forever enslaved to our sin, that we'll never gain victory.

But there's a better way, provided by Jesus. When we sin, we simply tell Jesus about it. We express how sorry we are, and we choose to rest not in our own righteousness, but in Jesus'. Because of his sacrifice on the cross, we have the beautiful gift of forgiveness.

What's even more astounding is that Jesus' death on the cross covers the whole world's sin. What an amazing God we serve!

Jesus, I don't want to hide my sin or ignore it either. But I also don't want to be defined by it and hang my head in shame wherever I go. I choose now to confess my sin to you and rest in your forgiveness. Amen.

Jesus, Who Bears Our Sin and Pain

He himself bore our sins in his body on the tree,
that we might die to sin and live to righteousness.
By his wounds you have been healed.

—1 PETER 2:24 ESV

Jesus did two things on the cross. Not only did he take upon his sacred shoulders every sin we've committed, as well as the sins of the entire world, but he also takes our pain too. His wounds on the cross mean healing for us.

In that way, Jesus is our sin bearer *and* our pain bearer. He takes our sin, bears the weight of it on the cross, then removes it as far as the east is from the west. But he also, by nature of his sacrifice, empathizes with our pain.

This also means that when someone sins against us, we can go to Jesus and ask him to bear the sin the other person committed. And it means we can ask him to bear the pain we endured as a result of that sin. What sometimes happens when we're sinned against is that we can harbor bitterness and revenge, which makes us sin.

The only way out is Jesus. He will take their sin, your sin in response, and the pain created by the situation.

Jesus, thank you that you are the sin bearer and pain bearer, not only for me, but for those who hurt me. I give you my sin, their sin, and the pain in the middle. Take it, please. Amen.

Day of Reflection

For God so loved the world that he gave his
one and only Son, that whoever believes in him
shall not perish but have eternal life.

—JOHN 3:16 NIV

THE OLD RUGGED CROSS

On a hill far away stood an old rugged cross;
the emblem of suffering and shame.
And I love that old cross where the dearest and best,
for a world of lost sinners was slain.

To the old rugged cross, I will ever be true;
its shame and reproach gladly bear,
Then He'll call me some day to my home far away,
where His glory forever I'll share.

So I'll cherish the old rugged cross,
til my trophies at last I lay down;
I will cling to the old rugged cross,
and exchange it someday for a crown.

—GEORGE BENNARD, 1913

Your space—a poem, prayer, thoughts . . .

Walk *with* God

Enoch walked with God.

—GENESIS 5:22 NASB

Enoch had a special relationship with God, so much so that he didn't die. Scripture says, "And he was not, for God took him" (Genesis 5:24). Moses used the word *with* to describe his walk, not other prepositions like *to, under,* or *above.*

If he walked *to* God, it would mean God seemed far off. I wonder how many of us walk to God, always striving to get closer but never really making it. God then becomes like those awful dreams when you're running to safety, but the closer you get, the farther safety moves away.

If he walked *under* God, the connotation would primarily be fear. While we are to fear God with reverence and awe, we are not to cower beneath him, viewing him as an angry parent, always afraid of getting smacked for our behavior.

If he walked *above* God, he'd be elevating himself above the God of the universe, the One who spoke the stars into existence.

Enoch walked alongside God—*with* him. God remained the God of all things yet still enjoyed the camaraderie of one of his creation, much as a mother connects to her children as they grow up.

Are you striving to find God when he's already promised his nearness? Can you shed the belief that he is an angry parent? Can you let go of control?

Dear Jesus, help me walk with you today. Please show me that you're closer than my breath, kinder than the kindest person I know, and are capable of directing my life. Amen.

A Gentle Blowing

So He said, "Go forth and stand on the mountain before
the LORD." And behold, the LORD was passing by! And
a great and strong wind was rending the mountains
and breaking in pieces the rocks before the LORD; but
the LORD was not in the wind. And after the wind an
earthquake, but the LORD was not in the earthquake.
After the earthquake a fire, but the LORD was not in
the fire; and after the fire a sound of a gentle blowing.

—1 KINGS 19:11–12 NASB

When Elijah met with God, he most likely had expectations
about his voice. He imagined it to be powerful like wind, or devastating like the earthquake, or all consuming like the fire. But
God didn't come to Elijah in a show of power and might. No, he
spoke to Elijah in a counterintuitive way—as a gentle blowing, a
whisper.

While it is true that God is big and mighty and amazing and
powerful, it is also true that we serve a relational God who knows
us well and knows best how to communicate with us. How beautiful this picture is of God's gentleness.

Sometimes we fail to hear God's gentle whispers because
we're waiting for the wind, earthquake, or fire of his majesty.
God's best communication isn't through the clatter and clamor,
but in the stillness of life.

How do you hear a gentle blowing? You must be quiet and
still. What in your life today prevents you from being alone and
quiet? Take some time out to be utterly silent right now. Ask God
to send his gentle blowing your way. Be willing to hear from him.

Jesus, thank you for coming to Elijah in the gentle blowing of the breeze.
I admit that my life feels more like windstorms or earthquakes or fires.
Life's been crazy. Help me to slow down enough to hear your whispers.
Amen.

Grow Deep Roots

And now, just as you accepted Christ Jesus as your
Lord, you must continue to follow him. Let your roots
grow down into him, and let your lives be built on him.
Then your faith will grow strong in the truth you were
taught, and you will overflow with thankfulness.

—COLOSSIANS 2:6–7 NLT

The Christian life doesn't consist merely of one prayer prayed.
Once we've invited Jesus to take over our lives, we've only just
begun the long journey. The word for that journey is a long one:
sanctification. Basically it means the lifelong process of walking
out our salvation.

Paul reminds the Colossians of this truth. He tells them to
continue to follow Jesus. He gives simple instructions to help
them do this. He tells them to have deep roots.

Roots that grow deep are roots that are nourished by the sun
and the rain and even stress. In a similar way, we need the Son
to shine down on us. We can't grow without him. We need the
rain of the Holy Spirit to refresh us when we're dry and tired. But
we also need stress to strengthen our roots. The trees with the
deepest roots are those that block the wind, that strain against
resistance.

So we grow deep roots in order to grow a faith that is strong.
Paul says a strong faith is built solely on Jesus. And the result of
our faith in him is overflowing thankfulness.

*Jesus, I want my roots to grow deep. While I like the idea of sunshine,
and even rain, I'm not as sure about the stress roots need to grow deeper.
Help me to welcome the trials in my life and see them as good things to
help strengthen me. Amen.*

Valleys and Mountains

> Yea, though I walk through the valley of the
> shadow of death, I will fear no evil: for thou art
> with me; thy rod and thy staff they comfort me.
>
> —PSALM 23:4 KJV

When the disciples left the valley and joined Jesus on the Mount of Transfiguration, they experienced such a rush of joy that they wanted to stay there. But Jesus let them know they had to go back down, down, down to the people and the problems—because that's where our faith is forged. The valleys are littered with lessons; the wise lean in and learn. The sights are spectacular from the rocky pinnacles, and we get a great overview of the orchards, but we also want to hold the pear in our hand and taste its sweet offering. That happens in the lowlands.

From the peaks, we see the lakes; but in the valley, we can explore the water's refreshing depths. From the crest, we see the canopy of trees; but in the valley, we can sit in the cool shade and listen as the wind sings through the branches.

We live the majority of our lives in the lowland; yet, if we look close enough, we'll find fruit, catch breezes, and hear music as we learn lessons along the way. This can make the jolts of valley life more bearable and, at times, downright joyful.

Lord of my valleys, thank you for your guiding presence. And thank you for the bumper crop of blessings amid the low places. Give me eyes not to miss your kind provisions. And when you guide me to the peak, Jesus, may I be as willing to topple off and try my wings as I am to rest on the rocks and enjoy the view. Amen.

Come Away

After telling everyone good-bye, he went
up into the hills by himself to pray.

—MARK 6:46 NLT

When asked about the most significant retreat in her life, a woman said, "Actually, it was when I went away with a group from our singles ministry and we spent an entire day without speaking. Several strongholds in my life were severed there. And I wonder why I don't take time to be alone with God like that."

Jesus, who was God in the flesh, had to pull away from others to pray. How much more do we who are surrounded by noise and clamor have to make that kind of prayer!

The story's been told of an overwhelmed pastor with too many counseling appointments. In exasperation, he told folks to spend one hour of quiet in the sanctuary before the scheduled appointment. To his surprise, most of his appointments cancelled. There's power in quiet.

What about you? How noisy is your life? Is there ever a time of complete silence? How can you carve out time right now to spend time with God in prayer? Not only will strongholds be taken down, but your problems might just melt away through your sincere conversation with the Almighty God.

Don't shortchange your walk with him by giving him the scraps of your day. He deserves your full attention.

Jesus, I appreciate the modeling you provided in taking time away from the busyness of ministry to talk to your Father. I want to do that too. But sometimes I feel torn between my busy life and you. Help me choose a quiet moment today to pour my heart out to you. Amen.

Holy Rest

Remember to observe the Sabbath day by keeping it holy.
You have six days each week for your ordinary work,
but the seventh day is a Sabbath day of rest dedicated
to the LORD your God. On that day no one in your
household may do any work. This includes you, your
sons and daughters, your male and female servants,
your livestock, and any foreigners living among you.

—EXODUS 20:8–10 NLT

While we may not have foreigners living among us, or livestock or servants, we can still heed this important commandment today by living in a holy rhythm.

God's intention in this commandment isn't restriction, but freedom. He knows our propensity to do-do-do, to trust in ourselves for making money, for becoming our own provision. God in his all-sufficiency gave us a supreme example of rest by resting himself on the seventh day, though he didn't need it. He is sufficient in himself.

If God provided the example and Jesus often pulled away from the crowds to be alone and rejuvenate, how much more do we need Sabbath rest? A day of rest is simply a day set apart to be with Jesus, to replenish that which has been depleted. To trust God enough to provide regardless of our workload.

Resting brings refreshment. It's for our own good. It reminds us that God is God and we are not. It helps us find perspective for the upcoming rest. And it is a beautiful gift from God. What prevents you from taking rest this week?

Jesus, thank you for pulling away from the crowds when you walked the earth. Thank you for the example of God the Father resting on the seventh day. Help me to return to rest, to trust you for everything including provision. I need rest! Amen.

Day of Reflection

She turned around and saw Jesus standing there.
—JOHN 20:14

IN THE GARDEN

I come to the garden alone,
while the dew is still on the roses;
And the voice I hear falling on my ear,
the Son of God discloses,

I'd stay in the garden with Him,
though the night around me be falling;
But He bids me go; through the voice of woe,
His voice to me is calling.

And He walks with me and He talks with me
and He tells me I am His own;
And the joy we share as we tarry there,
none other has ever known.

—C. AUSTIN MILES, 1912

Your space—a poem, prayer, thoughts . . .

Drunk in Other Ways

Do not get drunk on wine, which leads to debauchery.
Instead, be filled with the Spirit, speaking to one
another with psalms, hymns, and songs from the
Spirit. Sing and make music from your heart to the
Lord, always giving thanks to God the Father for
everything, in the name of our Lord Jesus Christ.

—EPHESIANS 5:18–20 NIV

It's interesting to note the juxtaposition here of drinking and being filled with the Spirit. We are not to be mastered by drink because it causes us to live uncontrolled. And yet, Paul makes the contrast for a reason. When we are drunk, another substance creates our behavior. In a similar manner, when we are filled with the Spirit, God controls our behavior.

Our drunkenness must be in Jesus, to so imbibe in the Holy Spirit that he controls us and gives us the ability to be uninhibited as we share him with others. We are not to be worried about what others think, but to be fully in tune with God's presence.

A life filled with the Spirit is a worshipful one, full of music. When we drink deeply of God's presence, we cannot help but sing, sing, sing. We may create our own songs, or we may hum along to worship music—all because of the joy of knowing Jesus.

The end result of our connection to the Holy Spirit is a life of gratitude. Paul encourages us to give thanks for everything, even our trials or the things that perplex us. So whether we're sad or happy, whether we're tired or energetic, we can praise God and thank him for filling us up with his presence.

Lord Jesus, I don't want to get drunk on other pursuits. Instead I want to drink deeply of the Holy Spirit, experiencing his life and control. Help me to sing and praise, no matter what comes my way today. Amen.

God's Perfect Way

This God—his way is perfect; the word of the LORD proves true; he is a shield for all those who take refuge in him.

—2 SAMUEL 22:31 ESV

We may not always see God's ways as perfect. Job, the righteous man who lost everything including family and health and wealth, wondered at God's goodness, though he held onto God through his awful ordeal.

It's not easy to understand the perfect ways of God in a fallen world where poverty, disease, family discord, addiction, slavery, and oppression seem to jump off the page of our Internet browser. If we let those things ensnare us, we may give into hopelessness.

But God's way is perfect. He has a plan. From the moment sin entered this world, God had already provided victory for mankind. When he came to the earth as Jesus, he bore the weight of all the ills of society. He experienced Job-like chastisement so that he not only appeared to lose everything, he also lost his life.

If that is how the story ended, we'd all have to embrace despair. But his way proves true because of the glorious, surprising, powerful resurrection.

Life might not be what we want. This world continues to be a dark place. But ultimately God's way is perfect, and someday we'll understand the unfolding.

Jesus, help me to truly believe your way is perfect. Sometimes when I look around at this world, I despair. But you overcame death. I want to settle my heart with that truth. Your plan is amazing, though I may not understand right now how it unfolds. Amen.

Jesus, Impartiality Personified

And they sent their disciples to Him, along with
the Herodians, saying, "Teacher, we know that You
are truthful and teach the way of God in truth, and
defer to no one; for You are not partial to any."

—MATTHEW 22:16 NASB

To be impartial means to be unbiased, to treat everyone equally. It means to be exactly fair in every evaluation of a situation or a person. Jesus personified impartiality. He sees everyone, every motive, every hidden thing. And he treats everyone fairly.

But even more, he treats us better than fair. Because of his death on the cross for our sin, he gave us the gift of a clean slate before the Father. When the Father looks at us, he sees the perfection of Jesus. What a gift!

If we want to live lives of grace like Jesus, we, too, must learn the art of unbiased judgment and sacrificial living. When we hear stories about other people, instead of jumping to conclusions, we pray and ask God to give us wisdom and insight. We choose to believe the best about others, to view them as God views them, in our dealings with people we differ with.

And when a friend hurts us, it means we choose to see her in light of how God sees us—perfected in Jesus Christ, well loved. We cannot be fully impartial. We are tainted by our senses and gossip. But we can choose to set aside our prejudices, asking God for wisdom as we love others.

Jesus, thank you that you were impartial in the way you dealt with the people you met on earth. Teach me to be that way. Thank you for dying on the cross so that when God sees me, he sees you. I cannot thank you enough for that. Help me live in light of that, both for myself and the people in my life. Amen.

The Gospel

> I passed on to you what was most important and what had also been passed on to me. Christ died for our sins, just as the Scriptures said. He was buried, and he was raised from the dead on the third day, just as the Scriptures said.
>
> —1 CORINTHIANS 15:3–4 NLT

In this passage Paul tells the Corinthian believers the simple truth of the gospel. Jesus died. They buried him. He rose again. Simple, profound truth.

The question is, do we live by the power of this gospel? Do we truly grasp what it means that Jesus died on our behalf? How many people in your life would die for you? And what about your enemies? Would they die for you?

When Christ died for us, we were enemies to him. Our sin made it so. And yet, he chose to die for us, his enemies, because of his great redemptive plan.

In the words of infomercials, "But wait, there's more!" He didn't stay dead. The crucifixion didn't finish Jesus. God the Father raised him from death to life. No breath to breathing. No heartbeat to thump, thump, thump. The glory of the gospel is our risen Savior! Alive, alive, alive forevermore!

Though sin entangled us and brought death, Jesus conquered death. In light of that, let's choose to live astonished lives.

Jesus, I want to always put your gospel at the forefront of my mind and live in light of it. Thank you for dying for me; thank you for rising again. Give me opportunity today to share that great news with others. Amen.

When Doubt Creeps In

All things are possible to him who believes.

—MARK 9:23

Do we really, at the core of our being, believe what we say we believe? If our behavior does not reflect our beliefs, we are either well-practiced phonies or possibly persons plagued with doubts about what we claim to believe. More than likely we are both. The person who struggles with major doubts about her beliefs also struggles with her behavior because the two don't mesh; there isn't a fit. She thinks, This is how I'm supposed to believe. But secretly she admits, Sometimes I don't think I believe any of it. These doubts affect not only our peace but our actions.

Let's talk about some faulty thinking concerning the role of doubt in a believer's life. A common assumption is that doubt is sin. That is not true. Doubt is sin only if it translates into an action that rejects God. Otherwise, doubt is to question the truth of something. Doubt is not rejecting truth; it is questioning truth. To doubt is to leave room for ultimate belief. Is it possible for the Christian to doubt and still maintain heavenly citizenship? Of course. To be human is to at times doubt even the most basic elements of our faith. In fact, doubt can be an instrument for the building of faith.

You may have kept your doubts secret or shared them with everyone who would listen. And now your doubts have caused you to cry out. Psalm 94:19 is a tender reminder of God's love for the doubter: "When doubts filled my mind, your comfort gave me renewed hope and cheer" (NLT).

Lord, strengthen my faith through my doubts. Even when I don't have all of the answers, you comfort me and lead me along. Thank you. Amen.

Christ Is Risen

Now if Christ is proclaimed as raised from
the dead, how can some of you say that there is
no resurrection of the dead? But if there is no
resurrection of the dead, then not even Christ has
been raised. And if Christ has not been raised, then
our preaching is in vain and your faith is in vain.

—1 CORINTHIANS 15:12–14 ESV

If Christ had not been raised from the dead, all of us would be following a great teacher, a miracle man. But Jesus was far more than that. After his outrageous act of forgiveness on the cross as he chose to die for our sins, people buried Jesus in a tomb. He stopped living, breathing, moving. All life had drained from him.

In that tomb, he became stiff and cold. He no doubt started decaying. And had he not resurrected, his bones would have been taken to an ossuary later and perhaps been enshrined.

But those bones were enlivened. His heart beat again. God the Father exerted the greatest strength of love in the universe and gloriously raised Jesus back to life. And because of that, we worship a risen Savior.

Your faith is not in vain. He who was dead is now alive and lives this very moment. Whatever you do for his kingdom is not wasted but is chronicled by the living, breathing, resurrected Jesus.

Thank you that you are real, Jesus. I forget sometimes. You are alive! And because of that, when I doubt, I can choose to remember that you see me right now and are available to me. Thank you for rising from the dead. Amen.

Day of Reflection

He is not here; he has risen, just as he said.
—MATTHEW 28:6 NIV

CHRIST THE LORD IS RISEN TODAY

Christ the Lord is risen today, Alleluia!
Sons of men and angels say: Allelulia!
Raise your joys and triumphs high, Alleluia!
Sing, ye heavens, and earth, reply: Alleluia!

Love's redeeming work is done, Alleluia!
Fought the fight, the battle won, Alleluia!
Death in vain forbids Him rise, Alleluia!
Ours the cross, the grave, the skies, Alleluia!

—CHARLES WESLEY, 1739

Your space—a poem, prayer, thoughts . . .

Resurrection Power

I pray also that the eyes of your heart may be enlightened
in order that you may know the hope to which he has called
you, the riches of his glorious inheritance in the saints,
and his incomparably great power for us who believe. That
power is like the working of his mighty strength, which
he exerted in Christ when he raised him from the dead
and seated him at his right hand in the heavenly realms.

—EPHESIANS 1:18–20 NIV

If you've ever been to a funeral of a loved one and longed for them
to still be alive, you understand the impossibility of that longing. But imagine what it would be like to experience a friend's
resurrection. Once casketed, now dancing. Once breathless, now
singing. Once cold, now alive with warmth.

That's the power of the resurrection. Jesus died for our sins.
We say it in passing as if it were a casual thing. But it's not. He
suffered then died. No more heartbeat. No more life. No more
speaking. Dead.

But God had a different "the end" to Jesus' story. The period
at the end of his sentence became a comma before brand-new
life. God raised Jesus to life in an astounding, mind-bending
resurrection.

Paul promises here that the same power that reignited life in
Jesus' dead body is the same power that works within us. Oh, if
only we could grasp that and really live that truth. There is hope!
Why? Because resurrection power lives within us.

Jesus, I'm amazed that you died for me. And I'm even more amazed that
you rose again. Help me live today in light of that resurrection truth. In
my fatigue and need, please be the splendid power within me. Amen.

The Bigness of God

Moses and Aaron went into the tent of meeting. When
they came out and blessed the people, the glory of the
LORD appeared to all the people. Then fire came out
from before the LORD and consumed the burnt offering
and the portions of fat on the altar; and when all the
people saw it, they shouted and fell on their faces.

—LEVITICUS 9:23–24 NASB

Moses and Aaron met with God in the tent of meeting; then they
exited to be with the people. In that hiccup of a moment, God's
glory appeared to every single person in the community. In a
flash, fire devoured their offerings. Their response? Hollering
and falling.

When we see the glory of God, whether it be in the face of a
child or the grandeur of a redwood tree or the star-pocked sky,
do we holler? Do we proclaim to others what we've seen? Do we
amplify God's greatness? Is praising God our first response?

And what about falling facedown? Are we willing to acknowledge that he is God and we are not? To, in a physical way, portray
the bigness of God?

What would it look like today to have those twin virtues of
hollering and falling? In this crazy-busy life, how can we naturally
share how great God is and live our lives so that we demonstrate
that by our actions? The secret is learning to walk closely with
Jesus because when he walked the earth, he hollered God's greatness and humbly submitted himself to his Father's will.

*Jesus, help me dance the dance of hollering and falling. Sometimes I holler
about my problems more than I shout about you. Sometimes I want to
do things my own way, and I forget how big you are. But today I want to
holler about you and submit to you. Amen.*

Fill Your Mind with Truth

Thy word is a lamp unto my feet, and a light unto my path.

—PSALM 119:105 KJV

Build an arsenal of Scripture verses tucked into your mind, ready for use at all times. If you have never made Scripture memory a practice, focus on two key things as you begin:

The first is to dwell on who God says he is—and who he is for you. You need to build an arsenal particular to you and specific to your challenges and needs. Here is a popular favorite: "The Lord is my light and my salvation; whom shall I fear? The Lord is the stronghold of my life; of whom shall I be afraid?" (Psalm 27:1 ESV).

Once you have a clearer understanding of the true nature of God, you need to fortify yourself with a clearer understanding of your new nature in Christ. Again, the verses you choose should speak strongly to your own soul.

But in case you'd like a few potent examples, here are two:

- "I can do all things through him who strengthens me." (Philippians 4:13 ESV)
- "There is therefore now no condemnation for those who are in Christ Jesus."(Romans 8:1 ESV)

Lord, thank you for the Word and for all the comfort it gives to me. Help me to immerse myself in it daily so as to become closer to you. Amen.

Fear God

> I tell you, my friends, do not fear those who kill the body,
> and after that have nothing more that they can do. But I will
> warn you whom to fear: fear him who, after he has killed,
> has authority to cast into hell. Yes, I tell you, fear him!
>
> —LUKE 12:4–5 ESV

We've heard it said that our fear of God must be reverence and awe—that we're not really supposed to fear God in the traditional sense. But the essence of this verse is the opposite. God has the authority to cast people into hell. Let that sink in for a moment.

God created everything we see and every person who has ever lived. He is in sovereign control of the universe. He has the final say about every person's fate. He is God. We are not.

So, yes, we are to fear him. Just as we might tremble in the presence of the president of the United States, tongue-tied and nervous, so must we tremble in God's presence out of fearful respect.

The reverse is true also. When we learn to fear God, to see him as lofty and amazing and gigantic, other people pale in comparison. We no longer need to fear our enemies. They cannot touch our souls.

Jesus, since you are so approachable, it seems difficult to fear you. But the Scripture says you have the power over hell. I choose today to fear you that way. And as I do, would you lessen the fear I have of other people? Amen.

Holy God

> I saw the Lord sitting upon a throne, high and lifted up;
> and the train of his robe filled the temple. Above him stood
> the seraphim. Each had six wings: with two he covered his
> face, and with two he covered his feet, and with two he
> flew. And one called to another and said: "Holy, holy, holy
> is the LORD of hosts; the whole earth is full of his glory!"
>
> —ISAIAH 6:1–3 ESV

Imagine seeing God.

Imagine fire and light and noise and smoke and grandeur. Imagine seeing angels who revere God, swirling around his throne. Isaiah had this experience. He saw the Lord on his throne, lofty.

The song the seraphim sang was a song of God's holiness. To be holy simply means to be "other." To be set apart and completely different. God is "other" than us. He is not like us. He is all consuming, all knowing, all able, all perceiving, all creating. Before him there was no God. He is the only sovereign deity in the universe.

When we forget how "other" God is, we can begin to think he's our chum, a friend who helps us when we're down. While that is true, he is also the Holy One, fully God, and awesome in the right sense of the word. Picturing God as holy will help us stay in a position of reverence and awe.

Jesus, I want to remember today that you are holy, completely "other" than me. Help me picture that and live my life in hushed reverence of you. Amen.

God's Wonderful Ways

O LORD, I will honor and praise your name, for you are
my God. You do such wonderful things! You planned
them long ago, and now you have accomplished them.

—ISAIAH 25:1 NLT

Isaiah elevates God in his prayer. Note how selfless and God-centered his words are. He praises God for what he does, how he plans, what he accomplishes. So often our prayers are laundry lists about us—our concerns, our worries, our frustrations.

When we take our eyes off our situation and begin to search for what God is doing in the world and then express our gratitude for his actions, our focus shifts like Isaiah's. Then we begin to see our lives as part of a greater tapestry, woven not merely for our good but for the good of God's colorful kingdom.

It's then that we can discern God's plans and recognize the wonderful things he does not only in our lives, but also in the lives of those around us. God has accomplished much. To realize that is to praise much.

Look back over your month. Trace the things God did on your behalf. List his accomplishments, then praise him for his work.

Jesus, I want to pray like Isaiah, fully focused on what you do and what you will accomplish. Give me faith like that. Open my eyes to your wonderful ways. Amen.

Day of Reflection

Each of the four living creatures had six wings and was covered with eyes all around, even under its wings. Day and night they never stop saying: "Holy, holy, holy is the Lord God Almighty," who was, and is, and is to come.

—REVELATION 4:8 NIV

HOLY, HOLY, HOLY! LORD GOD ALMIGHTY

Holy, holy, holy, Lord God Almighty!
Early in the morning our song shall rise to Thee.
Holy, holy, holy! Merciful and mighty!
God in three Persons, Blessed Trinity!

—REGINALD HEBER, 1826

Your space—a poem, prayer, thoughts . . .

Lay Down Your Life

I have told you these things so that you will be filled
with my joy . . . This is my commandment: Love each
other in the same way I have loved you. There is no
greater love than to lay down one's life for one's friends.
You are my friends if you do what I command.

—JOHN 15:11–14 NLT

Jesus told the disciples these words because he longed for them to
live a joyful life. What makes a life joyful? When we lay down our
lives for our friends. When we sacrifice for the sake of another.
When we step outside our comfort zones so we're inconve-
nienced for someone else. There is true, abiding joy that comes
from our abandonment.

How can we learn to live such radical lives? From Jesus'
example. In the New Testament we read how he constantly
poured his life out for people's sakes. He, who was the creator of
everything, stooped to serve those he created.

And when he gave his life for you and the entire world, he
ushered in a new era, where we could be friends with God. As his
friends, we are to be like him in everything, particularly in the
way we love.

Remember, too, that Jesus chronicles every ounce of sacrifice you've performed. He sees. He knows. He's aware. Nothing
escapes him. So lay down your life, then find the joy that results.

*Jesus, help me to remember the power of sacrifice, both of yours on the
cross and mine on behalf of others. Sometimes I grow weary of giving up
my rights for the sake of others. Renew me as I serve. Amen.*

Joy and Gladness

The Lord will surely comfort Zion and will look
with compassion on all her ruins; he will make her
deserts like Eden, her wastelands like the garden
of the Lord. Joy and gladness will be found in
her, thanksgiving and the sound of singing.

—Isaiah 51:3 niv

Joy is the hallmark of the Christian life. Not doldrums or morbid
introspection. Joy. Gladness. Thanksgiving. Singing.

What if we don't feel like singing? What if the joy has ebbed
out of us? We simply need to remember God's goodness to us, to
count our blessings, and trace the faithfulness of God throughout our lives. When we spend time taking our eyes off negative
circumstances and instead focus them on God's care for us, we
can't help but sing.

It's a discipline to sing when life pushes against you. It's
a choice to find joy in the mundane. It's work to choose praise
instead of complaint. But the rewards of a grateful heart are many,
including a lightening of your mood when you do.

Next time you're tempted to wallow in the negative, reorient
your mind to remember what Jesus has done in your life. He has
saved you. He has rescued you. He died for you. He made a way
for you to be in perfect relationship with God the Father. He sent
the Holy Spirit to be your always companion. He has taken care
of you.

In light of that, rejoice!

*Jesus, I choose right now to sing. I want to wallow in thanksgiving, not
crabbiness. I want to experience the joy and gladness that come from
counting all your blessings, not detailing my shortcomings. I love you
Jesus. Amen.*

His Glory Covers

For the earth will be filled with the knowledge of
the glory of the LORD as the waters cover the sea.

—HABAKKUK 2:14 NIV

No matter what we do or what we think or how we react, the truth is God's glory will make itself known everywhere. That takes a lot of pressure off us. It's no longer up to us to make sure his glory reaches everywhere. It simply stretches out to the outermost parts of the earth. The knowledge of God's glory is so gigantic that it's like the ocean, a never-ending stream of God's beauty.

When life feels stretching or our circumstances career out of control, we can rest in knowing that God is at work. He covers us as the seas cover the earth. He can't help but reveal himself to the cosmos. And yet, even as he holds the universe together by his glory and power, he concerns himself with the minutia of our days.

Our glorious, light-filled, amazing God is ever mindful of every detail. He clothes the fields. He feeds the birds. He watches over creation. And yet he understands parts of us we can't comprehend, and he comes alongside us to help us when we ask. That's the beauty of his glory—all encompassing, all consuming, ever present.

So if you're bothered today and you feel small, think of the ocean, how relentless it is, and remember that God is bigger still. And he is mindful of you.

Jesus, it's hard for me to look at the ocean and consider just how big you are. Help me to remember that you are bigger than my biggest thought, that your glory covers this entire earth. In that, I choose to rest in the fact that you're also mindful of me. Amen.

Help Through Many Voices

*Then Jesus said, "Come to me, all of you who are weary
and carry heavy burdens, and I will give you rest."*

—MATTHEW 11:28 NLT

Many times we have to work through challenges to get past the
edge that separates us from the blessings God wants to give us.
Amid those challenges, large or small, our best hope is to accept
the aid of those ready-to-help rescuers waiting on us.

Since the dawn of time, he has stood ready to put the pieces
of our lives back together again when we heed and accept the
help he's offered us through so many voices.

The prophet's voice: "This is God's Message, the God who
made earth, made it livable and lasting, known everywhere as
God: 'Call to me and I will answer you. I'll tell you marvelous
and wondrous things that you could never figure out on your
own'" (Jeremiah 33:2 MSG).

Jesus' voice: "Are you tired? Worn out? Burned out on religion? Come to me. Get away with me and you'll recover your
life. . . . Keep company with me and you'll learn to live freely and
lightly" (Matthew 11:28, 30 MSG).

And finally, the apostle Paul's voice: "Don't fret or worry.
Instead of worrying, pray. Let petitions and praises shape your
worries into prayers, letting God know your concerns. Before
you know it, a sense of God's wholeness, everything coming
together for good, will come and settle you down. It's wonderful
what happens when Christ displaces worry at the center of your
life" (Philippians 4:6–7 MSG).

*Lord, thank you that I can turn to you for help. And thank you for the
encouragement from the prophet's voice, Jesus' voice, and the apostle
Paul's voice. Amen.*

The Power of the Lord

While the harp was being played, the power
of the LORD came upon Elisha.

—2 KINGS 3:15 NLT

While music is a great way to encounter God, the point of this
quick verse is that God's power came upon Elisha in the first
place. In the Old Testament the Holy Spirit came upon people
in spurts and different times. He didn't permanently stay within
people.

How much more do we have the power now that the Holy
Spirit lives within us? It's enough to make us sing, to declare his
sufficiency in our lives. Elisha was a powerful man of God whose
prayers moved mountains and who saw miracles in his life. And
yet, we have more power available to us today.

Do we live as if the power of the Lord lives within us? The
very unction that made Jesus rise from the dead resides in our
hearts. Yet we forget. We live powerless lives, fretting, worrying,
and walking backward.

What in your life makes you forget God's available power?
Look back on your life where you experienced the power of the
Lord. What happened? Why do you think God's strength helped
you through? What position were you in to receive God's power?

*Jesus, thank you that you sent your Holy Spirit to live within me, to give
me power to live this daily life. Help me not take that for granted, but to
remember that you are strong within me. Amen.*

Open Arms

> But you, dear friends, carefully build yourselves up in
> this most holy faith by praying in the Holy Spirit, staying
> right at the center of God's love, keeping your arms open
> and outstretched, ready for the mercy of our Master,
> Jesus Christ. This is the unending life, the real life.
>
> —JUDE VV. 20–21 MSG

Picture yourself open-armed in a field, spinning, laughing, and waiting. That's a small picture of the abundant life God desires for you, to be so fully healed from the past that today is full of anticipation of what God will say and do. Real life comes on the heels of understanding God's very present love for you, his affection transforming the way you view yourself.

In this Jude passage, there's a beckoning to a life of anticipation and readiness. We must be open to the next delightful encounter with Jesus. How? By building into our faith through prayer, understanding afresh how much God loves us, and then cultivating a holy openness.

Where are you right now? Do you sense unending life or do you feel small? Would others categorize you as someone who brims with joy? Would your friends call you someone who actively seeks Jesus?

The good news is that we live in the great right now. We have a choice to live this kind of exuberant life. It's simply a matter of making ourselves open-armed and open-hearted. It's God's job to fill our arms and hearts with himself. He promises to fill us until we overflow.

Jesus, I feel tired today. I want to be your daughter spinning with open arms in a field, ready to hear from you and be refreshed. Help me pursue you today. Amen.

Day of Reflection

I'm thanking you, God, from a full heart, I'm writing
the book on your wonders. I'm whistling, laughing, and
jumping for joy; I'm singing your song, High God.

—PSALM 9:1–2 MSG

JOYFUL, JOYFUL, WE ADORE THEE

Joyful, joyful, we adore Thee, God of Glory Lord of love;
Hearts unfold like flowers before Thee, opening to the sun above.
Melt the clouds of sin and sadness; drive the dark of doubt away;
Giver of immortal gladness, fill us with the light of day!

Mortals join the mighty chorus, which the Morning Stars began.
Father love is reigning o'er us, Brother love binds man to man.
Ever singing march we onward, victors in the midst of strife;
Joyful music lifts us sunward, in the triumph song of life!

—HENRY VAN DYKE, 1907

Your space—a poem, prayer, thoughts . . .

Heeding God's Voice

The stone the builders rejected has become the capstone;
the LORD has done this, and it is marvelous in our eyes.

—PSALM 118:22–23 NIV

L. L. Barkat, in her book *Stone Crossings: Finding Grace in Hard and Hidden Places*, wrote these penetrating words: "Or maybe, in a kind of selfish pride, I prefer the Master side of God better than the Child, so I look for the big ministry opportunities while neglecting hundreds of opportunities presented every day—in the fields of my common relationships."

Sometimes we prefer the spectacular to the mundane. And yet, God came to us in the form of a baby. He reconfigured his majesty in the womb of a peasant. He stooped lower than we'll ever stoop.

While you may dream of doing big things for God, don't forget the pebble, the humility, the stark reality of God becoming child. In the greatest reversal of history, God traded opulence for ordinariness—for the sake of us who walk with him.

Perhaps worshiping the baby in a manger has more to do with loving folks in ordinary, pedestrian ways. Of lowering ourselves enough to see who it is he places before us. If God so lowered himself to relate and commune with us, shouldn't we follow in his footsteps?

To stoop? To empty? To open our eyes to the divine possibilities in our daily lives?

Jesus, forgive me for trying to be grandiose. For forgetting the humility you portrayed by emptying yourself of accolades. What a holy risk you took by becoming a pebble. Help me to pick up a pebble today and consider what you've done. Help the weight of it in my pocket remind me to walk humbly and simply with you, being attuned to your whispers, no matter what they say. Amen.

God, Our Garden Supply

Now He who supplies seed to the sower and bread
for food will supply and multiply your seed for sowing
and increase the harvest of your righteousness.

—2 CORINTHIANS 9:10 NASB

Gardeners need several things to be successful. They need good dirt, full of minerals and fertility. They need sunshine and rain. And they need seeds to plant in the first place. The apostle Paul reminds us that God supplies everything we need to garden well in this life, to produce crops for Jesus.

Not only that, but he multiplies what little we have. We are like the boy who gave Jesus five loaves and two fishes, everything he had, and waited to see what would happen. In miraculous strength, Jesus multiplied that meager offering into a catered feast for a crowd of thousands. All that was necessary was the boy's willingness to entrust his last morsels to Jesus.

In that same manner, we offer our lives to Jesus—our hopes, ambitions, aspirations, worries, everything—knowing that he can take what little we have and make something beautiful. He will supply, and as his children, we trust he will supply.

Not only that but as we continue to depend on him, he promises to multiply our righteousness. This is something we can't do on our own. All we can do is obey him. But his sweet gift back to us is exponential growth.

Jesus, thank you that you provide the seed, the bread, and everything I need to bless others and grow. Please increase my righteousness. I choose to give you everything on my heart today. I pour it out as my offering to you. Amen.

Only by Faith

For in the gospel a righteousness from God is revealed,
a righteousness that is by faith from first to last, just
as it is written: "The righteous will live by faith."

—ROMANS 1:17 NIV

We don't get righteousness by conjuring up enough goodness to be good. We don't find it by pulling ourselves up by our bootstraps and determining never to sin. We don't live godly lives based on campaigns we embark on. Nor do we find true life in spiritual to-do lists.

The secret of righteousness is a little word called *faith*. Faith is simply believing. Whom or what we choose to believe in determines what kind of faith we have. If we believe in money to solve our problems, then we'll have a small faith based on something that can be taken away from us. But if we believe in God, our faith enlarges because he cannot be taken from us.

Paul tells us that we are to live solely by faith. We entrust ourselves to God, believing that he is great enough to help us live our daily lives. We give God our sin, and he grants us refreshing forgiveness. We give up trying to live the Christian life in our own strength and instead ask the Holy Spirit to live victoriously through us.

Walking by faith has more to do with believing in our capable God than trusting in our incapable selves.

Jesus, thank you that I don't have to conjure up righteousness by myself. Help me to shift from trying to live this life on my own, to giving you full control. I want to have faith in you. Amen.

You Smell Good (or Not)

But thank God! He has made us his captives and continues
to lead us along in Christ's triumphal procession. Now he
uses us to spread the knowledge of Christ everywhere, like
a sweet perfume. Our lives are a Christ-like fragrance rising
up to God. But this fragrance is perceived differently by
those who are being saved and by those who are perishing.
To those who are perishing, we are a dreadful smell of death
and doom. But to those who are being saved, we are a life-
giving perfume. And who is adequate for such a task as this?

—2 CORINTHIANS 2:14–16 NLT

Because Jesus has captured our hearts, he leads us toward great
adventure. Part of that adventure is his infusing us with his perfume. He gives us the Holy Spirit when we meet him, and the
fragrance of the Spirit lets other people know we are his.

In light of that, consider that there's nothing you need to do
to make yourself smell good. You simply do, by nature of Christ's
gift. What a relief knowing you don't have to try to make that
happen by yourself!

On the other hand, realize that while you smell amazing to
folks who believe in Jesus, the perfume turns rancid in the noses
of those who don't know him. Your Jesus scent becomes a sickly
reminder of where they are and where they're headed. So don't
take offense if someone recoils from you once they realize you're
a Christ follower. Just rejoice in the fact that you're truly wearing Jesus perfume. And see that as a sweet opportunity to share
about the most important relationship of your life.

*Jesus, thanks for the perfume. I so appreciate it. When others don't like
the scent, help me this week to share you and your sweet fragrance. Amen.*

Living Water

When a Samaritan woman came to draw water,
Jesus said to her, "Will you give me a drink?"
—JOHN 4:7 NIV

In John 4:5–30, we meet a woman drawing water from a well. At that well she encountered a man sitting nearby who forever changed her life.

The man asked her for a drink. Sounds simple enough, right? But then he said that God could give her living water, and she would never thirst again. Who wouldn't want that kind of water? Who wouldn't want the burden of daily responsibility lifted off her head, back, and shoulders—much less have the ache of her thirst relieved?

The Samaritan woman was searching for something that would quench her longing and perhaps fill her loneliness, but she obviously was having trouble finding it. No wonder Jesus' offer of living water captured her attention—and the empty cistern of her heart. We know it did, because she couldn't wait to tell others about him.

That's how it is when our hearts begin to overflow; we have enough to offer others. The woman at the well couldn't believe that Jesus would speak to her. Yet Christ knew everything the Samaritan woman had done (v. 30), and he still spoke to her. And, knowing everything about us, he still speaks to us. Jesus' offer to give us living water is as clear and pure now as it was that day at Jacob's well. He doesn't withhold his offer because we are empty, broken, or contaminated. In fact, he understands our condition, and he comes with the cleansing water of forgiveness, inviting us to drink and be forever refreshed.

Are you thirsty?

Lord, ladle to our lips your living water, that we might never seek fresh water again in the polluted pools of our own making. And may we go forth and splash the world. Amen.

Thrive Where He's Placed You

But now God has placed the members, each one
of them, in the body, just as He desired.

—1 CORINTHIANS 12:18 NASB

God arranges folks into churches and local congregations. Isn't that encouraging? Sometimes he places us in a church that needs our encouragement. Other times he gives us a church that serves to heal us from past ministry heartache. Sometimes he calls us to be agents of change, though that can be painful. No matter what the purpose, he does call each and every one of us to thrive in the midst of his people.

We were never called to isolation, to "me + Jesus." Instead the formula for exponential growth as a Christian is "us + Jesus." You and others and Jesus. Why? Because folks rub us the wrong way, and we find we have to exercise the muscle of forgiveness. Or other people have needs and we discover the joy of sacrificial giving. Or we find a circle of unlikely friends who walk us through dark times.

Some of us, though, have been burned. Folks in church have hurt us or our families. And we want to run one thousand miles away from that. Yet, God's paradoxical way of healing us from the wounds of caustic community is to use healthy community. It's a risk, to be sure, but we will never grow if we withdraw into bitterness and isolation.

May it be that we can embrace the community God gives us or have discernment to know when to seek healthy community.

Jesus, thank you that you've placed me in your body. I trust you to lead me to people whom I can love, serve, and sacrifice for. And where I'm scared to trust others, please lead me to healthy, loving people. Amen.

Day of Reflection

All those the Father gives me will come to me, and
whoever comes to me I will never drive away.

—JOHN 6:37 NIV

JUST AS I AM

Just as I am, without one plea,
But that Thy blood was shed for me,
And that Thou bidst me come to Thee,
O Lamb of God, I come, I come!

Just as I am and waiting not
to rid my soul of one dark blot;
To Thee whose blood can cleanse each spot,
O Lamb of God, I come, I come!

—CHARLOTTE ELLIOTT, 1836

Your space—a poem, prayer, thoughts . . .

Wait for God

Therefore the LORD waits to be gracious to
you, and therefore he exalts himself to show
mercy to you. For the LORD is a God of justice;
blessed are all those who wait for him.

—ISAIAH 30:18 ESV

What a beautiful picture in Isaiah that God exalts himself in order to show us mercy. He can't wait to be gracious to you. He is just and longs to give to those who wait for him.

When we wait for him, anticipating the next cool thing he will do, we live with a holy expectation. No longer are we living in the doldrums of today, but in the hope of the future. We're no longer shackled to the regret of the past, but instead look forward to the new things God will do.

This passage also shows God's happy anticipation of graciousness. He can't wait to give to us, particularly when we're patient. Like a parent who purchases a unique and perfect gift for a child on his or her birthday, God delights in the anticipation of the gift.

But sometimes we snoop. We want his gifts now. We don't want to wait. So we shortchange our blessing in our impatience. Today, choose to rest. Choose to believe that God has great things in store. And then ask him for deep, abiding patience.

Jesus, I want to learn the art of patience, of living in holy anticipation of what you will do. I'm normally not very patient, so I even cast my impatience at your feet. Please bless me, but please also help me wait patiently for your blessing. Amen.

Do Right

Who may worship in your sanctuary, LORD?
Who may enter your presence on your holy hill?
Those who lead blameless lives and do what is
right, speaking the truth from sincere hearts.

—PSALM 15:1–2 NLT

To be in close communion and communication with God, we need simply to do right. But what about when we fail? What if we don't lead a blameless life today? What if we speak untruth? Does that mean we're cut off from God's presence?

Yes and no. If sin has taken hold of us, we naturally are separated from God in terms of our fellowship with him. But in the larger sense, because of what Jesus did on the cross, we are never far away from God because of that sacrifice.

The solution? Apologize. When you've done something to hurt someone else or God or haven't lived in light of God's grace, tell him. Share what's on your heart, that you're sorry for walking the way you walked, and that you need his perfect forgiveness.

The beauty is that, because the Holy Spirit lives imbedded in our lives, God's presence is never far away. Our relationship can always, always be restored. Just as there may be discord between you and a child, nonetheless you love that child. And when the child comes back to you apologizing, the relationship is renewed.

Jesus, thank you for dying on the cross for my sins. I don't always lead a truthful life, nor do I always choose to do what is right. I'm sorry. I want to be in close contact with you, so I rest in your forgiveness right now. Amen.

No Meddling!

Do not contend with a man for no reason,
when he has done you no harm.

—PROVERBS 3:30 ESV

When she received secondhand information from a friend about another person, she got angry. Her first instinct was to attack, to fix the problem, to confront the friend of a friend. Thankfully, mercifully, she read this verse first.

When we jump into someone else's fight, guess what happens? We get beat up. When it's not our fight to begin with, we only add to the problem and usually make it worse by intervening. The more people get involved, the more danger we run into for slander and gossip and blowing the whole situation out of control.

This doesn't mean we can't be a sounding board for our friend. Nor does it mean we can't pray. Both those practices are healthy and needed. But unless someone is breaking the law or causing true harm, it's not your fight to get involved.

When you're trying to discern whether a fight is yours, pray. Seek God to see if he is directing you to get involved. Share the situation privately, without names, to a spiritual mentor. The key is this: don't meddle in someone else's fight.

Jesus, help me know when it's wise to help a friend in a fight and when it's right to back away and let you take over. I don't want to contend with someone who hasn't directly hurt me. Keep me prayerful and available. Amen.

Seeing God as God

Hear, and I will speak; I will question you, and you
make it known to me. I had heard of you by the
hearing of the ear, but now my eye sees you; therefore
I despise myself, and repent in dust and ashes.

—JOB 42:4–6 ESV

Job lost everything: family, fortune, health, perspective. Before
he did, he heard God. And in that hearing, God counted him as
a godly, amazing man. And yet God allowed Satan to sift him, to
take much away from him.

During his time of testing and pain, when his wife told him
to curse God and choose death, when his friends said he must've
brought all that pain on himself, Job remained steadfast. He
stayed close to God even though the trials bewildered him.

But at the end of Job, when he comes to the end of himself, he
reveals something he learned through all that testing. He learned
he only knew God through one sense: hearing. After the trials,
he saw God.

We may despise the trials we walk through, but take heart.
At the end of the trial, you will see God in ways you've never seen
him before. You will know him more deeply. You will realize that
he is God and you are not.

*Jesus, I want to have a better perspective the next time trials come knock-
ing at my door. Help me to realize that the more I endure, the more I will
experience you. Amen.*

The Shame Monster

There is therefore now no condemnation
to those who are in Christ Jesus.

—ROMANS 8:1

The reason it is so hard for us to admit to the secrets hidden in our hearts is that we're ashamed of them. We think that if we keep denying our ugly stuff, then maybe we'll look better than we fear we actually are. We keep it a secret. And those secrets can fester and swell until they consume our happiness and our hope. No matter how carefully we guard the secrets, no matter how creatively we scramble in our efforts to look good, we still suffer from that deep-seated sense of shame and will do almost anything to avoid it. But here's an important truth: shame is not what we do; it's who we perceive ourselves to be.

Shame is a core indictment of our very essence. But when our secrets become too powerful, shame becomes an identity, a state in which we feel different, despairing, and helpless. It then creates an interior environment in which the balance is lost between the healthy shame and unhealthy shame. This kind of unhealthy shame indicates that we've lost our true identity and value as God's creation whom he called into being out of love and with pleasure.

In spite of the preaching of grace, shame is still an imperious presence in many of our hearts and our churches today. The good news is there is a cure for imperfection that leads to shame, which causes us to live in denial and fear. The cure begins when we open our hearts to the light of God's love—and share what's hidden in that dark, secret corner.

Jesus, help me to remember that my identity is in you. Thank you that you have paid for my sins on the cross and I am now free to serve you with joy. When I am overtaken by shame, help me to remember your words: "It is finished." Amen.

God Is Near

The Lord is near to the brokenhearted and
saves those who are crushed in spirit.

—PSALM 34:18 NASB

When we walk through trials, we sometimes forget God's nearness. Yet this scripture is clear: God is actually near brokenhearted and crushed people. In the midst of pain, we always have a choice—to access God's presence, or buckle down and try to grit our teeth through it.

While we may be applauded for our stoicism and our ability to tackle pain on our own, God promises us so much more than a grit-your-way-through-trials life. He walks beside us during stress. When we feel utterly crushed by circumstances or people, he rescues us.

In light of the New Testament and Jesus' life, we have even more assurance of this truth. Because Jesus walked the earth as a man, he experienced every single pain known to man. He was abandoned, mocked, in pain, hungry, tired, overwhelmed, forsaken, gossiped about, envied, backstabbed, and ultimately murdered. Because of all that, he is uniquely equipped to help us when we walk through our own painful valleys.

Ask yourself, *What does it cost me to try to do this all on my own?* And, *What do I gain by running away from God in my trial?* Answering those questions may help unearth shreds of pride and self-sufficiency in your life.

You were not made to walk alone. If you feel alone right now, get on your knees and ask God to come near to you and rescue you.

Jesus, I'm tired. And I feel distant from you. But you promise to be near to me and save me when I feel utterly crushed. I choose right now to hope in you, to trust you for your perfect empathy and strength. Amen.

Day of Reflection

He had a dream in which he saw a stairway resting
on the earth, with its top reaching to heaven, and the
angels of God were ascending and descending on it.

—GENESIS 28:12 NIV

NEARER, MY GOD, TO THEE

Nearer, my God, to Thee, nearer to Thee,
E'en though it be a cross that raiseth me!
Still all my song shall be, Nearer, my God, to Thee
Nearer, my God, to Thee, Nearer to Thee!

—SARAH F. ADAMS, 1840

Your space—a poem, prayer, thoughts . . .

Religious Sales Talk

Don't let yourselves get taken in by religious smooth
talk. God gets furious with people who are full of
religious sales talk but want nothing to do with
him. Don't even hang around people like that.

—EPHESIANS 5:6—7 MSG

There are people around the church who are wolves in sheep's
clothing. They talk a good talk and say all the right things, but
their hearts are far from Jesus. Paul instructs us to have nothing
to do with fakers like this. Our response to charlatans is to stay
away.

When people have religious smooth talk but don't know
God, they are all about their agenda and fame. They want to be
praised for what they know, and they long to be served because
of their eloquence.

How do you spot someone like this? It's not easy. Usually
they are marked by accepting others' praise without giving it to
Jesus. Or they say all the right holy words, but you catch them
constantly living differently as hypocrites. Or they're enslaved to
popularity or money.

Genuine believers are those who say things and mean them.
Their words on the outside match their hearts on the inside, and
their actions confirm their beliefs. May it be that we are not full
of smooth talk, trying to decorate our outsides, but that we are
authentic, showing more of Jesus and less of our abilities.

*Jesus, help me discern folks who want nothing to do with you but sweet
talk as if they do. I need your perspective. And please enable me to be
authentic, where my inside and outside match, and my walk confirms my
talk. Amen.*

My Pain + His Comfort = Your Comfort

Blessed be the God and Father of our Lord Jesus Christ,
the Father of mercies and God of all comfort, who
comforts us in all our affliction so that we will be able
to comfort those who are in any affliction with the
comfort with which we ourselves are comforted by God.

—2 CORINTHIANS 1:3–4 NASB

God is so good. He comforts us in every circumstance, not only
for our own good, but also for the sake of others. His comfort, no
matter what form or for whatever malady, is universal. In other
words, we don't have to experience the same heartache as our
friends to be able to come alongside them.

We don't have to be alcoholics to empathize with alcoholics. We don't have to be sexually abused to comfort those who
have experienced that devastation. We don't have to have walked
through divorce to shoulder the pain of a friend's divorce.

The important words in this passage are *all* and *any*. God
comforts us in all our pain so that we can love well those who
have any pain. Once we've experienced God's salving comfort,
we are uniquely qualified to be his ambassadors of comfort to
anyone walking through trial.

In light of that, see your pain and God's subsequent comfort
as training grounds to become the hands and feet of Jesus to this
comfort-needy world.

*Jesus, thank you that you comfort me in every single trial I face. I grab
for your hand right now, trusting that you will comfort me deeply. Make
me empathetic and responsive to those who are walking through their own
pain. And may I be an ambassador of comfort this week. Amen.*

A Holy Flashlight

All Scripture is inspired by God and is useful to teach
us what is true and to make us realize what is wrong
in our lives. It corrects us when we are wrong and
teaches us to do what is right. God uses it to prepare
and equip his people to do every good work.

—2 TIMOTHY 3:16–17 NLT

The Bible is not merely an instruction manual. It is a living, breathing document that reflects the heart and words of God. Because it contains his perspective, when we read it and devour it, we begin to see our lives in light of his viewpoint.

The Bible cannot help us live great lives. Only the Holy Spirit working within us can do that. But it can be a holy flashlight on our hearts, exposing the things we'd rather hide, highlighting areas of weakness, or revealing our motivations. It instructs us in every area—money, relationships, time management, family, work, and play.

God provided the Bible as an equipper. It's the toolbox we go to when we're bewildered or needy. But it's not helpful to us if we ignore it or don't put into practice what we've learned from it. To be a blessing to us, the Bible must be our passion, and we have a joyful obligation to do what it commands.

Jesus, thank you for the Bible. I want to be passionate about its message. I want to be a follower who actually obeys what it says. Help me be receptive to the Bible's ability to shed light on the dark areas of my life. Amen.

Forgiving Yourself

As far as the east is from the west, so far has
he removed our transgressions from us.

—PSALM 103:12 NIV

Have you messed up? Do you wonder if God still hears and cares about you? Perhaps you are ashamed to even face what you have done. It may have been something that caused harm not just to you but to others. You may fear facing the truth and beginning the process of restoration because it seems like such a long path home. If so, have the faith to remember that with God all things can be made new. Your past is just that. But your future in him is limitless.

All God looks for is a desire to begin moving in the right direction, and he will be there. And not just passively but waiting to embrace you. Just say the name of Jesus, and the condemnation of the enemy, who would love to keep you in the belly of the whale for the rest of your life, will have to go. You are loved; you are loved; you are loved!

You have to be willing to forgive not just others but yourself too. Of all of us who run into the arms of a gracious, forgiving Father this day, you might be the only one individually named on the invitation. Welcome home!

Lord, thank you for healing all wounds. Help me to remember that you
died so that I could be made new again. Thank you for forgiveness. Amen.

Fruitful

My Father is glorified by this, that you bear
much fruit, and so prove to be My disciples.

—JOHN 15:8 NASB

God is most glorified when we bear a lot of fruit. The first part of this verse implies, then, that our prayers shouldn't be for favor or escaping our lot, but for fruitful lives. God delights to answer prayers like, "Jesus, will you please help me grow today? I want to bear more fruit for you."

In order to be fruitful, the key is the word *abide*. Because we can do nothing significant in the kingdom of God in our own efforts, the way to growth comes through our relationship with Jesus Christ. Abide means to spend time with, to be near, to dwell with. So the more we're near to Jesus and his ways, listening to his voice, the more we'll produce fruit.

What would it look like in your life if you were your most fruitful? What would change to make that happen? What prevents you from making that change today?

Remember that Jesus is amazing and helpful and endearing and loving. When we're near to him, we receive all of his direction and comfort. It's not a sacrifice to abide in him if we view it that way, and the by-product will be fruitful, living the life of a disciple.

Jesus, I want to be fruitful. I want to learn the art of abiding with you. Would you please make my life fruitful? Forgive me for trying to produce fruit on my own. I realize that my nearness to you is what makes me fruitful. Amen.

He Moves You

> I will give you a new heart and put a new spirit in you; I
> will remove from you your heart of stone and give you a
> heart of flesh. And I will put my Spirit in you and move
> you to follow my decrees and be careful to keep my laws.
>
> —EZEKIEL 36:26–27 NIV

In the Old Testament, the Holy Spirit fell upon people for a specific task or period of time. Never was someone fully filled at all times. We as New Testament believers forget how amazing it is that we have 100 percent access to the Holy Spirit at all times.

In this passage, Ezekiel foreshadows this delightful gift. Instead of a dead heart, weakened and atrophied by sin, God will give his children himself! He'll take out the decay and replace it with life. And not only that, he will give us the will and desire and power to live out a godly, infectious life.

Take a moment to think about the enormity of that. God in you. With you. Always empowering. Always listening. Always pardoning. There is great joy and hope in that realization.

If you're feeling behind or lacking or needy, spend some time right now thanking God for granting you the Holy Spirit, the gift he first gave the moment you surrendered your life to him. Ask him to show you specifically this week how powerful yet intimate he is. If you're having a hard time obeying, ask him to move you to follow him.

Jesus, I want to be moved by your Holy Spirit this week. Convince me afresh of the reality of the Spirit's presence in my life. I am grateful that he lives within me. Amen.

Day of Reflection

If you remain in me and my words remain in you, ask whatever you wish, and it will be done for you.

—JOHN 15:7 NIV

ABIDE WITH ME

Abide with me!
Fast falls the even tide.
The darkness deepens; Lord with me abide!

When other helpers fail and comforts flee,
Help of the helpless,
O abide with me!

—HENRY F. LYTE, 1847

Your space—a poem, prayer, thoughts . . .

Pray and Praise

Is anyone among you suffering? Let him pray. Is anyone
cheerful? Let him sing praise. Is anyone among you sick?
Let him call for the elders of the church, and let them pray
over him, anointing him with oil in the name of the Lord.

—JAMES 5:13–14 ESV

The solution to our problems and the aches and pains of our
friends and family is always prayer and praise. Often our first
response to suffering is whining to others or uttering complaints
under our breath. Sometimes it's to push against the suffering or
allow it to make us bitter.

James encourages us instead to be proactive with our pain
and the pain of others. He instructs us to pray if we are suffering,
to give it all to Jesus. And if we happen to be joyful in the midst
of our days, to offer that joy to God as an offering of praise. We
neglect God if we don't pray or praise in sadness or joy.

The end result of prayer and praise is peace. When we pray
for ourselves, our burdens lift and we sense God's presence.
When we pray for others, we lift the burden from their shoulders
and take a bit of it on ourselves while giving the rest to Jesus.

When we praise God in quiet moments of the day, we redirect our hearts away from our own agendas and self-absorption
and place our minds fully on God, his beauty, his provision, and
his protection.

*Jesus, I want to be someone who prays and praises. Whatever comes my
way today, help me to give it all to you, to thank you for whatever you
send. I want to be fully connected to you. Amen.*

Selfish Ambition

Some indeed preach Christ from envy and
rivalry, but others from good will. The latter do
it out of love . . . The former proclaim Christ
out of selfish ambition, not sincerely.

—PHILIPPIANS 1:15–17 ESV

Have you ever been puzzled by these verses? What does it mean
to preach Jesus with rivalry or selfish ambition? Isn't preaching
Jesus devoid of those things?

Preaching Jesus with selfish ambition means folks use Jesus
to further themselves. They use the platform of Jesus to better
themselves or gain financially because of him.

Going a little deeper into our own hearts, though, we must
look in the mirror and ask ourselves, when do we preach Jesus out
of selfish ambition? Do we ever try to appear more spiritual than
we are to attract friends? Do we put on Jesus masks hoping others
don't see who we really are?

We preach Jesus with good will when we are wholly who we
are, humble, warts and all, when we truly want Jesus elevated. We
preach Jesus with a sincere heart when we utter words that John
the Baptist uttered—about our decreasing and Jesus increasing.
When we fret far more about Jesus getting the glory than finagling our own applause, we preach Jesus out of love.

*Jesus, I want to preach you with a good heart, the right motives—out of
love for you. Show me if there are any parts of me that use you for my
gain, or where I hide to try to impress others with my Christianity. No,
I want it all to be for you alone. Amen.*

No Other God

I am the LORD, and there is no other; apart from me
there is no God. I will strengthen you, though you have
not acknowledged me, so that from the rising of the sun
to the place of its setting men may know there is none
besides me. I am the LORD, and there is no other.

—ISAIAH 45:5–6 NIV

Resting in the truth that there is no other God will revolutionize our walk with him. Why? Because we won't turn to false gods or idols to satisfy us. Though we live in a modern culture where idols are not easily discerned, we actually are surrounded by thousands of gods.

The god of culture. The god of money. The god of youth. The god of fame. The god of career. The god of beauty. The god of skinny. The god of quick fixes. The god of everything I want. The god of I want it now.

All these gods vie for our attention. But Isaiah reminds us that there is no other God. And that God is available to us to give us power to live an obedient, reverent life. He who created the sun and controls its rising and setting deserves our adoration and allegiance. He deserves our full attention.

Jesus, there is no other God. I know that. Forgive me when I try to fill myself up with lesser gods. I don't want to live for stuff or looks or fame or success. What I really want is to wholly live for you. Amen.

Me Monster or God Glorifier

*Not to us, O LORD, not to us, but to Your name give glory
because of Your lovingkindness, because of Your truth.*

—PSALM 115:1 NASB

A "Me Monster" is someone who uses the words *I* and *me* in every conversation. They seek ways to insert themselves into important crowds. They find ways to talk about their accomplishments, accolades, and awards. They seldom listen to others, and they certainly don't trumpet someone else's wins. And they can't bring themselves to acknowledge God.

But the psalmist here speaks of a different kind of person. A God Glorifier. A person who orients her conversations not on her own accomplishments, but on God's. A God Glorifier seeks to chat about God's lovingkindness, His steadfast, amazing love. She loves God's truth. And if glory comes her way through praise, she is careful to thank the person giving the praise, but gently redirects that worship to the One who truly deserves it.

God deserves to receive our praise. Because he utters truth and showers us with love, he should be the center of every conversation we have. May it not be that we speak only to share our brilliance, but that we find ways to point to the Brilliant One.

Jesus, I don't want to be a Me Monster. Make me a God Glorifier, one who actively praises how amazing you are. Amen.

Drinking in the Fresh Air

In the beginning God created the heavens and the earth.

—GENESIS 1:1 NASB

Creation causes us to stand and celebrate. Not to worship creation, which we willingly applaud, but to worship the Creator—he who was before the sun, moon, and stars.

God's handiwork declares him day after day, and the declarations become our education, our inspiration, and our restoration. When we have ears to hear and eyes to see, we're left breathless by his visual power displayed throughout the universe, and we're silenced when we detect his whispers in a meandering brook. That a holy God would speak through river pebbles to our stony hearts is humbling.

People travel the world over to applaud creation's art and to stand amazed when they visit Victoria Falls, the Grand Canyon, Mount Everest, Niagara Falls, Antarctica, and the ocean's edge. Just think. All that and more was wrought from God's creative hand with us in mind.

If you ever want to brighten your day, just head outside where you can see the trees, birds, flowers, and hear the church bells wafting favorite old hymns through the maple's branches. Remember running barefoot in the cool grass as a kid? Not so much anymore. But we should never tire of the restoration to mind and soul that comes with a good dose of nature. Take two swigs and call the doctor in the morning.

Lord, your majesty is found all throughout the earth. Thank you for the beauty of your creation. As I take in all that you have created, bring to my mind your great love for me. Amen.

Loyalty

*For the eyes of the LORD run to and fro throughout
the whole earth, to show Himself strong on
behalf of those whose heart is loyal to Him.*

—2 CHRONICLES 16:9

God looks for loyal people. The Scripture today says he actively searches for folks like that. And when he finds them, what does he do? He shows himself strong on their behalf.

What does it look like to have a heart that is genuinely loyal to God? It means we spend time studying who God is, learning what he loves, then doing things that please him. It means we discover what breaks his heart and try to alleviate that pain by addressing injustice. It means we cultivate an intimate friendship with God. It means being faithful in the small tasks he assigns us so he can entrust us with bigger things. It means telling God our secrets, entrusting our reputations to him, and taking moments throughout the day, telling him how much we love him.

If we draw near to God, he will draw near to us. And as he does that, he shows himself strong in our lives. To experience more and more of this amazing strength, we must learn to let go of our self-will and control and entrust everything to him.

God is not after perfect women who appear to have everything all together. He simply looks for loyal women whose hearts beat for him. Which will you be?

*Jesus, help me to have a truly loyal heart that beats for you. Thank you
for pursuing people whose hearts are fully yours. That takes the pressure
of me to perform or act like a perfect Christian. I just need more of you.
Amen.*

Day of Reflection

. . . and on His head are many crowns . . .
—REVELATION 19:12

CROWN HIM WITH MANY CROWNS

Crown Him with many crowns,
the Lamb upon His throne.
Hark! How the heavenly anthem drowns
All music but its own!

Awake my soul and sing
Of Him who died for Thee;
And hail Him as thy matchless King
through all eternity.

—MATTHEW BRIDGES / GODFREY THRING, 1851

Your space—a poem, prayer, thoughts . . .

Welcome Trials as Friends

When all kinds of trials and temptations crowd into your
lives my brothers, don't resent them as intruders, but
welcome them as friends! Realise [*sic*] that they come to test
your faith and to produce in you the quality of endurance.

—JAMES 1:2 PHILLIPS

J. B. Phillips translated this familiar passage in James with a perfect metaphor—that of intruders and friends. And he uses the
word *crowd* to describe trials and temptations. Isn't that the way
of life? We're walking along our merry way only to be inundated
with way too much pain and worry.

James' heart in these verses is to change the way you think
about those trials. Instead of barring the door and pressing
against it hoping they'll go away, we're given the uncanny picture
of friendship.

Welcome trials as friends? You mean shake hands with them,
give them tea, and let them have dessert? How can that be? Why
would we ever want to welcome trials as friends? Isn't that pure
masochism?

The secret to that conundrum is in the last part of the verse.
Once we realize that trials are the means God uses to grow us
and make us enduringly strong, we can then welcome them as
friends.

*Jesus, I don't see trials as friends right now. I'd rather see them as awful
intruders bent on my destruction. Reorient my thinking so I shake hands
with the trials, befriending them, so I can grow deep and wide and strong.
Amen.*

God Means It for Good

As for you, you meant evil against me, but God
meant it for good in order to bring about this
present result, to preserve many people alive.

—GENESIS 50:20 NASB

Joseph said these words to his brothers in the book of Genesis after he'd become Pharaoh's righthand man. His journey to this place was full of deception and manipulation on the part of his brothers who sold him into slavery, triggering a long struggle in Potiphar's house and then in prison.

Joseph could've said so many things. He could've rightfully condemned his brothers for selling him into slavery. But he didn't. Instead he looked back at his story from God's viewpoint. He saw that although his brothers did mean to harm him, God used their very defiance to bring about something very good.

Which proves to us that God isn't always interested in making our circumstances the way we want them. He sees the entire picture for everyone. Not merely interested in Joseph's happiness, God brought him along the journey for the sake of Israel's good, to save many starving people.

When you're in the midst of a trial, remember that God means good. It may not feel good, but ultimately he has the greater good of the entire world in mind. God will do what he wants and accomplish things far beyond our comprehension if we let him.

Jesus, I have had people be mean to me and hurt me. Help me to see your hand in that. I need to understand better that you are out for the greater good, not necessarily my relief and comfort in the moment. Train me to trust you even now. Amen.

Come as You Are

O LORD, how my adversaries have increased! Many are
rising up against me. Many are saying of my soul, "There
is no deliverance for him in God." But You, O LORD, are a
shield about me, My glory, and the One who lifts my head.

PSALM 3:1–3 NASB

A passenger in a taxi leaned over to ask the driver a question and
tapped him on the shoulder. The driver screamed, lost control
of the cab, nearly hit a bus, drove up over the curb, and stopped
just inches from a large plate-glass window. For a few moments
everything was silent in the cab, then the still-shaking driver
said, "I'm sorry, but you scared me to death." The frightened passenger apologized to the driver and said he didn't realize a mere
tap on the shoulder could scare him so much. The driver replied,
"No, no, I'm sorry. It's entirely my fault. It's just that today is my
first day driving a cab . . . I've been driving a hearse for the last
twenty-five years."

Sometimes we act as if God might be like that cabdriver.
Were we to tell him our secrets, share with him how we really
feel, he might be so startled and horrified by what we say he'd
jump the curb and hit a light pole.

David, writer of the Psalms, did not tiptoe around God out of
fear that God would judge him, reject him, or hold his thoughts
against him. David whined, fussed, and praised, depending on
how he felt and what his circumstances were. He was secure in
his relationship with God.

David modeled for us the kind of honest communication it is
possible to have with God, the kind that trusts God to receive our
feelings and not judge us for having them.

*Lord, you know me fully, in all my sin, but you still chose to save me. You
still chose to die for me. Teach me to come to you freely and openly. Amen.*

He Carries Our Sorrows

Surely he has borne our griefs and carried our sorrows; yet
we esteemed him stricken, smitten by God, and afflicted.

—ISAIAH 53:4 ESV

Think about your closest friend. What do you like about her?
How has she been a blessing to you? No doubt she's learned the
secret of bearing your grief when you've walked through a dark
time. And she has an uncanny way of making you see your painful situation in a new light, carrying away the pain.

Your closest friend is a sweet representation of God. He, too,
wants to bear our grief, to shoulder the pain that life inevitably
brings. He knows how to carry away our sorrows because he
created us and knows us intimately. Because of that, we should
praise him.

But we must remember that when Jesus came to earth to bear
our grief and empathize with our sorrows, he paid a tremendous
price. Because he didn't come as a conquering king, folks didn't
consider him favored by God. He not only bore our grief, but he
eventually bore God's wrath against sin on the cross.

Jesus did all that for us, for the sake of God's renown, for
redemption. Because of that, he deserves our affection. Much
like we have deep love for our closest friend, our friendship with
God must have depth and respect.

*Jesus, thank you for suffering on my behalf. I'll never, ever get over that.
I want to see you as my best friend. I love you. I choose today to move
closer to you. Amen.*

No More Tears

Therefore, they are before the throne of God and serve
him day and night in his temple; and he who sits on the
throne will shelter them with his presence. Never again
will they hunger; never again will they thirst. The sun
will not beat down on them, nor any scorching heat.
For the Lamb at the center of the throne will be their
shepherd; he will lead them to springs of living water.
And God will wipe away every tear from their eyes.

—REVELATION 7:15–17 NIV

On this earth, we will cry. We'll experience hunger. We'll sweat.
But that is not the reality of the new earth promised to us in the
book of Revelation. God will create a new reality where Jesus will
be the center of the entire cosmos, portrayed as a lamb leading
his people toward eternal refreshment.

It's hard to picture that kind of joyful peace when we're in the
middle of stress on this earth. It's hard to envision a tearless eternity when our eyes spill right now. It's hard to picture abundance
when our lives feel barren. It's hard to envision refreshment when
we're burdened by money issues. But not impossible.

The reality is this life is just a vapor. The problems we face
today will be faded memories in light of Jesus' cleansing, healing
presence. We have a sure hope that pain will eventually cease.
Living in light of that will help us endure whatever it is we face
right now.

*Jesus, help me remember the new heavens and the new earth, where my
tears are wiped away and all that pain is washed in cleansing streams.
Right now I'm overwhelmed, but help me realize its insignificance in
light of eternity with you. Amen.*

God, Our Defender

Yes, you came when I called; you told me, "Do not fear." Lord, you are my lawyer! Plead my case! For you have redeemed my life.

—LAMENTATIONS 3:57–58 NLT

When we are wronged, we tend to want to clarify our case. We want everyone to know that what we did or didn't do had been misunderstood. We like to plead on our behalf for the sake of our reputation.

But Jeremiah the prophet says something entirely freeing in this passage. God is our lawyer. He is our defender. We don't need to fret about our reputation or run around micromanaging it. The question becomes, do we trust him as our lawyer or do we take our case back?

What would your life look like today if you truly believed God was your defender? And not only does he plead on your behalf, but he also takes your broken life and redeems it. Because of that truth, God tells us, "Do not fear."

Fear rushes back in when we wrestle the pleading and redemption from God, when we try to live in our own strength and become our own savior. A life like that is constantly lived in fear because everything is on our shoulders.

Instead, why not let God be both your lawyer and redeemer today? He is more than capable. You can put your hope in him.

Jesus, sometimes it seems easier to defend myself to others, or to try to make my life right in my own strength. But right now I want you to be my lawyer and redeemer. Take the stress from me. Be my strength. Amen.

Day of Reflection

Do not be anxious about anything, but in every
situation, by prayer and petition, with thanksgiving,
present your requests to God. And the peace of
God, which transcends all understanding, will guard
your hearts and your minds in Christ Jesus.

—PHILIPPIANS 4:6–7

WHAT A FRIEND WE HAVE IN JESUS

What a Friend we have in Jesus,
All our sins and griefs to bear!
What a privilege to carry,
Everything to God in prayer!

Oh, what peace we often forfeit.
Oh what needless pain we bear.
All because we do not carry
Everything to God in prayer!

—JOSEPH M. SCRIVEN, 1855

Your space—a poem, prayer, thoughts . . .

Oh, How God Gives!

For the LORD grants wisdom! From his mouth come
knowledge and understanding. He grants a treasure
of common sense to the honest. He is a shield to those
who walk with integrity. He guards the paths of the
just and protects those who are faithful to him.

—PROVERBS 2:6–8 NLT

God is the supreme, final source for wisdom, knowledge, understanding, and common sense. And yet he is often not the source
we go to first when we face a problem. We read books. We consult
friends. We try new paths on our own. We look to the business
world. And yet God promises that he will supply the knowledge
we need to live our lives.

In this verse, the promise is that he chooses to grant what we
need. In addition, when we walk closely with him and consult
with him daily, he promises to shield us from the crazy world,
particularly when we actively walk with integrity. When we are
faithful, he protects us.

How can we slow down enough to remember that God will
give us treasures like these? What can we do that will help us
automatically turn to him when we are perplexed or befuddled?
What would it look like if we viewed God's wisdom as the most
precious commodity on earth?

Spend a moment listing your current stresses to God. Ask
for discernment and common sense. And as you ask, genuinely
desire God's response. Remember, he loves to come alongside his
daughters.

*Jesus, I love that you grant wisdom. I need it today, along with a huge
dose of common sense. Please shield me and protect me from myself, my
agenda, and my ways of doing things. I want to live a you-inspired life.
Amen.*

The Next Generation

And even when I am old and gray, O God, do not
forsake me, until I declare Your strength to this
generation, Your power to all who are to come.

—PSALM 71:18 NASB

Despite our desire to turn back the clock, the truth is we're getting older every day. And hopefully, as we grow older, our souls are becoming more beautiful and our minds wiser. As we grow up and learn to follow Jesus more closely, we have a mandate from God: to tell about him and his ways to the next generation.

In this verse, the psalmist encourages us to declare God's strength to the next generation. This means we've had a lifetime of understanding that we are weak and he is strong, that anything we do in our own strength is nothing compared to the life lived in his power.

Determine today to tell your story of God's strength to the next generation. This may be your children, kids in your church, or your neighborhood friends. They are the future, and if they meet Jesus and live in his strength, they become the ambassadors to the following generations in our stead.

Sharing Jesus with those younger than you is a strategic, godly investment in the future of the kingdom of God. Even if you're afraid or timid, choose to love those younger folks God puts in your life, and as you love them, tell your story.

Jesus, I do want to share your strength with the next generation, but I don't know exactly how to go about that. Help me to see opportunities to share you, then take advantage of them. I'd love to see your kingdom advance beyond me. Amen.

Be Humble

In the same way, you who are younger, submit
yourselves to your elders. All of you, clothe yourselves
with humility toward one another, because, "God
opposes the proud but shows favor to the humble."

—1 PETER 5:5 NIV

It's always right to be kind to those older than us and offer
respect. It's also a sign of that respect when we choose to submit
ourselves to those who hold the office of "elder" in our church.
They are responsible for overseeing our well-being and growth,
so to submit to them means growing.

But beyond our relationships with older people and church
elders, Peter gives us a pathway to every single relationship in our
lives. It's called humility. If you are a humble person, you've recognized your tendency toward pride and have actively chosen to
turn away from that.

You're more interested in hearing than saying. You're more
excited about serving than being served. You're passionate about
seeing others promoted instead of yourself. You pray for others
when you'd rather be preoccupied with yourself.

To be humble is to be in God's favor. But to give into pride
places you squarely in God's opposition. Which place would you
rather be?

*Jesus, I admit that sometimes I'd rather have my own way. I'd like things
done my way. But instead of that today, help me to choose to be humble
instead. To take the last seat. To joyfully promote others. To walk the way
you walked. Amen.*

Taking Off the Mask

But whenever anyone turns to the
Lord, the veil is taken away.

—2 CORINTHIANS 3:16 NIV

We are all are broken at some level. Some of us know it and have no idea what to do about it, while some are deeply unaware, although at times we feel a distant rumble in our souls. To each one of us, God's answer is Christ.

When our loving Father saw the pathetic attempt Adam and Eve made to cover themselves, he said, "That will never do." Scripture says, "And the Lord God made clothing from animal skins for Adam and his wife" (Genesis 3:21 NLT). They would indeed be covered, but something had to die to accomplish that. Such a beautiful foreshadowing of Christ, who would shed his blood to cover us all!

You don't have to hide anymore. You are loved as you are. You needn't wear a mask; God sees you as you are. You don't have to pretend to be okay; Christ is our righteousness, and we get to be human after all, to be real, to be loved, to be free. You don't have to deny the truth; the Lord knows it all and offers you Christ. If you will dare to try on this outfit that God has made for you, in no time at all you will begin to see the truth: it's a perfect fit.

Lord, thank you for accepting me as I am but also for loving me enough to refuse to let me stay that way. Help me to remember that I don't have to wear a mask for you or for others. Amen.

He Loves Us

Jesus looked at him and loved him. "One thing you lack," he
said. "Go, sell everything you have and give to the poor, and
you will have treasure in heaven. Then come, follow me."

—MARK 10:21 NIV

When you think about this story of the rich young ruler who
tells Jesus he's obeyed every command, you might forget this
line, "Jesus looked at him and loved him." Jesus loved that man.
And he knew what enslaved him. So he offered him complete joy
and freedom by giving him the perfect remedy: get rid of what
enslaves you.

The man didn't perceive of Jesus' words as loving. Instead
he loved Jesus less and coveted stuff more. Or perhaps he felt he
needed the security of wealth more than he needed Jesus.

It's important to note that Jesus' love for us sometimes looks
like discipline. But inevitably, the hard things he asks us to do
are for our good. In like manner, when we love the people in our
lives, we won't always say things they'll perceive as kind. The
most loving thing we can do is set good boundaries and help our
friends or family members see that the things they cling to will
be their ruin.

It is loving to rescue others from their vices, to speak the
truth in utter love. Jesus did here, and he set a perfect example for
us as we navigate our relationships.

*Jesus, thank you that you love me. I don't always see your commands to
me as easy or even an indication of your love. Instead I see what I'm asked
to give up. Instead of seeing the lack, Lord, help me to understand your
love behind the words, and help me extend truly loving words to others.
Amen.*

When God Smiles

The LORD bless you, and keep you. The LORD make His
face shine upon you, and be gracious to you; The LORD
lift up His countenance on you, and give you peace.

—NUMBERS 6:24–26 NASB

How many of us picture God radiant over us? That his face lights up at the thought of us? It's hard to believe that God has that kind of sure affection toward each one of us. After all, we're well aware of our frailty, neediness, and failure. Why would a perfect God smile when thinking of us?

To understand that kind of extravagant love better, consider how a parent loves a child. That child may climb the furniture, tell lies, or smear pudding on the wall, yet still the parent loves. She disciplines, yes, but she continues to love. No matter how far a child strays or rebels, the constancy of the parent's love lives on.

Earthly parents may grow weary. They may even stop loving. But God in his infinite kindness and patience bears with us even when we're smearing pudding all over our lives. God blesses you with life. He keeps you close to him. He shines his radiant face upon you. He graces you. His expression brightens when you come to mind. And above all that, he gives peace to you.

Do you struggle believing that today? It's the truth. God created you and loves you wildly. Rest there with that hope right now.

Jesus, is it true? Do you really smile down upon me? Sometimes I don't feel that way. Would you help me understand your smile and favor and grace in a tangible way today? Amen.

Day of Reflection

I pray that you, being rooted and established in love, may have power, together with all the Lord's holy people, to grasp how wide and long and high and deep is the love of Christ, and to know this love that surpasses knowledge.

—EPHESIANS 3:17–19 NIV

JESUS LOVES ME

Jesus loves me! This I know,
For the Bible tells me so;
Little ones to Him belong,
They are weak but He is strong.
Yes, Jesus loves me.
The Bible tells me so.

—ANNA WARNER, 1860

Your space—a poem, prayer, thoughts . . .

Kids Get God

Assuredly, I say to you, unless you are converted
and become as little children, you will by no means
enter the kingdom of heaven. Therefore whoever
humbles himself as this little child is the greatest
in the kingdom of heaven. Whoever receives one
little child like this in My name receives Me.

—MATTHEW 18:3–5

In this passage, Jesus reminds the disciples that unless they have a childlike view of the world and his kingdom, they won't "get" God. And he reminds us to welcome people like that into our lives because when we do, we welcome Jesus.

But how do we become like kids? Not in a childish, immature way, but in the sense that Jesus is talking about here?

First, kids are trusting. They believe what others say. In the same way, if we are to interact closely with God, we must trust him, believing what he says through his Word.

Second, kids live with wonder. They are innately curious about the world, and discovering new things brings them joy. If we are to be like that, we have to actively shed our cynicism and dull routines.

Last, kids take risks. They climb trees taller than their houses. They jump over creeks. They play tag late at night. Similarly, if we want to be living for the kingdom of God, we have to be willing to take new risks.

How about you? What prevents you from being a kid today?

Jesus, I want to be more like a child today, more trusting, more wonder-filled, more in love with risk. I can't do that on my own. I need your help. Amen.

Lights in the World

Do all things without complaining and disputing, that
you may become blameless and harmless, children of
God without fault in the midst of a crooked and perverse
generation, among whom you shine as lights in the world.

—PHILIPPIANS 2:14–15

Simply living the first phrase of this verse would change not only our world but the entire world. We are a people of whining and argumentation. We actively find fault with others and share those faults openly.

But we are called to be light in this crooked world. We are to be utterly different. God calls us to be blameless, meaning we choose not to hurt others. He wants us to be harmless, particularly with our thoughts and words. He wants us to stop our arguing, pushing for our own way. And he desires we become a thankful, content people.

Yes, this world is crooked and perverse on every single level. But we are daughters of God. We must stand out as different, new, changed. We must shed pettiness, envy, getting our own way, enacting our own revenge, bitterness, and gossip. Why? So that the world will know that God makes all the difference in our lives and our behavior.

Jesus, forgive me for arguing, for complaining yet again. I want to be blameless and harmless. By your grace, help me to be a light in this crazy, mixed-up world. Amen.

Boasting

> For if anyone thinks he is something when he is nothing, he deceives himself. But each one must examine his own work, and then he will have reason for boasting in regard to himself alone, and not in regard to another. For each one will bear his own load.
>
> —GALATIANS 6:3–5 NASB

Paul says that if we think we're all that, we're caught in the act of deceiving ourselves. Sure, we are wildly loved by our Creator. But we are not the Creator, so our boasting makes no sense. Everything we have, even our personality, is a gift God gives us. To boast as if we created ourselves is deceptive.

Paul encourages us to look at what we do, not at others. Often, boasting involves comparing ourselves to others. "Well, I may be angry, but not as angry as So and So." Instead we're simply to examine ourselves and see how far we've personally come in our journey toward Jesus. Then we can accurately say, "I used to be an angry woman, but by God's grace, today I'm less angry."

We are to bear our own load in terms of our growth. No one can make us grow. No one can examine us quite the way we can. Nor can comparing ourselves to others cause us to grow. Essentially, we're to look inside, ask God for help, and then grow deep and wide.

Jesus, I don't want to think I'm all that. Nor do I want to keep comparing myself to others so that I come out looking better. Help me have a realistic view of where I am in my journey with you, and to trust you for growth. Amen.

A Sign from God

Gideon knew it was the angel of God! Gideon said, "Oh no!
Master, God! I have seen the angel of God face-to-face!"
—JUDGES 6:22 MSG

Many of us grew up hearing the story in Judges 6 about Gideon,
who was called by God to attack the enemy Midianites—at least
he thought that's what God was telling him. To make sure he
was getting the right message, he asked God for confirmation.
He told God he was leaving a wool fleece on the threshing floor
overnight. In the morning, if the fleece was wet with dew but the
floor around it was dry, then he would know he'd understood
God correctly. Sure enough, the next morning "he wrung out
the fleece—enough dew to fill a bowl with water!" (v. 38 MSG).
But what God was asking Gideon to do—attack a much larger
army—was a pretty drastic action. Gideon wanted to make sure.
So he put out the fleece the next night too. "Don't be impatient
with me," he said to God. "But this time let the fleece stay dry,
while the dew drenches the ground" (v. 39 MSG). The next morning, "only the fleece was dry while the ground was wet with dew"
(v. 40 MSG). Gideon had his marching orders.

We can't manipulate God or tell him what to do. We may
ask him for some signal communicating a message to us, but
that doesn't mean he's going to play the game. Still, we can be
watchful and prayerful, hoping he will guide our steps in quiet or
dramatic ways so that we constantly walk in his will.

*Lord, help me to be watchful and prayerful like Gideon. Thank you for
allowing me to walk in your will. Amen.*

Displaying Strength

By smooth words he will turn to godlessness those who
act wickedly toward the covenant, but the people who
know their God will display strength and take action.

—Daniel 11:32 NASB

In this verse, Daniel utters a warning to those who take lightly
God's covenant (promise). In other words, those who turn away
from God will get the fill of their actions and experience more
godlessness.

Thankfully, there's a wonderful conjunction in the sentence—the word *but*. God will display his strength and take
action on behalf of people who know God.

Notice it doesn't say that he will show his strength, but display it. When we know God and humbly bow before him, he not
only supplies strength, but parades it around on the stage of our
weakness. To know God is to know we're not God. And the more
we know we're not him, the bigger the stage for him to work.

So it's not a detriment to feel weak. It's not bad to experience failure. Those help us to know God better, to ask him for his
strength and victory. With a yielded heart like that, God is able to
take action on our behalf.

*Jesus, sometimes I think I have to be strong for you to like me. Help me
realize that you love me simply because you created me. I want you to
display your strength in my weakness. Amen.*

The Money Monster

He who loves money will not be satisfied with money, nor he who loves wealth with his income; this also is vanity.

—ECCLESIASTES 5:10 ESV

We've heard it said that the last thing converted is our purse. Why? Money represents control. If we have money, then we can solve almost any problem. If we're sick, we can head to the doctor. If we're hungry or thirsty, we can venture to the grocery store. If we're bored, we can purchase a movie ticket. *Almost* any issue we might have can be solved with money.

Which is why God wants us to ultimately be satisfied first in him. When we love and serve money, we'll never be fully satisfied, and we'll be guilty of trusting the almighty dollar instead of the almighty God.

Money is an idol that Solomon says never, ever fills us up. No matter what we have, our tendency is to want more. So how do we shift our allegiance from trusting in our checkbook to trusting in Jesus?

It starts with a belief in the greatness of God. He is big. He sees every single worry we have. He is a provider. When we truly believe this, our attachment to money wavers because we realize he ultimately is responsible for us. Great relief and peace come from truly trusting in God.

Jesus, help me shift my perspective from thinking money will solve all my problems to realizing you see everything in my life. Help me to trust your provision so I won't chase after the money monster. Amen.

Day of Reflection

He did not enter by means of the blood of goats and
calves; but he entered the Most Holy Place once for all
by his own blood, thus obtaining eternal redemption.

—HEBREWS 9:12 NIV

JESUS PAID IT ALL

I hear the Savior say, "Thy strength indeed is small;
Child of weakness watch and pray, find in Me thine all in all."

And when before the throne, I stand in Him complete;
"Jesus died my soul to save," my lips shall still repeat.

Jesus paid it all. All to Him I owe.
Sin had left a crimson stain, He washed it white as snow.

—ELVINA M. HALL, 1865

Your space—a poem, prayer, thoughts . . .

Embrace God, Not Your Culture

So here's what I want you to do, God helping you: Take your
everyday, ordinary life—your sleeping, eating, going-to-
work, and walking-around life—and place it before God as
an offering. Embracing what God does for you is the best
thing you can do for him. Don't become so well-adjusted
to your culture that you fit into it without even thinking.
Instead, fix your attention on God. You'll be changed from
the inside out. Readily recognize what he wants from you, and
quickly respond to it. Unlike the culture around you, always
dragging you down to its level of immaturity, God brings
the best out of you, develops well-formed maturity in you.

—ROMANS 12:1–2 MSG

God asks us for everything. Not parts of us that are convenient.
Not leftovers. Not scraps from the tables of our lives. No, he asks
us for our lives—every single part. Why? Because he has the ability to rejuvenate our lives. Only he can sustain us and bring us
joy in the journey. Living in our own strength just wears us out.

Instead, the apostle Paul encourages us to not only give him
our lives, but also be cautious about how much we allow the culture around us to shape us. In this crazy-busy me-first world,
it's hard to take our eyes off trends, famous folks, diets, or even
worldviews. But we must.

When we do, God brings out his best in us. He helps us grow
up, to stand out against the culture as a beacon of light. Instead of
blending in, he gives us the ability to be wildly, blessedly different.

*Jesus, I want to give you everything—my life, my will, my heart. Help
me to see where the culture has hijacked me. I want to stand out from the
culture and be made stronger and wiser by you. Amen.*

Love Your Enemies

But I say, love your enemies! Pray for those who persecute
you! In that way, you will be acting as true children of your
Father in heaven. For he gives his sunlight to both the evil
and the good, and he sends rain on the just and the unjust
alike. If you love only those who love you, what reward is
there for that? Even corrupt tax collectors do that much.

—MATTHEW 5:44–46 NLT

Jesus says something quite simple here. We've heard it so many
times we might be tempted to gloss over his words. He tells us to
love our enemies. Later he issues a stern correction to those who
only love those who love them, equating them with corrupt tax
collectors. *Ouch.*

Yet when we look at our lives, isn't that what we do? We
actively love those folks who love us well. We dote on them, give
them our attention, and help meet their needs. All good things.
But Jesus calls us to something more radical. Even corrupt folks
love people who love them back. Jesus calls us to actively love our
enemies.

Who are our enemies? Folks who say mean things about us,
spread gossip, who have taken advantage of us or scammed us.
Those folks are hard to love. Jesus says we must pray for those
people too. And while we do, we are more like God because he
loves every single person on this earth, even the rapscallions.

*Jesus, help me to bless my enemies, to pray for them, to not become like
them or do unto them what they've done unto me. Help me have a higher
love, a bigger heart, a sweeter disposition. Only you can help me be that
way. Amen.*

Promoting Others

Let someone else praise you, not your own
mouth—a stranger, not your own lips.
—Proverbs 27:2 NLT

When we're trying to sell something or succeed in a job, we sometimes have to toot our horns or chat about how cool our product is. While that may be an important part of business, the writer of this proverb speaks of a better way.

This way takes a lot of humility. We choose to stop talking about ourselves and simply wait and see how others might do it. Holding back like this takes extreme patience, and it allows others to promote us. When someone else praises us, his or her praise carries more weight than our own self-promotion.

The reverse of this is what makes life fun and interesting. Why not, instead of being quiet and waiting for others to say nice things about us, actively seek to praise others? Why not be proactive, looking for ways to encourage our friends and acquaintances we see doing great things?

Praising others and finding ways to point out their strengths will bless them and keep you humble.

Jesus, show me ten people this week to praise specifically. Next time I want to toot my own horn, stop me and help me think of someone else to praise. Amen.

Confront (Kindly) and Forgive

Pay attention to yourselves! If your brother sins, rebuke
him, and if he repents, forgive him, and if he sins
against you seven times in the day, and turns to you
seven times, saying, "I repent," you must forgive him.

—LUKE 17:3–4 ESV

It's vitally important that we don't neglect the first part of this
verse. Before we crusade to tell another about her sin, we must
first examine ourselves to see if we are walking on crooked paths.
Or, to use Jesus' metaphor, take the log out of our eyes first so we
can see those pesky specks in our friends' eyes.

But notice that we are still called to take action. Once we've
examined ourselves, we are to kindly confront those who are
in error or harbor sin. That's the loving thing to do because
we deeply value our friend's relationship to Jesus. Any sin in
between her and Jesus is something that will ultimately harm
that relationship.

The verse gets harder to obey. When a friend sins against us
more than one time, Jesus calls us to forgive—even up to seven
times in one day. That's radical, painful forgiveness, and it even
seems foolish.

Yet think back over your day. How many times did you sin
against Jesus? How many times did he forgive you? We are most
like Jesus when we forgive people.

*Jesus, help me to examine myself. And in that, if you want me to confront,
give me the strength to be kind and brave. And above all that, help me to
become more like you—forgiving folks a lot. Amen.*

He Leads the Humble

He leads the humble in what is right,
and teaches the humble his way.

—PSALM 25:9 ESV

In this passage we see the kind of person God leads. He doesn't lead the all-together folks or the people who find strength in themselves. He shies away from the proud and self-sufficient.

He is attracted to those who are humble, and he actively teaches those people his surprising ways. Think on some of the synonyms for humble: *modest, respectful, low in level, meek, unpretentious, submissive, unassuming, plain, common*. In light of that list, who do you know who personifies those words? What attracts you to that person?

Now consider the antonyms to humble: *proud, noble, exalted, rude, insolent, arrogant*. Who do you know to be like that? What repels you about that person?

If you are attracted to humble people and repelled by proud people, imagine God's interaction with both sets of people. The beauty is that he actively pursues those who live submissive, reverent lives. The more we exemplify the synonyms of humility, the more we'll learn God's ways.

Jesus, I want to be more humble. Help me to see where I'm prideful or arrogant. I give you permission to help me become humble so I can learn your ways. Amen.

He Holds Your Hand

The steps of a man are established by the LORD, And He delights in his way. When he falls, he will not be hurled headlong, because the LORD is the One who holds his hand.

—PSALM 37:23–24 NASB

There is great peace in truly realizing that God establishes our steps. Nothing we've done takes him by surprise. And he knows the way we will take tomorrow. Not only that, but this verse says that he delights in the way we take.

It's hard to believe that God loves us that much, that he delights in our future journeys, even though we're bound to fail and stumble. But beyond that, God also promises that he will catch us as we fall because he holds our hands.

Picture an older woman trying to cross a busy street. Alone, she is tentative—maybe even a little scared. Now watch as a younger man dashes into the street to take her hand and steady her across the street. The woman now feels safe and has confidence she'll make it to the street corner.

That's a picture of God with us. We can't do life on our own. We feel scared, isolated, and worried, so God dashes into our lives, grabs our hand, and helps us to the next spot on our journey.

Jesus, thank you that you know the steps I take even before I stumble to take them. Thank you for holding my hand and protecting me. Thank you for always being with me. Help me to live joyfully in light of that ever-present truth. Amen.

Day of Reflection

He guides me along the right paths for his name's sake.

—PSALM 23:3 NIV

HE LEADETH ME

He leadeth me, O blessed thought!
O words with heavenly comfort fraught!
Whate'er I do, where'er I be,
Still 'tis God's hand that leadeth me.

He leadeth me, He leadeth me,
By His own hand He leadeth me;
His faithful follower I would be,
For by His hand He leadeth me.

—JOSEPH H. GILMORE, 1862

Your space—a poem, prayer, thoughts . . .

Hot-Tempered People

Do not make friends with a hot-tempered person,
do not associate with one easily angered, or you
may learn their ways and get yourself ensnared.

—PROVERBS 22:24–25 NIV

When we engage with people who are constantly angry, we run the risk of becoming like them, or at least retaliating in kind. Sometimes we can't always avoid angry people as the proverb describes, but we can always control our level of engagement with them.

The verse also warns us not to pursue someone who is prone to outrage. So if you see someone constantly combating the people around him or her, it's a helpful sign from God to politely step away.

The verse has a flipside too. What if we are the hot-tempered people we're warned about? What if we are easily angered? What's the direct result of living hotheaded? According to this verse, it's friendlessness. People don't like to associate with someone in a constant stage of rage.

If you have a raging friend, ask God to show you how to love that person, whether that means distancing yourself, bringing their anger to their attention—be careful!—or praying from afar. You don't love your friend well if you enable anger or dismiss it.

If you fear you are someone who shouts too much and is easily set off, ask God to show you why. What is the root issue that causes all the anger? It's nearly impossible to treat the symptoms of anger successfully unless you know the why behind it. God is gracious and will show you, and he is more than capable of setting you free.

Jesus, show me how to love the anger-prone in my life. Do I distance myself? Say something? Pray? And please show me the roots of my own anger. What is it that causes my angry reactions? I trust you to show me and heal me. Amen.

Wanting Others' Stuff

You must not covet your neighbor's house. You must not
covet your neighbor's wife, male or female servant, ox or
donkey, or anything else that belongs to your neighbor.

—EXODUS 20:17 NLT

This passage is one of the Ten Commandments. Why did God
take coveting so seriously? Because ultimately when we covet—
or lust after—someone else's stuff or their relationship or status,
we are placing our allegiance in them rather than God. We're
basically saying, "God, you are not enough to fill me up, but I'll
finally be happy if you give me something someone else has."

When we give in to covetousness, we no longer live care-
free, happy lives. We become consumed by what consumes our
thoughts. We obsess over getting things that aren't ours in the
first place. And in that tyranny of wanting what we can't have, we
become enslaved.

The cure for coveting comes in communion—to find our
ultimate satisfaction in God and his presence. With him, we have
everything we need: relationship, provision, sustenance, joy.
When we find contentment in God, we learn to be joyful for what
he has given others.

There is freedom in letting others have what they have and
being thankful for what we do have. We escape the sin that would
cause us to steal or wish ill on our neighbor. And as we're content,
we experience joy in Jesus.

*Jesus, I don't want to covet what my friend has, whether it be looks or
stuff or relationships or success. I want to be content with where I am
right now. Ultimately I want to find my satisfaction in you alone. Amen.*

Stronger Than Lions

The lions may grow weak and hungry, but those
who seek the LORD lack no good thing.

—PSALM 34:10 NIV

When we think of the king of the beasts, we think of sinewy power, cunning, and abundant strength to fight and kill. Lions are mighty, and they are fierce. Meeting one in any other place than a zoo would most likely end in the lion devouring us as prey.

The psalmist wants to contrast the lions' power with God's supernatural ability. The way to tap into that power, which is infinitely greater than the lions', is this little word *seek*. When we seek the Lord, we are stronger than a lion.

Even lions grow weak. They suffer hunger, but when we choose to seek God, he becomes our provider. He supplies us with the strength we need for this moment and every moment. When we grow weak, his strength undergirds us.

When we seek God, we lack nothing. What would it look like today to see God as bigger than lions?

Jesus, thank you that you give us every good thing. I acknowledge that you're stronger than lions and your power is available to me whenever I seek it. You fill my heart with hope. Amen.

Less Really Is More

*In the morning, O LORD, you hear my voice; in the morning
I lay my requests before you and wait in expectation.*

—PSALM 5:3 NIV

It's often said, "Expect more and you get more," but sometimes if we expect less, we get more. This may sound counterproductive to positive thinking but read on.

Let's assume you had a high expectation for your family vacation. But on the second day out, two of your children come down with stomach flu, which quickly spreads to everyone else in the family. In addition to that, you have a flat tire, ruin the tire driving on it, and your spare is flat. No one is happy.

How could lowered expectations for this trip have helped your happiness potential? You know sickness is always a possibility, so while hoping against it you prepare for it anyway, packing medicine for the trip. When the flu erupts, you and your family are grateful for your provision. Your car's tires are showing signs of wear, so you make sure your spare is aired up and ready to go before you leave, and you also carry a can of flat-fixer. Plus, you bring along the Old Maid cards to play while you're waiting for the flat to be fixed, increasing the happiness of your children because you inevitably picked the Old Maid card.

Expecting less does not mean we prepare less, we try less, or we are less determined to live out our potential. It means less can become more, and when that happens, it produces joy.

*Lord, I stand amazed at you. Even though life may sometimes fail my
expectations, you always exceed them, and for that, I thank you. Amen.*

Sing Praises

God has ascended with a shout, The LORD, with the
sound of a trumpet. Sing praises to God, sing praises;
Sing praises to our King, sing praises. For God is the
King of all the earth; Sing praises with a skillful psalm.

—PSALM 47:5−7 NASB

Our response to God's greatness is song. Because of God's place
as King of the entire earth, the subject of our songs is his sovereign reign over everything. He owns it all. He created it all. He
rules over all.

So let's sing today. Let's look beyond the concerns of the day
and lift our eyes heavenward and holler to everyone how great
our God is. When we choose to lift our gaze from the craziness
of life and elevate to the bigness of God, our problems melt away.

When we praise the sufficiency of God, we recognize our
insufficiency. We are saying that God deserves our allegiance in
every little part of our lives. And when we sing praises to God, we
delight his heart.

Just as a child praises his mother for a great dinner or a sweet
present, so must we bring a smile to God's face by praising him
for his gifts. We bless him when we slow down enough to recognize that everything we see and experience is a gift from him.
And when we praise, we place our hearts in submission under his.

*Jesus, I want to sing, sing, sing. Not of my greatness. Not of my fame.
But of yours. You've done so much in my life. It would take me years to
share all the stories of your redemption. I choose right now to praise you.
Amen.*

Praise Him!

*Let everything that has breath praise
the Lord. Praise the Lord!*

—Psalm 150:6

This verse implies that every living creature on the earth has an opportunity to praise God. How can an elephant praise God? By simply being an elephant, one of God's creations. We, too, praise God just by being alive, serving as a testimony to the wild creativity of our Creator.

Praising is a choice we make too. When life careens crazily and things don't go as we planned, we can decide in the moment to grumble or praise. We can do this because praising God is not based on our circumstances, but on his attributes. He will never change, though our situations and trials shift constantly.

Today is a particularly wonderful day to praise God. We have air to breathe, a mind to think, and if we are mobile, legs to walk. God has fully forgiven us and invited us into relationship with him. We have constant access to his presence every moment.

We also have creation all around us, hollering his praise. The flowers, trees, grass, mountains, sky, oceans, stars—all proclaim him and shout his significance and ability. All we need to do is open our eyes and train our hearts in gratitude.

Jesus, I'm alive! And since I'm alive I choose to praise you right now. Not for stuff. Not to complain. But to rejoice in how very amazing you are. Amen.

Day of Reflection

Will You not revive us again,
that Your people may rejoice in You?
—PSALM 85:6

REVIVE US AGAIN

We praise Thee, O God, for the Son of Thy Love;
For Jesus, who died and is now gone above.
Hallelujah! Thine the glory! Hallelujah! Amen!
Hallelujah! Thine the glory! Revive us again!
                              —WILLIAM P. MACKAY, 1863

Your space—a poem, prayer, thoughts . . .

Scrubbed Clean

"Come now, let us settle the matter," says the
LORD. "Though your sins are like scarlet, they
shall be as white as snow; though they are red
as crimson, they shall be like wool."

—ISAIAH 1:18 NIV

A bloodstained garment is not easy to whiten. We must take
detergent and bleach, scrubbing it clean, laying it out in the sunshine to bring it back to its white glory. In a similar manner, God
takes our sin-stained lives. He scrubs us with Jesus' sacrifice, and
lets us bask in the sunshine of his favor.

The stain does not remain when the great Stain Remover
takes it away. It is gone forever, never to return. What would it look
like if we internalized that truth? That our dirtiness is cleansed
forever, that we are deemed white before a white-holy God?

This is God's work, not ours. We cannot scrub ourselves clean.
When we do, we dirty ourselves with more sin and self-effort.
Only a perfect God can bring our perfection. And only a perfect
sacrifice can secure our right standing before God.

Jesus made the way for us to be as white as wooly snow. His
blood was the cleansing agent that removed our guilt forever. He
covered our sins—past, present, and future. In light of that, we
can live clean, joyful, free lives. We are brand-new, as if sin never
tainted us. Amen!

*Jesus, thank you that you removed my sins from me, that you scrubbed me
clean with your blood. I can't thank you enough. You did what I could not
do. I want to live freely in light of your cleansing. I want to dance through
this life because of that freedom. Amen.*

What God Wants

*The sacrifices of God are a broken spirit; a broken
and a contrite heart, O God, You will not despise.*

—PSALM 51:17 NASB

God is not interested in our perfect offerings. We're not to be
mannequins, flawless, yet without soul. Our offering shouldn't
be us trying to tidy ourselves up so he'll love us. Guess what? God
loves you. As you are. Right now. Even as you feel small.

The sacrifices God delights in are a broken spirit, a broken
and contrite heart. He is the God of the needy, of those who know
their need for him. If you feel you don't have anything of value to
offer him, chances are your very brokenness is what he's after. He
loves taking the broken pieces of our lives and making us whole.

Why? Because God can intervene in people's lives when they
share their need with him. If we are capable and don't need him,
we won't reach heavenward. But when life breaks us, or we live
under the condemnation of our own mistakes, we realize we cannot live this life with victory unless we hold his hand.

God does not despise you. He loves you affectionately. And
he longs, like a good father, to pick you up after you fall, dust you
off, and gather you into a huge embrace.

*Jesus, thank you that you love me when I fail. You love me when I'm bro-
ken. I need you to fix me, Lord. In my own strength, I fall apart. But you
are my strength. I trust you again. I fall into your arms! Amen.*

Your Specific Race

But I do not consider my life of any account as dear
to myself, so that I may finish my course and the
ministry which I received from the Lord Jesus, to
testify solemnly of the gospel of the grace of God.

—ACTS 20:24 NASB

Paul wrote this at the end of his ministry, as his imprisonment
eventually led to his death. He didn't count his life as something
to grab at, point at, or revel in. No, he viewed his life only in terms
of how it related to God. His life was dear to God. He lived a life
that wooed God's smile.

Paul had single-minded focus on his mission, to proclaim
the gospel to the world. His specific mission was loving Gentile
people to Christ.

God gives us all a specific us-shaped mission. It's a joy to
discover it. If you're having a hard time figuring out your place
in God's redemptive plan, look back over your life and see what
common threads God has woven through. Do you always rescue
the hurting? Are you bent toward art?

As you discover what motivates you, hold it loosely. Don't
make your pursuit an idol. Instead, forge ahead as Paul did to finish the specific race God has called you to run. Don't look to the
left or the right, but take one step, then the next. Your life is dear
to God.

*Jesus, I want to be like Paul in my singular pursuit of the ministry you
have planned for me. I want to testify to your amazing power in this
world. And I want to love you as I walk. Help me see your mission for
me, even today. Amen.*

Hope for the Nations

For this, O LORD, I will praise you among the
nations; I will sing praises to your name.

—PSALM 18:49 NLT

God's great intent for the nation of Israel was to be a beacon to
all the nations of the earth. He blessed them in order that they
would be a blessing to everyone. But they shrunk inside themselves, turning inward, cherishing their blessing. They forgot
God's plan and intent.

God commands us to sing about him to the entire world
because his salvation is intended for everyone. He has grace
aplenty, and a desire to see every single person come to a saving
knowledge of him.

We become like the introspective Israelites when we hoard
our faith to ourselves, when we forget our great outwardly
focused God. He blesses us so we can be a blessing to the nations.

When we spend our time absorbed in our own lives and
problems and go to Jesus solely for those issues, we forget that
we're part of the great redemptive plan of God to bring every
nation to him. It's God's heart that instead of navel-gazing, we
constantly look outward, singing salvation's song to everyone.
When we live in light of that, there's no room for selfishness or
prejudice.

*Jesus, I want to praise you among the nations. I don't want to forget your
plan to save the entire world. I don't want to hoard your blessings. Help
me to share with many what you've done in my life. Amen.*

How to Live in This Evil World

> And we are instructed to turn from godless living and
> sinful pleasures. We should live in this evil world with
> wisdom, righteousness, and devotion to God, while we
> look forward with hope to that wonderful day when
> the glory of our great God and Savior, Jesus Christ,
> will be revealed. He gave his life to free us from every
> kind of sin, to cleanse us, and to make us his very own
> people, totally committed to doing good deeds.
>
> —TITUS 2:12–14 NLT

There are two ways to live in this evil world—to turn away, and to turn toward. Paul instructs Titus to turn away from godless living—living as if God didn't exist—and from sinful pleasures, those things that take our attention off God.

And we are to turn toward wisdom—the kind that comes directly from the throne of God. We are to orient our hearts toward righteousness, which simply means right living in the strength God provides. And we are to fixate on devoting ourselves to God, to have hearts that run first to him.

When we turn away and turn toward, we find hope. We fix our eyes on Jesus, who will eventually return to this earth. He is the reason we live well on this earth because he is the only One who can free us from sin's tyranny.

Jesus, help me to turn away from godless living and sinful pleasures. I want to live with wisdom, righteousness, and devotion. Keep my heart close to yours so I'll remember again and again that you love me, and that I am your daughter. Amen.

Knowing Joy, Knowing Pain

> I have told you these things, so that in me you may
> have peace. In this world you will have trouble.
> But take heart! I have overcome the world.
>
> —JOHN 16:33 NIV

In Genesis chapter 50, we read where Joseph was unfairly convicted of a crime and spent many years in jail. But when he was released, God had a high position in the Egyptian nation awaiting him. When his brothers—who, out of jealousy, sent Joseph to Egypt to be a slave—found themselves kneeling before him for a handout during a season of famine, Joseph said, "You meant evil against me; but God meant it for good" (Genesis 50:20).

Gratitude requires us to be investigative agents. Joseph sure had to be one to find gratitude when he knew his spiteful brothers had plotted against him. He could have sought revenge, but Joseph knew God had used his hardships for Joseph's own good and for a higher purpose. It isn't natural to look for good in bad. It's far more human, when bad rears its ugly head, to gaze upon it stymied. But when we believe that God designs and redesigns all things for our good, even when the intent of others is for our demise, it allows us to let them off the hook and look up. Our task is to detect and embrace the good, which means we will have to be alert and discerning if we are to benefit from the windbreaker of gratitude.

Someone once said, "We can only know joy to the degree we have known pain." Hardships have the potential of carving out greater space for God's grace within us. And grace helps us to live with life's inequities without the disabling residuals of anger, bitterness, and disillusionment.

Lord, forgive my blustering. Regardless of what tumultuous winds bring my way, you are the prevailing one, and I am the recipient of your goodness. I acknowledge your constancy and your supremacy. Amen.

Day of Reflection

Blessed is the nation whose God is the LORD.

—PSALM 33:12

MY COUNTRY, 'TIS OF THEE

My country, 'tis of Thee, Sweet land of liberty,
of Thee I sing:
Land where my fathers died, Land of the pilgrims' pride,
From every mountainside, Let freedom ring!

Our fathers' God, to Thee, Author of liberty,
to Thee we sing:
Long may our land be bright with freedom's holy light;
Protect us by Thy might, Great God, our King!

—SAMUEL F. SMITH, 1831

Your space—a poem, prayer, thoughts . . .

Biblical Confidence

Such confidence we have through Christ before God.
Not that we are competent in ourselves to claim
anything for ourselves, but our competence comes
from God. He has made us competent as ministers
of a new covenant—not of the letter but of the Spirit;
for the letter kills, but the Spirit gives life.

—2 CORINTHIANS 3:4–6 NIV

Some of us shrink back, giving in to inferiority, believing everyone else is more important, more capable, more intelligent, more worthy. Others swing to the other extreme, boasting in our abilities and looking down on those who don't measure up to our standards. Both are forms of pride and don't equal biblical confidence.

It's not biblical confidence to shrink away. Nor is it biblical confidence to neglect Jesus when we think of our worth. Biblical confidence, according to Paul, comes from God. He enables us to be bold, yet humble—an interesting paradox. He gives us the wherewithal to stand up to injustice with a boldness not our own. But he humbles those who exalt themselves.

The kind of confidence that blesses God is a dependence on him. It's in saying, "I know I'm not everything I should be, but God is everything I need."

The latter half of this verse gives us a final treasure. When we have godly confidence, one of the greatest indications that we have it is life and freedom. When we are confident in the right way, we have the freedom to serve God with joy, not shrinking back afraid, but confident in his ability to walk us through.

Jesus, I want to be confident in you and what you do. Forgive me for shrinking away. And if I've been proud, please humble me. I love you. You are everything I need. Amen.

Healing Prayer

*Therefore, confess your sins to one another and pray
for one another, that you may be healed. The prayer of
a righteous person has great power as it is working.*

—JAMES 5:16 ESV

Do you believe God can heal? Is he capable of healing people?
We only need to watch how he worked as Jesus on the earth. He
healed every form of disease and blessed many with eyesight,
cured deafness, and cast out evil spirits. God is certainly big
enough to do all those things.

But Jesus didn't heal every living person on the earth when he
walked it. His sovereign plan is mysterious. Just as Jesus can heal
today—and may—he also may choose not to. Either way, we're
to pray to him and ask for healing, believing in his capability.

James 5:16 encourages us to do two things: pray and be righteous. When we are sick, we must pray. When others are in pain,
we must pray. And all the while, we must strive to be what James
calls a "righteous person," one who is in right standing with God.

Our righteousness, we realize, doesn't come from our doing
a bunch of good things. No, it's tied to our centered reliance on
Jesus Christ. So when we pray, we rely on Jesus, remember his
miracles, and ask him to heal our friends. But after that, we leave
the outcome in his sovereign hands.

*Jesus, I want to believe you are big, and pain and sickness are small. Grow
my faith. Help me become a righteous woman who fully relies on your
power and strength. As I pray for my friends and family, I pray I'll be
satisfied to rest in your answer. Amen.*

Finding Strength in God

And David was greatly distressed, for the people
spoke of stoning him, because all the people were
bitter in soul, each for his sons and daughters. But
David strengthened himself in the LORD his God.

—1 SAMUEL 30:6 ESV

David faced a mighty personal battle in this passage. The very
people he loved spoke of stoning him. They'd given in to bitterness and wanted to blame someone. David became their
scapegoat.

He had nowhere to turn in his anguish and stress because
the people he would confide in now wanted him dead. So what
did he do? He chose God.

It would be amazing if every time we felt betrayed or abandoned that God would send us a sweet friend to carry the burden.
Sometimes he does. But sometimes he allows wilderness experiences like David's to help us to turn solely to him and him alone.
In the wilderness, we have to rely on God for provision, direction, comfort, and safety. David chose, though his circumstances
were dire, to turn to God.

We, too, can make a choice to strengthen ourselves in God
alone. How? By reading his Scripture and replacing the fears we
might have with his truths. By turning on worship music in the
car and singing our cares away, sending them heavenward. By
dropping to our knees and asking God for perspective and help.

Remember, it's his delight to be there for you.

*Jesus, I want to be like David who made a choice to be strengthened by
you, even when his life was falling apart. Teach me how. I need you; and
I love you. Amen.*

God, Our Liberator

He shatters the doors of bronze and
cuts in two the bars of iron.

—Psalm 107:16 ESV

Not only does this scripture speak of God's amazing strength, but it also indicates that God is the God who liberates. Bronze doors prevent prisoners from escaping. Bars of iron separate imprisoned people from the outside world. And yet God in his great capability can shatter bronze and cut iron.

In what areas of your life do you need God's liberation? Where do you need his strength? Are you stuck spiritually? In what ways are you imprisoned?

Some people need to be set free from the tyranny of living for others' expectations. Others need to be liberated from an unhealthy attachment to food and body image. Others can't seem to forgive an enemy. Some are enslaved to pop culture. And some women need to be delivered from apathy.

Whatever your imprisonment, the truth remains. God is bigger still. Spend some time seeking him today, asking him to shatter the bronze doors and cut the bars of iron that prevent you from living an abundant, joyful, hope-filled life today.

Jesus, thank you that you're strong enough to liberate me. I give you the things in my life that hold me captive right now. Please set me free. Amen.

On Our Knees Together

Everything in the world is about to be wrapped up, so
take nothing for granted. Stay wide-awake in prayer.
—1 PETER 4:7 MSG

God has always called us to walk out our faith as a people—not as individuals but as a group. When he called the Israelites out of Egypt, he called them to come out together, not one by one. The Psalms were written as corporate liturgy to be sung together as a community. Jesus told us that he is returning for a bride, who is all of us in the body of Christ. This means that not only is prayer our personal means of communication with God, but it is a way for us believers to come together as one.

Never, ever underestimate the power of praying together. There is nothing like it. It is fellowship at its barest and most powerful. And it is life changing.

Some of the closest relationships are formed with friends you pray with. Prayer is acknowledging the invisible in the presence of the visible, and the evil one trembles when he sees God's people on their knees together.

Perhaps, like many, you are afraid to pray in public or to offer prayer for a friend because you have no confidence in your prayer skills. But ponder this: a child you love with all your heart comes to you and with faltering words says, "I love you such a bunch!" Would you despise that sentiment because it wasn't articulated properly? Of course not! Your heart would be moved, and you would reach down and embrace that child.

That is how our Father sees us. Prayer is not about impressing other people. It's about loving God all the way home.

Lord, thank you for hearing my prayers even when they're not perfectly polished. Help me to remember to reach out to friends and family to pray together. Amen.

Truth Telling

Don't scheme against each other. Stop your
love of telling lies that you swear are the truth.
I hate all these things, says the Lord.
—Zechariah 8:17 nlt

Telling lies is our native language. When it's easier to tell a fib that will make us look better or smarter or cooler, we do. Bending truth is the foundation of the advertising that assails us every single day. If we want to stand out in this world of lies, God calls us to be brave and tell the truth.

That doesn't mean we run around telling truth to people in a way that hurts them—after all, the Scripture says that our truth must lead to peace (Zechariah 8:16). We always temper truth with love and say things the way we'd love to have them said to us. And we choose to relegate drama to the stage, choosing to step away from creating conflict.

God loves truth. And if we want to be like him, we will love it so much we can't help but tell it.

What can that look like today? One word: *encouragement*. Think about someone in your life who desperately needs to hear the truth about herself, the good truth. Make an effort to share it with her face to face, or if that's not possible, in a note, text, voice message, or e-mail. Truth, after all, breeds life.

Jesus, show me people today who need to hear the truth of their beauty and worth. Help me be someone who speaks and writes the truth in love. I want to love truth as you do. Amen.

Day of Reflection

Who is this King of glory?
The LORD strong and mighty,
the LORD mighty in battle.
—PSALM 24:8

BATTLE HYMN OF THE REPUBLIC

Mine eyes have seen the glory of the coming of the Lord;
He is trampling out the vintage where
the grapes of wrath are stored;
He hath loosed the fateful lightning of His terrible swift sword;
His truth is marching on.

With a glory in His bosom that transfigures you and me;
As He died to make men holy, let us live to make men free.
While God is marching on.

—JULIA WARD HOWE, 1861

Your space—a poem, prayer, thoughts . . .

You Were Made for Such a Time as This

If you keep quiet at a time like this, deliverance and relief for the Jews will arise from some other place, but you and your relatives will die. Who knows if perhaps you were made queen for just such a time as this?

—ESTHER 4:14 NLT

God created you for this time period on earth. He placed you in your family. He gave you your background, your passions, and your experiences to uniquely bless the generation you live within.

You are made for such a time as this. You were created for glory, to proclaim Jesus to this next generation. Though it may be scary to think this way, it's true. There is only one you on the face of this earth, only one you who interacts with the circle you hang out with, only one you who is gifted the way you are.

It's never easy to step out and help others. But God has placed you right here, right now, to do just that. It is not dependent on your pluck or ability. It's entirely dependent on your dependence on Jesus.

Dare to believe he will give you the power you need to bless the generation you live in. Don't shrink back from what he has for you. Don't stand in the corner while others suffer. Be all you can in every circumstance, rescuing folks who Jesus brings your way.

Jesus, sometimes I feel insignificant and small, and I have no idea why you'd want to use me. Still, I want to believe like Esther that I was made for this one time. Be my capability, Jesus. Amen.

Iron Friends

Iron sharpens iron, so one man sharpens another.
—PROVERBS 27:17 NASB

Everyone needs iron friends—those friends who love you enough to say hard things. If all our friends are easy to spend time with, never stepping on our toes, always bowing to our wishes, we will not have a growing friendship. We need folks who are so deeply entrenched in our lives that they can actually see our warts and love us enough to place a mirror in front of them.

True growth happens in the context of community. It does not happen in isolation. Relationships are the measure of our growth, and how we respond to criticism indicates how much we have grown.

In marriage, for instance, we learn the art of dying to self, to prefer another's wishes above our own. We also open ourselves up for scrutiny. In that deep relationship, we become more self-less, kinder, easier to live with.

But if we withdraw from relationships, we will not have the opportunity to practice our selflessness, nor will we have others in our lives who have an unbiased perspective of us. We absolutely need that perspective to grow.

Jesus, help me to be a friend who helps sharpen my friends. Help me to love others well, not nit-picking, but genuinely doing life with them. Also, please help me be willing to see the selfish parts of me that hurt others. I truly want to grow. Amen.

The Perfect Getaway

I'm asking GOD for one thing, only one thing: To live with him in his house my whole life long. I'll contemplate his beauty; I'll study at his feet. That's the only quiet, secure place in a noisy world, the perfect getaway, far from the buzz of traffic.

—PSALM 27:4–5 MSG

We live in a noisy world. Our lives buzz out of control with tasks and media vying for our attention. We can't seem to find quiet. But this psalm provides hope. When we stop long enough to rest in God's presence, we'll have the space we need to think about how beautiful he is. We can be like Mary who studied and worshiped at Jesus' feet.

Eugene Peterson calls this house of God "the only quiet, secure place in a noisy world." But sometimes we're so consumed by the business of our own houses and lives that we neglect to open the door to God's house.

Our joyfulness, though, depends on our willingness to hang out in God's house. There, he can shelter us. There, he can heal us. There, he can rejuvenate us. There, he can make us ready for the battle outside the front door.

Take a moment to still your heart. Ask God to be your quiet, secure place. Ask him to silence the buzz from your life. Breathe in. Breathe out. Lay everything that concerns you at his feet. He will comfort and renew you in his house.

Jesus, thank you that you are so hospitable, welcoming me into your haven of a house. Still me. Quiet me. I want to spend time in your perfect getaway today. Amen.

A Beautiful Heart

But the LORD said to Samuel, "Do not look on
his appearance or on the height of his stature,
because I have rejected him. For the LORD sees
not as man sees: man looks on the outward
appearance, but the LORD looks on the heart."

—1 SAMUEL 16:7 ESV

We judge others. We look at what others wear and form an opinion about their affluence, economic status, and even their potential as a friend. But friends actually come in surprising packages, don't they? Think back on your friendships. What friends seemed to be perfect for you initially but then didn't work out? What people did you initially avoid but who became invaluable allies?

God doesn't look at appearances. He knows us all from the inside out. While we may make judgments and inaccurate perceptions about others, his opinions are always right. And they don't deal at all with what's on the outside.

How can you be more like God in the way you evaluate people? By simply remembering that the heart is what matters. By pursuing people who don't always fit your preconceived notions. By listening well. By watching behavior before you make a judgment.

And alongside that, strive to be—through the strength of the Holy Spirit—a person whose heart is beautiful.

Jesus, I want to see people as you do, from the inside out. Help me look beyond appearances to the person on the inside. And, too, would you clean me up on the inside? I want to have a beautiful heart. Amen.

Unity, Not Factions

Now I do beg you, my brothers, by all that Christ
means to you, to speak with one voice, and not allow
yourselves to be split up into parties. All together you
should be achieving a unity in thought and judgment.

—1 Corinthians 1:10 phillips

In this passage, Paul reminds us of the devastation that comes
from dividing into factions. And he emphasizes the importance of unity in the way we think and judge. He entreats the
Corinthian believers to change their ways because of Christ and
what he means to them.

Jesus came to earth to bring all people to himself. Because
of this, within his church, there are all sorts of people with thousands of different agendas, personalities, and quirks. And with
that recipe of diversity, there are bound to be disagreements.

While it's normal to disagree with other Christians—we
are not robots!—the way in which we handle our disagreements
must always be filtered through love. Because Christ loves us, we
can now extend that same kind of love to others. And how did he
demonstrate love? By serving others.

When we serve others, particularly those who disagree with
us, we no longer need to divide into factions. We see how having
warring parties devastates people, how it harms them individually and also reflects badly on the church.

Jesus, I don't want to form a faction. I don't want to be a part of the prob-
lem. Help me instead to serve those who differ from me. I want to operate
with love as my motivation, not trying to assert my rightness. Amen.

The Golden Rule

Do to others as you would have them do to you.
—LUKE 6:31 NIV

There is no doubt that if everyone on the planet followed the "Golden Rule" from Luke 6:31, we could live out our time in harmony and peace. But some people didn't get the memo, and as a result, harmony and peace are rare commodities for most cultures.

Too often the world's thinking seems to be, I want your [fill in the blank], so I'll fight for it. I want your technological formulas, so I'll steal them. I want your power, so I'll manipulate to get it. I want your money, so I'll cheat you out of it. I want your wife, so I'll seduce her. The list is endless, and the golden rule is nowhere to be seen.

In contrast, our daily lives offer plenty of opportunities for living out the rule simply and quietly: water the neighbors' plants during their vacation, walk the dog until a friend's leg heals, take hot meals to shut-ins, donate food to a food bank and clothes for the homeless. Again, the list is endless.

We are designed to do good things for others. God embedded that instinct within each one of his creation because yielding to it is a good use of our time. There is a definite personal payback when we "do unto others," and it feels good to extend kindness beyond ourselves.

Lord, please remind me to treat others as I would want to be treated.
Amen.

Day of Reflection

Then the angel showed me the river of the
water of life, as clear as crystal, flowing from
the throne of God and of the Lamb.

—REVELATION 22:1 NIV

SHALL WE GATHER AT THE RIVER?

Shall we gather at the river,
where bright angel feet have trod;
With its crystal tide forever flowing by the throne of God?

Soon we'll reach the shining river,
soon our pilgrimage will cease,
Soon our happy hearts will quiver with the melody of peace.

Yes, we'll gather at the river, the beautiful, beautiful river;
Gather with the saints at the river
that flows by the throne of God.

—ROBERT LOWRY, 1864

Your space—a poem, prayer, thoughts . . .

Finding Hope in a Crazy, Fallen World

The fundamental fact of existence is that this trust in God,
this faith, is the firm foundation under everything that
makes life worth living. It's our handle on what we can't see.

—HEBREWS 11:1–2 MSG

Our life pivots on this fulcrum: God. And everything we do depends on him. To have faith in God, the beautiful object of our faith, is to trust him for everything, to depend on him to walk us through life, to lean on him for hope in this crazy, fallen world.

The difficult thing about faith is that it is not often placed in what is seen. We cannot see God. We can't always discern his ways. But we hold to him anyway, which can make us look foolish or faith-filled, depending on who is observing us.

You can exercise your faith right now by filling in the blanks. Jesus, I trust you to _____. I believe you are big enough to _____ in my life. Whether or not I see a direct answer to this prayer about _____, I ask you to help me trust you anyway, to praise you regardless.

It's counterintuitive to have faith in a God who can seem far off, but it's entirely rewarding. Why? Because he sees you. He is intimately acquainted with every care you have. And he knows the needs of every human on this earth. He is available, and he is sovereign.

Jesus, sometimes it's really hard to see that you are trustworthy. It's hard for me to put my faith in what I cannot see. And sometimes I'm curious as to why you don't answer my prayers in my timetable. Even so, I choose right now to put my full faith in you because you are the perfect object of faith. Amen.

Put Away Bitterness

And do not grieve the Holy Spirit of God, by whom
you were sealed for the day of redemption. Let all
bitterness and wrath and anger and clamor and
slander be put away from you, along with all malice.
Be kind to one another, tenderhearted, forgiving
one another, as God in Christ forgave you.

—EPHESIANS 4:30–32 ESV

To put away something is to banish it forever, to make a holy declaration that certain qualities cannot take up residence in your heart. For the believer, we must lock the door to these things: *bitterness, wrath, anger, clamor, slander, and malice.*

Bitterness means seeing the world only through the lens of pain turned to anger. It's a punitive position, bent on asking "Why me?" Wrath is unremitting anger with a desire to inflict harm. Anger is wrath to a lesser degree, a view of the world that tends to evaluate everything in terms of how it affects you. If your expectations aren't met, anger rears its head. Clamor is simply a grabbing at and hollering about your perceived injustices. Slander is saying mean, untrue things about others to discredit them. And malice is acting and saying this with evil intent.

In light of that, what parts of that list resonate with you? What do you struggle with? As you endeavor to lock the doors on those traits, the best way to shoo them out is to embrace the latter virtues: *kindness, tenderness, forgiveness*—as they are the opposite traits of the first list. May it be that we hold these three virtues as dear, that they typify our lives. When they do, we will be free to love and forgive others.

Jesus, I don't want to welcome bitterness, wrath, anger, clamor, slander, and malice. Show me when I've let those take hold of me. Instead, by your grace, infuse me with kindness, tenderness, and forgiveness today. Amen.

Honoring Others

Love each other with genuine affection, and
take delight in honoring each other.

—ROMANS 12:10 NLT

For some of us, genuine affection is difficult. We may have been injured in the past, or we grew up in homes where affection was absent. Paul would've known this about the human condition, but he still asked the Roman believers to love others with genuine affection.

How do you do that which you don't know how to do? Or, conversely, how do you love someone who struggles with affection? The answer lies at the end of the verse: *honor*. When we love people in our lives, we will naturally want to honor them.

To honor means to esteem people, to think highly of them, to find ways to bless them in specific them-shaped ways. When we love someone, we become a student, uncovering what makes each happy.

To love others with genuine affection may come naturally, or it may not, but a deep desire to honor another, coupled with God's affection, will help us love and honor them in new and sacrificial ways.

Spend some time today thinking about the five most significant people in your life. How can you love each specifically? What would make each person feel honored? If you're afraid you can't offer what each one needs, simply ask Jesus to help you.

Jesus, I do want to have affection for my friends and family. Help me to be affectionate and connected. I long to bring honor to those I love. Would you show me how to do that in specific ways this week? I truly want my loved ones to feel loved and honored. Amen.

He Will Quiet You

The LORD your God in your midst, the Mighty One, will
save; He will rejoice over you with gladness, He will quiet
you with His love, He will rejoice over you with singing.

—ZEPHANIAH 3:17

When we're under duress, we chatter. We call up a friend or maybe
talk to a spouse and share our anguish. We protest and worry.
Nothing is wrong with talking; it's human; it's healthy. But consider the beauty of this verse: "He will quiet you with His love."

Picture a hurting toddler who just skinned her knee. She is
crying, rightfully so. She runs to her mommy, tears and limbs fly-
ing akimbo, racing into Mommy's arms. Instinctively, Mommy
soothes her little one, maybe singing a song, stroking her hair,
looking at the boo-boo, bandaging it, and speaking gently to her.

Eventually the toddler stops crying and melts into the
embrace of her mother. This is a picture of God's love toward
you. While you may holler and cry and point to your pain, God
scoops you into his arms, sings over you, settles you down, and
listens to your cries until your sobbing becomes a whimper.
Eventually your tears cease, and you find yourself utterly safe in
your Father's arms.

He will quiet you. Even now. Even when the crying seems
long and longer. His delight is to calm his children.

Jesus, thank you that you quiet me with gentle songs, a warm embrace.
Help me to see you as a good parent who soothes a child after injury. And
instead of running away from you when I'm in pain, reverse my direction
so I run open-armed into your embrace. Amen.

He Will Deliver You from the Fowler

Surely He shall deliver you from the snare of the
fowler and from the perilous pestilence.

—PSALM 91:3

A fowler is a hunter who studies his prey enough to know their habits. Because he so deeply knows the weaknesses of his prey, he knows exactly how to snatch them. The traps he sets work because of his hunting skills.

We have a very real enemy who acts as a fowler in our lives: Satan. He is well acquainted with humanity, knows our weaknesses, and has discerned the best traps to snare us. He lurks as a conniving hunter.

But God sent Jesus to defeat Satan and his fowler ways. He is able to frustrate the fowler's evil intent. All we need to do is call out to him.

This scripture promises that God is our ultimate protector. If we are his children, he delights in delivering us from enemies and disease. That doesn't mean we won't face problems, temptations, and failures in this life, but it does mean that God is near and will help us.

Thank you, Jesus, for delivering me from Satan's schemes. I choose today to rest in your power and ability to conquer him. Thank you for all the beautiful protection you've given me over the course of my life. Amen.

Living Freely and Lightly

Come to me, all you who are weary and burdened,
and I will give you rest. Take my yoke upon you
and learn from me, for I am gentle and humble
in heart, and you will find rest for your souls.
For my yoke is easy and my burden is light.

—MATTHEW 11:28–30 NIV 1984

Resting—learning to weave practical Sabbaths into our schedules—isn't a punitive decree; it's God's generous endowment for our protection and perseverance. In the verses above, Matthew narrates Jesus' words regarding this gift better than anyone else.

Our heavenly Father is not some insensitive CEO pushing his minions for more billable hours. He cares far more about the posture of our hearts than our productivity. Even "good" things can become the enemy of God's best for us. Furthermore, our Creator encourages us to make time for rest because he knows we tend to get burned out when we have too many irons in the fire. Take more deep breaths. Pray. Listen to God's guiding voice. And pay closer attention to the anxious thoughts running through your mind and the selfish feelings lodged in your soul, which are contrary to what God says.

Our Redeemer's gift of rest allows us to fulfill our responsibilities while maintaining inner peace and intimacy with God. Aren't you glad Jesus advocated rest for his followers? He doesn't guilt us into overdoing it even when it comes to ministry. Instead, he teaches us to find a balance between going out and doing and being still and knowing.

*Lord, thank you that I can always come to you and rest in your arms.
Amen.*

Day of Reflection

And he took the children in his arms, placed
his hands on them and blessed them.

—MARK 10:16 NIV

SAFE IN THE ARMS OF JESUS

Safe in the arms of Jesus, safe on His gentle breast,
There by His love o'ershadowed, sweetly my soul shall rest.
Hark! 'tis the voice of angels, borne in a song to me,
Over the fields of glory, over the jasper sea.

—FANNY J. CROSBY, 1868

Your space—a poem, prayer, thoughts . . .

Success Is a Platform

Does the servant get special thanks for doing what's expected of him? It's the same with you. When you've done everything expected of you, be matter-of-fact and say, "The work is done. What we were told to do, we did."

—LUKE 17:10 MSG

Any "fame" we receive in this life is for the sole purpose of building up others, of serving those God places in our lives. And beyond that, if we think of ourselves as simply servants who serve a Master, we won't mire ourselves in pride.

It's that simple. When people thank us for simply being obedient, we graciously say thanks. And then we remind ourselves that we're just stewarding the gift God's given us. We're merely doing what he's told us to do. No fanfare. No parades. Just simple obedience.

Fame is simply a platform to proclaim Jesus' fame. No matter where you are, what "fame" you find, view your success as a way to shout Jesus' beauty and glory and power, and you will do well.

We all have the potential to struggle with being praised. We have to push down pride. Sometimes we fret too much about our careers. And there are times we like seats of prominence. But there's more to life than being recognized. And if, by chance, we're recognized, Jesus makes it clear that any position just gives a broader base to serve and to shine his fame.

Dear Jesus, help me withstand the trial of praise. I lay my ambitions at your feet. And if any of my wildest dreams come true, help me to steward them as I serve others and point out your deserving fame. Amen.

Staying with It

Staying with it—that's what God requires. Stay with it
to the end. You won't be sorry, and you'll be saved. All
during this time, the good news—the Message of the
kingdom—will be preached all over the world, a witness
staked out in every country. And then the end will come.

—MATTHEW 24:13–14 MSG

God's requirement of us as followers of Jesus is to stay with it.
To keep his kingdom at the forefront of our minds as we live our
day-to-day lives. As we do laundry or work hard on a project or
disciple our children, we must persevere, always keeping the end
in mind.

God's kingdom is expanding. Our job is to simply be faithful in the little things he asks us to do today. He entrusts us with
bigger tasks the more we are faithful to perform the small tasks
with joy.

God sees. He watches how we obey in the quiet places. He
will use us to expand his kingdom, but his ways may not always
be spectacular or up front. All he asks is that we stick with what
he's given us and stay with it to the end.

*Jesus, help me to be happy to be faithful in the small things. Even those
things that no one recognizes. I want to be a part of building Your kingdom. Amen.*

The Temporary vs. the Eternal

Therefore we do not lose heart. Though outwardly we are
wasting away, yet inwardly we are being renewed day by
day. For our light and momentary troubles are achieving for
us an eternal glory that far outweighs them all. So we fix
our eyes not on what is seen, but on what is unseen, since
what is seen is temporary, but what is unseen is eternal.

—2 CORINTHIANS 4:16–18 NIV

When we see ourselves in the mirror, chances are we look older
than we did ten years ago. Entropy has had its way, and age has
won. But God doesn't see things that way, and neither should we
deeply concern ourselves with our outward appearance.

The beauty that God wants to enact in us is one that can
always get better. We can be renewed every moment of every day.
Our souls can be more beautiful than they were ten years ago.

How does God give us beautiful souls? By walking with us
through trials. As we walk through them, we learn how to better
conquer the next mountain. We grow stronger. And the further
we walk holding his hand, the more we'll see the goal as he does.
Not the world's goals of fame, achievement, beauty, and stuff, but
his kingdom goals, which are not seen—things like honesty and
joy and holiness and dependence.

May it be that we look in the mirror today and see our souls
beautifying even as we age. And may we be more in love with
Jesus and his kingdom the older we get.

*Jesus, help me to see what you see. I want eternity eyes. Help me not
obsess over aging, but instead seek you to make me a beautiful soul. Amen.*

Needing Nothing

So let it grow, for when your endurance is fully developed,
you will be perfect and complete, needing nothing.

—JAMES 1:4 NLT

"So let it grow"—what we are to let grow is our endurance. Not our wit. Not our abilities to orate or lead. But our patient endurance. When we lean into endurance, James promises we'll need nothing.

Why will we need nothing if we've developed our endurance muscle? Because in doing so, we'll realize that whatever trial we are facing, we will endure it, not by our strength, but through the power Christ supplies. The more we endure, the more we see the availability of Jesus to meet our needs even when we're bowed under.

The more we walk when we feel like we can't, the less we'll rely on our own pluck and the more we'll see of the kingdom of God. As we walk through trials, God will also give us the gift of an eternal perspective, helping us realize that our trials aren't for nothing, and that they have deep significance not only on earth, but also in the afterlife.

What would your life look like if you needed nothing? If you'd developed the endurance muscle? How can you experience God's strength today? What do you need to let go of to find his power?

Jesus, I want to develop better endurance so I won't need anything. Help me to have an eternal perspective in my trials. I need you and your view of things to keep moving forward. Amen.

Hannah's Hope

And now, Lord, what do I wait for and expect?
My hope and expectation are in You.

—PSALM 39:7

Do you remember the story of Hannah from the Bible? Hannah was heartsick because she couldn't have a baby. She finally reached the point that she had stopped eating and cried continually. Yet she never gave up hope. How do we know Hannah still hoped? Because she continued to pray. Her hope was probably wobbly and threadbare and had lost most of its shiny wonder; yet she still beseeched God.

Bearing up under a great disappointment isn't easy, but then add a rival's taunting, and the situation feels heavy beyond bearing. In Hannah's case, her husband's other wife had borne him children. Hannah's emotional pain was so great it almost obscured hope. But Hannah cast herself once again on the altar of God's will and pled her case.

We don't know how long it was before Hannah gave birth, but Scripture tells us "it came to pass in the process of time that Hannah conceived and bore a son" (1 Samuel 1:20). Holding on to hope "in the process of time" can be most challenging. Hannah likely experienced moments when she thought she was too broken to be fixed. Over the years, Hannah must have found the waiting cruel. But after her prayers and her breakthrough moment with Eli, it appears that she was liberated and at peace.

Did God assure Hannah that she would have a child? Or did God assure her that her life was in his hands? Whatever the message, we don't find her agonizing again.

Lord, help me to remember that no matter how hopeless I feel, you're always there for me. You never leave my side even for a second. Amen.

Beyond Our Imaginations!

That is what the Scriptures mean when they say, "No eye
has seen, no ear has heard, and no mind has imagined
what God has prepared for those who love him."

—1 CORINTHIANS 2:9 NLT

When we live in light of pain or failures, we are guilty of a looking-back mentality. We filter everything through the lens of hurt. But God's call to us is a great looking forward, of anticipation.

While you may have been hurt in the past, the truth is that God is capable of healing you today. He is available in this very moment to shoulder whatever trial you're facing. He is the great I Am in that sense.

But he is also the great Not Yet. We won't experience every blessing on this side of heaven. We won't know the complexity of God's plan while we walk this earth. There are some questions that won't be answered. And yet, we can rest knowing that God will be bringing us amazing things.

He has prepared us for a future, joyful life with him and the people who love him. He has gifts and surprises galore. Let's live today in light of the Not Yet, trusting God's timing.

Jesus, thank you that you are the great I Am. I choose to give you my burdens right now. But even more than that I want to live as a woman who anticipates what you will do in the future. Thank you for preparing amazing things for me! Amen.

Day of Reflection

My Father's house has many rooms; if that
were not so, would I have told you that I am
going there to prepare a place for you?

—JOHN 14:2 NIV

SWEET BY AND BY

There's a land that is fairer than day,
and by faith we can see it afar;
For the Father waits over the way,
to prepare for us a dwelling there.

In the sweet by and by
We shall meet on that beautiful shore.
In the sweet by and by
We shall meet on that beautiful shore.

—SANFORD F. BENNETT, 1868

Your space—a poem, prayer, thoughts . . .

Abiding

I am the vine, you are the branches; he who
abides in Me and I in him, he bears much fruit,
for apart from Me you can do nothing.
—JOHN 15:5 NASB

It's a sobering thought that in our own efforts, we accomplish nothing. We who love to start campaigns or fill out petitions or bend over backward for a cause. If those endeavors aren't rooted in Jesus, they accomplish nothing of significance in the kingdom of God.

Jesus is the life of our lives. He is the vine to our branches. The more we realize that, the more we bear fruit. But if we live severed lives, happy in our own strength, what we produce will be burned up on the other side in heaven. What we do with impure motives will also mean nothing.

How can we possibly live this way, abiding in Jesus? If we examine our motives, we'll be sure to come up wanting. If we do things in our own strength, we'll accomplish nothing that remains. The only solution is to recognize once and for all that our ability is terribly small compared to God's great capability.

Jesus doesn't want our action or power. He wants our submission. He doesn't want us to erect monuments to him in our own strength, he wants to build his kingdom through us. All he desires is our humble dependence on him.

Jesus, I want to accomplish something for your kingdom. I'm tired of doing life in my own strength. Instead, help me to hope in you, to give you my life and trust you for the outcome. Be the strength in my weakness today. Amen.

Repentance and Trust

This is what the Sovereign LORD, the Holy One of Israel,
says: "In repentance and rest is your salvation, in quietness
and trust is your strength, but you would have none of it."

—ISAIAH 30:15 NIV

God has a way out for us, but it's not in a way we expect. We think
that trying harder and doing more will help us, but the counterintuitive is true. Realizing where we've gone wrong and repenting
of it is the first thing we must do to show God that we are no longer trusting in ourselves. And after that, trust, believing that God
will come through when we can't.

Our strength, according to Isaiah, derives from our ability
to repent and trust. But the problem was, the Israelites, much to
Isaiah's frustration, would have none of that. They would rather
live boastful lives in their own power. They would rather trust in
their own ability.

The implication is that God is truly available to us when
we're humble and willing to live as if we're not "all that." To live
with repentance and trust, we live in dependence on the God
who truly is "all that." We find God's sufficiency to be perfect
when we bow our hearts to those notions.

How can you practice repentance and trust today? Where
are you living in your own strength? Doing your own thing? Not
asking God for help? How have you trusted more in yourself than
in Jesus?

*Jesus, I choose right now to repent of my sin and my own ability. I want
to shift my allegiance from my strength to yours. I don't trust easily, but I
want to learn the art of trusting you for everything. Amen.*

Suffering for Doing What's Right

Now, who will want to harm you if you are eager
to do good? But even if you suffer for doing
what is right, God will reward you for it. So
don't worry or be afraid of their threats.

—1 PETER 3:13–14 NLT

Sometimes we suffer justly. We do something wrong or hurt a friend, and we feel the consequences. And because it's just, we learn to suffer with joy and humility.

But other times we suffer unjustly. We're accused of something completely untrue. We're misunderstood. We are threatened. What do we do in those circumstances? Do we peddle our message of rightness to the masses? Do we jump into hyperdrive, managing our reputations at every turn? Do we tell folks just how wrong their impressions are?

Those are certainly possibilities, but Peter here offers a different tact. He tells us not to be afraid of other people's threats, that if we suffer for doing something good, we have a different kind of mandate: receive a reward.

In this world, there will be misunderstanding. When Jesus walked the earth, he was often misunderstood and accused of all sorts of wrongdoing. But he learned the secret of entrusting himself to God. And God rewarded him.

If you suffer unjustly today, lean on Jesus. Trust him for your reward. He sees.

Jesus, I don't like to suffer for something I didn't do, or be perceived wrongly. Help me to endure this time so that I can trust you for reward. I need you and your help. Amen.

Wise and Innocent

For the report of your obedience has reached to all;
therefore I am rejoicing over you, but I want you to be
wise in what is good, and innocent in what is evil. And
the God of peace will soon crush Satan under your feet.

—ROMANS 16:19–20 NASB

Paul tells the Roman Christians that they have a reputation—a great reputation of obedience to Christ. This makes Paul jump for joy, but in that joy, he offers a caution. He advises the believers to be wise in good things and innocent in evil things.

What does it mean to be wise in good things? We get to know other believers who help us grow, who challenge us. We read God's Word. We pray and listen to God. We serve those who can't serve us back. We look for God's face on the distressing disguise of the poor. We give away our resources.

What does it mean to be innocent in evil things? It means we avoid coarse talk and ungodly websites. It means we walk away when gossip reigns, or change the subject. It means we confront evil instead of tolerate it. It means we actively choose to keep our minds full of good, pure things.

The promise is that if we can be wise and innocent, God will defeat the enemy in our lives and shower grace upon us. What an amazing promise!

Jesus, I want to be wise in what's good, and innocent in what's evil. Train me even today to know the difference. Help me be brave and strong. Amen.

Tangled-Up Messes

Why am I discouraged? Why so sad? I will put my hope
in God! I will praise him again—my Savior and my God!

—Psalm 42:11 NLT

Even if you'd been the only person on earth, Jesus would still
have done it. He would have come to earth and gone through the
crucifixion just for you. Jesus didn't go through that ordeal so
that we could merely survive. He said he did it so we could "have
life, and that [we] might have it more abundantly" (John 10:10
KJV). Or, as the Message version puts it, so that we could have
"more and better life than [we] ever dreamed of."

When we face some overwhelming problem or when we're
urgently trying to overcome some despised thing, we cry out to
him, begging him to help us. And in response, as the friend of
Job told his problem-prone pal, "God always answers, one way
or another, even when people don't recognize his presence" (Job
33:12 MSG). The apostle Paul instructed us to "be cheerful no
matter what; pray all the time; thank God no matter what happens" (1 Thessalonians 5:16 MSG). We should be thankful for the
problems we encounter because God may be using them to snap
us out of whatever distractions we've drifted into. As Job's friend
also said, God may use our difficulties to "get [our] attention
through pain" (Job 33:19 MSG).

When God finally gets our attention, we're wise to keep it
focused on him—because that's how we'll get through the next
challenge, which is probably waiting right around the corner.
And through it all, we have to remember that no matter what
kind of tangled-up mess we've landed in, God is going to use it
for our ultimate good.

*Lord, I will put my hope in you even in times of trouble. Thank you for
using my tangled-up messes for good. Amen.*

Saving Our Lives

Then Jesus said to his disciples, "Whoever wants
to be my disciple must deny themselves and take up
their cross and follow me. For whoever wants to save
their life will lose it, but whoever loses their life for
me will find it. What good will it be for someone
to gain the whole world, yet forfeit their soul? Or
what can anyone give in exchange for their soul?"

—MATTHEW 16:24–26 NIV

Jesus says some hard things in this passage. He speaks of denying
ourselves, choosing the way of the cross—which certainly means
dying to our old way of doing things—and actively following
wherever he leads. If we try to micromanage our lives and save
ourselves in our own strength, we will fail.

Stop and think about that a minute.

In our own small strength, there is nothing in us that can
save us from our sin. Nothing. Only Jesus can. Even if you were
the richest woman on earth, you couldn't buy eternity in heaven
for your soul.

The only avenue to salvation is through Jesus Christ. And
that takes humility on our part—a recognition that we cannot do
what he alone can do. The promise in this verse, though, is that
if we lay down our lives, wills, sins at the foot of his cross, we will
ultimately find abundant life.

*Jesus, I realize that I can't save myself. I know there's nothing I could
do or buy that will take care of my sins or my standing with you. Thank
you for taking on your cross willingly, then rising again. In you today, I
choose life. Amen.*

Day of Reflection

Not that we are sufficient of ourselves to think of anything
as being from ourselves, but our sufficiency is from God.

—2 CORINTHIANS 3:5

I NEED THEE EVERY HOUR

I need Thee ev'ry hour, most gracious Lord;
No tender voice like Thine can peace afford.

I need Thee ev'ry hour, most holy One,
Oh, make me Thine indeed, Thou blessed Son!

I need Thee, O I need thee; Ev'ry hour I need Thee;
O bless me now, my Savior I come to Thee!

—ANNIE S. HAWKS; ROBERT LOWRY, REFRAIN, 1872

Your space—a poem, prayer, thoughts . . .

Born Again

Thank God, the God and Father of our Lord
Jesus Christ, that in his great mercy we men
have been born again into a life full of hope,
through Christ's rising again from the dead!

—1 Peter 1:3 J.B. Phillips translation

We've heard the words "born again" strung together, not always in a flattering light. But reconsider the words. To be rebirthed. To start over fresh. To inaugurate life all over again. To be a part of the great do-over.

When we follow Jesus, we are born again. What used to be our lives now becomes brand-spanking new. All our sins are buried in the deepest sea. All our pain is swallowed up. All our regret is overcome. We have a new start.

That's why Peter calls it a living hope. Our new life is full of possibilities, of not-yets. It's permeated with hope because we truly follow a Living Hope. Jesus who was once dead for our sins is now, at the very moment, alive—breathing, walking, moving. His rising from the dead not only confirmed his power, but it gave us a living Savior, a constant companion on the journey we walk.

Let those words sink into your soul today. Born again. Living hope. What would your life look like if you truly lived by those words? The old is gone; the new is come. And hope reigns eternal.

Jesus, thank you that you enabled me to be born again. Help me not to live in light of my past, but in anticipation of a glorious future with you. Take my eyes off me and my regrets, and place them on you resurrected. I hope in you alone. Amen.

The Story of His Love

> Your love, GOD, is my song, and I'll sing it! I'm forever telling everyone how faithful you are. I'll never quit telling the story of your love—how you built the cosmos and guaranteed everything in it.
>
> —PSALM 89:1 MSG

Everyone who knows Jesus has a story of his love—a testimony. What is yours? How has God rescued you? When did he put a song in your heart? How have you experienced God's faithfulness in the past three years? Your answer to these questions is the story of God's love toward you.

May it be that we are ready at all times to sing and tell this story—to our families, to strangers, to specific people God prompts us to share with. Stories about God's faithfulness are full of danger, adventure, despair, redemption, and hope. And as we tell them, we invite others to experience God's story too.

Take some time to write down a recent story of God's love, maybe in your journal or a blog or in a letter to a friend. What was the setting of your story? Who were the characters? What was the main conflict? What difficulties did you encounter in the story? And how did Jesus rescue you? How are you different as a result?

Our stories are important. Living our stories well can be life changing. And God's overall story of humanity is one giant story arc of redemption.

Jesus, I want to live a great story, and I want to tell—or sing!—your story of love to others today. Would you put people in my path today with whom I can share my story? Give me boldness to tell it, no matter how scared I might be. Amen.

Singing to Our Bountiful God

I will sing to the LORD, because He
has dealt bountifully with me.

—PSALM 13:6

The word *bountiful* means generosity, liberal giving, abundance. It means having more than we need, an overflowing gift. God, in light of that, has dealt bountifully with us, though we don't always pause to consider it.

Look over your life today. Consider all the things God has graced you with: family, friends, provision, redemption, forgiveness, grace, hope, joy, new relationships, a church, a home. God's dealings with his children are bountiful. And when we have eyes tuned to see that, we'll also live with a bountiful perspective.

How do you cultivate a bountiful perspective? The psalmist gives one indication: singing, specifically to the Lord. To sing to the Lord is a sheer act of will. It means that despite how we perceive our circumstances in the moment, we are choosing to sing a song to him.

Whether that song occurs in the shower, in the car, off key, or a joyful noise, something dynamic happens when we pull our eyes off the world around us and focus solely on Jesus.

Jesus, you have dealt bountifully with me in so many ways. I can't even count them. Today I want to sing to you out of gratitude. Help me to sing with joy. Amen.

When Afraid: Trust in God

When I am afraid, I will put my trust in You. In God, whose word I praise, In God I have put my trust; I shall not be afraid. What can mere man do to me?

—PSALM 56:3–4 NASB

Often we worry about what others can do to us. Words we hear stifle us. Gossip that another friend has spread about us levels us. An enemy undermines us, and we see just how destructive other people can be. Someone we trust betrays or abuses, and we are left wounded and wanting.

But these verses give us an important reminder. God is bigger. Because he is bigger, we can trust him and entrust our hearts to him. No matter what people throw our way, they can never be bigger than God, nor can their words level us. They are mere men and women. They do not have ultimate authority.

We must settle our worth today. Our worth is not based on people's opinions of us. Our worth comes from God. He created us and he loves us. We can truly rest in his opinions of us.

Life should not be lived in fear of what others will do. Instead, we live our lives in confident hope that God is with us, sees us, and will sustain us if others throw words or insults our way.

Jesus, forgive me when I see people as bigger in my life than you. I want to see you as bigger, as the One who will take on all the words hurled my way. Really, it's only your opinion of me that counts. Remind me this week in a specific, tangible way that you see me and love me. Amen.

Guilt? Gone.

When I refused to confess my sin, my body wasted away,
and I groaned all day long. Day and night your hand
of discipline was heavy on me. My strength evaporated
like water in the summer heat. Finally, I confessed all
my sins to you and stopped trying to hide my guilt.
I said to myself, "I will confess my rebellion to the
LORD." And you forgave me! All my guilt is gone.

—PSALM 32:3–5 NLT

David wrote this psalm after he committed adultery with
Bathsheba, then essentially ordered her husband killed to cover
up his sin. When he kept everything quiet, he wasted away. He
groaned. He felt the heaviness of guilt like a wet blanket in a shivery winter. Every ounce of vitality drained from him.

The psalm hinges on the word *finally*. David *finally* let God
in on his terrible secret—even though God already knew. David
gave up trying to hide his guilt. He called his sin what it was:
rebellion. And most likely he expected severe and swift justice.

Instead he received surprising mercy. God forgave him. He
took the guilt away.

When we hide our sin, we're not fooling anyone, particularly
not God. The weight of the secret devours us like stage four cancer. Our hiding makes it so we can't bear to look in the mirror.

If you're suffering from this kind of guilt and hiding, now is
the time to get right with God. Give what was done in the darkness to God. Let the light of day shine on it. Then wait expectantly
for relief. Freedom. Joy. And no more guilt.

*Jesus, show me where I'm hiding. I don't want to waste away, harboring
my sin way deep inside. I want it out there, in your light, because I'm tired
and I desperately need your forgiveness. Amen.*

A Grace-Filled Throne

Let us then approach the throne of grace with
confidence, so that we may receive mercy and
find grace to help us in our time of need.

—HEBREWS 4:16 NIV 1984

Imagine being invited to meet the Queen of England. Through
a series of background checks and pre-meeting meetings, you
finally stand—bow!—in her presence, share a few words, then
leave. And what if before you leave, she asks you to come sit down
and have tea with her? She inquires about your life, your hopes,
your dreams. You spend an hour with her this way, she pouring
tea while getting to know you.

Now think about meeting a brutal dictator who is known for
killing his own people. The same protocol is in place: background
checks and meetings. But when you're ushered in, you feel yourself
shake under the pressure. This man sneers at you, says something
entirely impolite about your country of origin, then threatens to
torture you unless you leave his presence at once.

Approaching God is more like the first scenario. Yet sometimes we move closer to God, trembling, fearing him to be an
unfair, crazy tyrant. The Scripture says his throne is bejeweled
in grace, not scorn. He invites us, because of Jesus' blood shed on
our behalf on the cross, to have tea, to be known and validated.
He loves us and wants to spend time with us.

How about you? How do you view God and his throne? Is it
a place of safety or fear? Of joyful reverence or shrinking trepida-
tion? Rest today in knowing that God is for you and his desire is
to welcome you.

*Jesus, help me truly understand that you sit on a grace-filled throne.
Please show me today how extravagant your grace is. I want to revel in
it. Amen.*

Day of Reflection

That is why I am suffering as I am. Yet this is no
cause for shame, because I know whom I have
believed, and am convinced that he is able to guard
what I have entrusted to him until that day.

—2 TIMOTHY 1:12 NIV

BLESSED ASSURANCE

Blessed assurance, Jesus is mine!
Oh what a foretaste of glory divine!
Heir of salvation, purchase of God,
born of His spirit, washed in His blood!

Perfect submission, all is at rest,
I in my Savior am happy and blest;
Watching and waiting, looking above,
filled with His goodness, lost in His love.

This is my story, this is my song.
Praising my Savior all the day long.

—FANNY J. CROSBY, 1873

Your space—a poem, prayer, thoughts . . .

Garbage

What is more, I consider everything a loss because
of the surpassing worth of knowing Christ Jesus
my Lord, for whose sake I have lost all things. I
consider them garbage, that I may gain Christ.

—PHILIPPIANS 3:8 NIV

When we throw something away, we believe it is meaningless to us. An old orange peel holds no appeal. A torn item of clothing becomes a rag. A broken piece of pottery can no longer hold our cereal in the morning. So we discard.

The apostle Paul used the metaphor of garbage, which in the Greek actually means dung, to describe his life before Jesus. Paul had been a Super Pharisee, persecuting the church, zealous, and very high in religious ranking. He'd been popular and esteemed in his circles.

That all meant not only nothing, but it also meant refuse, garbage, dung. All that religious effort wasn't just neutral; it was odious, something to distance himself from.

The problem today is that much we see as valuable is actually garbage. We are attracted by trinkets and small worldly treasures, and we forget that none of it means anything. What is truly valuable isn't our effort, or things, or prestige, but Jesus Christ himself. When we gain him, we gain everything.

Jesus, I want to consider my own efforts and my striving for stuff as garbage. Help me to do that. Instead, I want to treasure you, to follow you, to be near you. Amen.

Forever

Having been born again, not of corruptible seed but
incorruptible, through the word of God which lives
and abides forever, because "All flesh is as grass,
and all the glory of man as the flower of the grass.
The grass withers, and its flower falls away, but the
word of the LORD endures forever." Now this is the
word which by the gospel was preached to you.

—1 PETER 1:23–25

We see death every year with the turn of the seasons. In spring,
the world erupts in color and fragrance, thriving through the
summer, only to turn orange, brown, and yellow and fall to the
ground. The flowers and grass all wither eventually, and winter
has its icy way.

But something will remain forever. It's God's Word. Whatever
he utters lasts eternally.

Think of the things God has said. He made the world with
four words, "Let there be light." He promised Abraham that he
would bless him so that the nation that sprung from him would
show that light to the entire world. He spoke the law into existence. Jesus was and is his ultimate Word, the best gift ever given.
And when Jesus sacrificed it all for us, he concluded with the
words, "It is finished." He promised to come again, then usher in
his kingdom forever and ever.

Stopping to ponder that will help us all reframe our days.
Yes, plants die. Yes, people die. Yes, dreams die. But God's Word
never does. It echoes throughout generations and shouts into
eternity.

*Jesus, help me to remember that your words are eternal. When my life
fades, or I watch the plants around me die in the winter, help that to serve
as a reminder that my days are fleeting, but you are forever. Amen.*

Jesus Stands with You

> God has said, "Never will I leave you; never will I
> forsake you." So we say with confidence, "The Lord is my
> helper; I will not be afraid. What can man do to me?"
>
> —HEBREWS 13:5–6 NIV 1984

In the verses above the writer asks, "What can man do to me?" Seriously? What kind of question is that? Man can do all sorts of things to me. He can bully me, insult me, threaten me. He can divorce me, abuse me, abandon me, injure me, cripple me. He can bankrupt me, jail me, kill me. But what he can't do, what he can never do, is make God leave me. No one in the universe can do that.

When God promises, "Never will I leave you; never will I forsake you," you never have to worry about being left alone, ever again. You will never, in time or eternity, be all alone. And when God says he will help you, he means that his constant presence goes far beyond merely spectating; he means that his ever-present hand is there to grab you, hold you, and give you whatever assistance you require, right up to and beyond the moment he uses that hand to bring you to heaven to live with him forever.

Nothing that happens surprises God, so trust him in the midst of your pain.

God loves you, and nothing can separate you from his love.

God will be with you always, and whatever you have to face, he will go through it with you.

Do you believe those things? If you do, then *stand* there. Stand on the Rock. Stand, when your knees buckle and your tears fall like rain. Stand when everything else gives way. You can do that because Jesus himself continues to stand with you. Forever.

Lord, thank you for never leaving me. Even in my lowest moments, you have always been there waiting to pick me back up. Thank you for your never-failing love. Amen.

Bad Circumstances
= Opportunity

I want you to know, brothers, that what has happened
to me has really served to advance the gospel, so that
it has become known throughout the whole imperial
guard and to all the rest that my imprisonment is for
Christ. And most of the brothers, having become
confident in the Lord by my imprisonment, are
much more bold to speak the word without fear.

—PHILIPPIANS 1:12–14 ESV

When we find ourselves in pressing circumstances, our first
tendency is to complain and ask God to remove us from those
situations. We forget about the apostle Paul's response to imprisonment when we do so.

While it's fine to give our requests for relief to God, perhaps
it would be better if we simply ask God how we can best glorify
and share him in the midst of our painful circumstances.

A woman with stage four cancer found a way to love others
while she underwent chemotherapy. She brought snacks and
blankets to the others suffering through their treatments. Instead
of seeing cancer as a prison, she viewed it as a way to further the
gospel.

Although it's never easy to walk through trials, having a Paul
perspective on them will help us see the valuable truth that God
can use even the most pressing things for the sake of his kingdom.

*Jesus, help me to discern how my current circumstances can be a part of
furthering your kingdom. Forgive me for only seeking solutions. Help me
instead to be proactive during this season, glorifying you however I can.
Amen.*

God Is *Always* There

Is there anyplace I can go to avoid your Spirit? To be out
of your sight? If I climb to the sky, you're there! If I go
underground, you're there! If I flew on morning's wings
to the far western horizon, You'd find me in a minute—
you're already there waiting! Then I said to myself, "Oh,
he even sees me in the dark! At night I'm immersed in
the light!" It's a fact: darkness isn't dark to you; night and
day, darkness and light, they're all the same to you.

—PSALM 139:7–12 MSG

We know God is everywhere, but often we live as if he's not. In
this psalm, we're beautifully reminded that God is wherever we
are, whether we find ourselves on the pinnacle of success or the
doldrums of despair.

What would your life look like if you truly lived out this belief
of God's omnipresence—God is everywhere?

Even in the dark of night, when you're woken up by an awful
dream—even then God is there. Even in hearing the diagnosis
you dreaded, God is there. Even when a loved one passes over to
heaven, God is there. Even when your dreams crash like waves on
the beach, retreating again, God is there. Even when your spouse
hurts, God is there. Even when the sun doesn't seem it will rise
because your sadness overwhelms, God is there. Even when you
get every single thing you want, yet find it empty, God is there.

He fills all and is in all. Because of that, we can trust him. We
can believe that he will be with us no matter what.

*Jesus, I forget that you're everywhere. Or sometimes I don't invite you into
my joy or pain. Please help me live my life believing you are there. I want
to have that kind of faith. I want to hope in your available presence. Amen.*

The Lord Is Peace

Gideon perceived that he was the angel of the LORD.
And Gideon said, "Alas, O Lord GOD! For now I
have seen the angel of the LORD face to face." But
the LORD said to him, "Peace be to you. Do not fear;
you shall not die." Then Gideon built an altar there
to the LORD and called it, The LORD Is Peace.

—JUDGES 6:22–24 ESV

Gideon had an amazing, life-altering encounter with the angel of
the Lord. His response to this was a deep sense of dread because
God's reply to him indicates Gideon thought he would die.
Gideon's response to his encounter was to erect a monument to
God about his peace.

When we face hardship and we worry about what will happen to us, God's perfect plan is for us to recognize him as the God
of peace. He is not the God who disturbs your heart or makes you
fret about the future. He is not the God of death and despair. No,
he grants peace even in the peace-less places.

Are you worrying today? Has your stomach clenched in fear?
Remember Gideon, and God's gentle response. God is peace. He
is *your* peace. Your trust in that, giving God everything and asking him to settle your heart, is your way of erecting a monument
to God's peace.

The world might swirl around you in anxiety, but God is stronger still. He and he alone can give you peace in the whirlwind.

*Jesus, thank you that you are my peace. When I'm slipping into worry,
please remind me afresh that you delight in giving me peace. I choose
today to build a monument to your peace by trusting you for the next step
in my journey. Amen.*

Day of Reflection

The righteous person may have many troubles,
but the Lord delivers him from them all.

—PSALM 34:19 NIV

IT IS WELL WITH MY SOUL

When peace like a river, attendeth my way
When sorrows like sea billows roll;
Whatever my lot, Thou hast taught me to say,
"It is well. It is well with my soul."
It is well. It is well. With my soul. With my soul.
It is well. It is well with my soul.

—HORATIO G. SPAFFORD, 1873

Your space—a poem, prayer, thoughts . . .

Don't Despise Discipline

He who neglects discipline despises himself, but he
who listens to reproof acquires understanding.

—PROVERBS 15:32 NASB

It seems the opposite would be true. If we love ourselves, we'll
avoid people who tell us the truth about ourselves. Why? Because
it hurts to hear the truth, and it's never fun to be on the receiving
end of discipline.

But the writer of Proverbs shows us a different story. If we
actively push away the people in our lives who speak the truth
in love to us, if we run from rebuke, we are actually despising
ourselves.

God wants us to be people of understanding and wisdom. He
longs for us to grow and mature. But we can't if we have rough
edges. The primary method God uses to sand down our rough
edges is other believers. It's being in community deep enough that
others can see those edges, lovingly talk to us about them, and
pray for us as we grow beyond them.

So do yourself a loving favor today. Be teachable. Be willing to
hear discipline-laden words from a friend. Their words are God's
gift of growth to you.

*Jesus, thank you for putting good folks in my life who dare to speak the
truth in love. I confess, it's not always easy to hear, and sometimes I push
back. Help me to be teachable when I hear words like that. Amen.*

Recipe for Living

Rejoice with those who rejoice; mourn with those
who mourn. Live in harmony with one another.
Do not be proud, but be willing to associate with
people of low position. Do not be conceited.

—ROMANS 12:15–16 NIV

Paul outlines a simple, yet difficult to follow recipe for living well with others in this passage. He reminds us of the importance of true empathy—that when a friend is hurting, we don't try to cheer her up, but simply cry alongside her. Or when a friend shares a victory, we don't silently envy her or try to demean her dream, but we genuinely celebrate. Becoming a friend who can rejoice and not secretly be jealous is a rare gift indeed.

Paul encourages harmony. The way to live that out is to let go of our pride. When we're proud, we only associate with people who will benefit us, or who make us feel more important. He warns us about becoming conceited, and he encourages us to hang out with people whom others overlook. When we do this, we're more like Jesus.

Take a look at your relationships as they exist right now. Do you have friends who will cry with you? Laugh with you? Rejoice with you? Are you that type of friend? When was the last time you hung out with someone on the fringes? Have you ever held yourself aloof from others?

The way you treat others reveals your heart.

Jesus, help me to be the kind of friend I desire others to be for me. I want to weep alongside. I want to genuinely rejoice with others who succeed. I want to look for the overlooked. Help me walk that way this week. Amen.

Pruning

I am the true vine, and my Father is the vinedresser.
Every branch in me that does not bear fruit he
takes away, and every branch that does bear fruit
he prunes, that it may bear more fruit.

—JOHN 15:1–2 ESV

Jesus reminds us in this passage that he is the vine and his Father is the gardener, or the One who tends the vine.

First let's reorient ourselves around Jesus being the vine. We forget this. We think we're the vine. We think everything that must be done must originate from our effort. But anything worth pointing to in the kingdom must always be originated in Jesus, our vine.

From those vines burst forth branches, and from those branches burst forth fruit. If our lives are connected to the vine, we will naturally bear fruit. But if we are dried-up branches unconnected to the vine, we will never produce fruit. Dead branches must be cut away for the sake of the rest of the plant.

That's why God the Father prunes us. He is best able to see where we are trying to create our own fruit in our own effort. He knows those efforts won't benefit us or bless the kingdom, so he kindly—and painfully—prunes them. He wants us to fully reflect the vine and the vine's action in our lives.

Jesus, forgive me for trying to be my own vine. Forgive me for trying to produce fruit all by myself. I give God the Father permission now to prune me so there's more of you, less of me. Amen.

Taking Time

But a Samaritan, as he traveled, came where the man
was; and when he saw him, he took pity on him.

—LUKE 10:33 NIV

The point of the parable of the good Samaritan was primarily
to illustrate the kindness of a Samaritan who saved the life of a
badly injured Jewish man. For some of us, the parable illustrates
an additional lesson: the need to simply take time to do the right
thing, the kind thing.

Psychologists conducted a Good Samaritan study with seminary students. They asked each one to prepare a sermon on the
parable of the good Samaritan. Each seminarian then was told to
walk to a building only a few blocks away and give his sermon to
a waiting audience.

The researchers sent each seminarian over to the building
with different instructions. Persons in the first group were told to
hurry because they were starting out later than planned. Persons
in the second group were told they need not hurry because they
were a few minutes ahead of schedule.

On the way to the building, each of the seminarians saw a
bloody, battered, and moaning person lying in an alley. The seminarians did not know this was a staged scene.

The results of this study revealed that those who thought
they had more time stopped to help the "victim." The other group
literally stepped over the victim in their haste to get to the building on time and deliver their sermon on the good Samaritan.

Would you have taken the time to do the right thing?

*Lord, I pray that I will be open to situations where I can be a good
Samaritan. Amen.*

The Art of Servanthood

So Jesus called them together and said, "You know that
the rulers in this world lord it over their people, and
officials flaunt their authority over those under them.
But among you it will be different. Whoever wants to be
a leader among you must be your servant, and whoever
wants to be first among you must be the slave of everyone
else. For even the Son of Man came not to be served but
to serve others and to give his life as a ransom for many."

—MARK 10:42–45 NLT

Jesus didn't come to this earth so important folks could serve and
crown him. He came to serve us and serve his Father's purposes.
Why is it that we think we're owed service?

The happiest people are those who spend their hearts and
wills and affections and resources for the sake of others. They
bend low, searching for opportunities to bless those less fortunate.
They make it a point to find a hurting person and then specifically
encourage her. They hear about a need, then quietly meet it.

When we look back at our lives, we'll be most satisfied when
we see those times we set aside our agendas for the sake of others.
Not that we're doormats, but that we, like Jesus, willfully choose
to love the people around us. May it be that we become more and
more like him, stooping low, joyfully serving.

In this world of me-first, let's ask God for the strength to be
him-first and others-first. May we love others as we'd love to be
loved. And may we understand the beauty of venturing outside
our comfort zones for the sake of others.

Jesus, lift my gaze from myself, my needs, my hurts, so I can see the rest of
the world you created. Help me be like you, seeking to serve others. I don't
want to be a Me Monster. Amen.

An Undivided Heart

Teach me your way, LORD, that I may rely
on your faithfulness; give me an undivided
heart, that I may fear your name.

—PSALM 86:11 NIV

The psalmist prays for an undivided heart so he can better learn to fear—reverence—God's name. What is an undivided heart?

It's a heart that only beats for God. A heart whose affections are solely on him.

In today's world, what is a divided heart? It's when our focus veers and we find other things to fill us other than God. Here are some tangible examples:

- We worry more about money than pray about God's provision.
- We spend time trying to make everyone like us.
- We climb the ladder of success, waiting for achievement to make us feel better about ourselves.
- We become addicted to things: food, drugs, porn, TV, the Internet, e-mail, Facebook, exercise.
- We let something from the past define us in the present and stayed emotionally tethered to "back then."

Having a divided heart prevents us from growing deep and wide in Jesus. Take some inventory of your heart today, asking God to show you where your loyalty is divided.

Jesus, I want an undivided heart, but it's so hard. I want things. I want relationships. I want my world ordered the way I like it. Turn my eyes and heart toward you today. I want to love you fully. Amen.

Day of Reflection

What is more, I consider everything a loss because
of the surpassing worth of knowing Christ Jesus
my Lord, for whose sake I have lost all things.

—PHILIPPIANS 3:8 NIV

TAKE MY LIFE AND LET IT BE

Take my life and let it be consecrated, Lord to Thee.
Take my hands and let them move,
at the impulse of Thy love, At the impulse of Thy love.

Take my love, my God, I pour at Thy feet its treasure store.
Take myself and I will be ever, only, all for Thee,
Ever, only, all for Thee.

—FRANCES R. HAVERGAL, 1874

Your space—a poem, prayer, thoughts . . .

The Enrichment Factor

Whoever brings blessing will be enriched, and
one who waters will himself be watered.

—PROVERBS 11:25 ESV

In this world of grab-everything-you-want, it's counterintuitive to read this proverb. We sometimes believe—whether we say it out loud or not—that those who are truly enriched are those who are rich in the first place. Those who take and keep are the wealthy ones.

But in God's economy, he reverses things. Those who let go of what they have in order to help someone else receive much from God. And those who look for parched people in need of water will eventually be watered themselves.

Who in your life needs blessing? Who is thirsty and dry? Has God pressed someone into your heart—a struggling friend, an elderly neighbor, a wayward child? If he has, love them lavishly. Seek ways to tangibly bless them, and ask God for creative ways to water each person suffering drought.

The promise is that we who live a giving lifestyle end up living in abundance.

Jesus, I want to exemplify a giving lifestyle. Place people in my path this week who need blessing and watering. I understand that anything I give is simply a regift from what you've already abundantly given me. Amen.

Freely Give

One gives freely, yet grows all the richer; another
withholds what he should give, and suffers only want.

—PROVERBS 11:24 ESV

This proverb points out the deprivation of a stingy life. Those who
hoard things in fear of losing everything end up suffering. Why?
Because things become an idol, and their hold on us only grows with
time. The longer we cling to money and possessions, the more we
hoard things out of fear; the more we withhold our love and possessions and money from those in need, the angrier and colder our
hearts become.

Contrast that with the woman who freely gives. She sees her life
and possessions, and even her energy and time, as gifts from God.
They aren't hers in the first place, so why hoard them? She actively
seeks out people who are in need so she can bless them.

What is the result of this kind of lavish perspective? Richness.
And growth. It's an interesting truth that what we grab at defines us
and deprives us. But what we let go of gives us wings in the meantime.

Who can you bless today? Who can you lavish God's abundance
on? May it be that you live a free life!

*Jesus, I want to live in freedom and joy and generosity. I give you permission
to step in when I'm trying to hoard or I'm living my life in fear. I love you and
I need your abundance in my life. Amen.*

Life's True Treasures

A bowl of vegetables with someone you love is
better than steak with someone you hate.

—PROVERBS 15:17 NLT

Some people marry for money. They figure having more stuff, coupled with the lure of security, is better than finding a true, suitable marriage partner. But eventually all the money or security in the world cannot replace joy or harmony.

The true mark of life isn't stuff. It's people. Whether we have little or a lot, if we have great relationships, we are rich. We're like George Bailey in *It's a Wonderful Life* who faces bankruptcy and jail time, but finds great wealth in the kindness of his friends.

Our lives should reflect that truth. Are we spending more time on chasing after money or on pursuing the relationships God has given us? Are we more inclined to think money will fill us, or have we realized that the richest people are those with good friends?

If you feel deprived today and you don't have the amount of money you'd like, take a moment to thank God for your family and friends who love you deeply. They are your treasure. They are better than money.

Jesus, open my eyes to your real blessings: the people in my life. I am sorry for thinking money can buy happiness. Make me a person who is a great friend, a supportive family member, a lover of people. Amen.

God Holds Success

He holds success in store for the upright, he is
a shield to those whose walk is blameless.

—PROVERBS 2:7 NIV

While it's hard to measure success because there are so many
ways to gauge it—financial, familial, relational, missional, personal, etc.—ultimately God's desire is for us to have a successful
walk with him.

But sometimes it's hard to walk forward when we face loss
or failure. It's hard to believe that God wants us to be successful spiritually, particularly when he sends trials our way. We get
caught up blaming him for our circumstances and forget he is
for our welfare.

This verse says he stores up success. It's held in his vast
reserve. Not only that, he promises to shield us when we've made
blamelessness a goal.

God is sovereign. That means everything in our lives filters
through his control. Nothing escapes his notice, even our current circumstances. We may not feel successful today. We may
be discouraged. But the good news is that God is near no matter
what happens to us. His nearness is what helps us walk through
trials, learn from them, and become stronger and more successful because of them.

*Jesus, is it true that you are holding success for me? Help me to remember
that when a trial comes my way. Be so near that your presence helps me
endure well, learn a lot, and grow spiritually. Amen.*

Bread of Heaven

The manna came down on the camp
with the dew during the night.

—NUMBERS 11:9 NLT

Manna is described as a small, round substance, which Moses proclaimed to be "the bread" God had provided for the Israelites in
the wilderness. It appeared on the ground every morning, sort of
like frost on a cool winter morning. Manna is referred to as "the
bread of heaven" (Psalm 105:40), which was literally true since
it rained down from heaven as provision for the Israelites (see
Exodus 16:4).

At first, the Hebrews were awed and grateful for this bounty
from heaven. But after, say, a month or two of the same fare, this
staple in their diet—which they ended up eating for every meal for
forty years—began to wear a little thin. The idea of finding milk
and honey in the promised land made them salivate. The Israelites
named this mysterious bread "manna," which in Hebrew means
"What is it?" We might take a look at the Lord's latest "gift" and
say, "What's this? God, I don't remember asking for patience. So
why is the driver in front of me dawdling like we're in a parade?"

Manna comes in forms we don't always appreciate. But we
regularly need to be reminded that manna is provision from God,
sustenance for the soul to be eaten with gratefulness. Rather than
responding to the item on your platter with the question, "What is
it?" we would be better off saying, "Well, now, what's this?!"

*Lord, thank you that you supply manna even when I don't always gra-
ciously receive it. Help me to remember, as your heavenly gifts float into
my life, that they come from your good hand. Amen.*

Foolish Things

Consider your calling, brethren, that there were
not many wise according to the flesh, not many
mighty, not many noble; but God has chosen the
foolish things of the world to shame the wise.

—1 CORINTHIANS 1:26–27 NASB

We tend to disqualify ourselves for God's service because of our
limitations. We know all too well what lurks in our hearts. We
can recount our failures. We look back and see our dumb mistakes and wish we could reverse time and correct them.

But God promises something shocking. It's actually our
foolishness and weakness that he sees as assets. Why? Because
when we realize our lack, we reach for his abundance. When we
know we're foolish or needy or incapable, we allow him to be
wise, strong, and capable in our stead.

He chooses us in our weakened state because then he'll get
the glory. We'll look back on what God did and have nothing to
say but, "Wow, look what he did. I couldn't have done it. But he
was big in my smallness."

Don't discount the foolish things in your life. They are the
very things God uses to build his kingdom.

*Jesus, when I look at my life, I see foolish things. Thank you that you're
in the resurrection business, taking all my failures and working through
them anyway. Thank you that you've chosen to take my foolish things and
shame the wise with them. I choose right now to give you all the glory.
Amen.*

Day of Reflection

The least of you will become a thousand,
the smallest a mighty nation.
I am the Lord;
in its time I will do this swiftly.

—ISAIAH 60:22 NIV

LITTLE IS MUCH WHEN GOD IS IN IT

In the harvest field now ripened, there's a work for all to do;
Hark the voice of God is calling, to the harvest calling you.

When the conflict here is ended and our race on earth is run;
He will say if we are faithful, welcome home my child, well done.

Little is much when God is in it, labor not for wealth or fame;
There's a crown and you can win it, if you go in Jesus' name.

—KITTIE LOUISE SUFFIELD, *c.* 1924

Your space—a poem, prayer, thoughts . . .

Deservedness

Judge not, that you be not judged.

—MATTHEW 7:1 ESV

While many of us know Paul's explanation of salvation by heart—"For it is by grace you have been saved, through faith—and this is not from yourselves, it is the gift of God" (Ephesians 2:8 NIV)—most of us still water the plant of self-righteousness on the windowsill of our hearts.

We may be thinking to ourselves that we're better than or spiritually cleaner than the chick who smells like cigarette smoke in our Beth Moore Bible study. We may be assuming that our regular church attendance is adding up like divine frequent-flyer miles. Or we may secretly believe that we somehow deserve God's acceptance and approval more than the stinkers we rub shoulders with on a regular basis.

Have you made a habit of stroking and feeding an inner pet idol of deservedness? Make a short list of the people in your life story who appear to be the least deserving of God's forgiveness. Pray for them by name—that they will stumble into the redemptive grace of Jesus Christ—at least once a week. Instead of praying for God to take them out if he's not going to save them, ask him to kill the idol of deservedness in your own heart.

Lord, I am so humbled and convicted and glad you don't give me what I deserve. Instead of taking me out, you take me into your loving arms. Please forgive me for smugly thinking I deserve more grace than the other sinners in my story. And help me to see them in the light of how precious they are to you, even on their worst days. Amen.

Trusting God in the Midst of Pain

[God says]: My purpose will stand,
and I will do all that I please.

—ISAIAH 46:10 NIV 1984

The Bible presents God as sovereign over all of history . . . including your history. While that doesn't necessarily mean that he
"caused" your difficult circumstances—God rarely privileges us
with that sort of information—it does mean he will strengthen
you to glorify him through whatever comes your way. He saw it
coming, he knows what's coming next, and he asks you to trust
him in the midst of it all.

Nothing catches God off guard. Nothing blindsides him.
Nothing derails his ultimate purposes. God knows "what is still
to come," and He declares about it, "My purpose will stand, and
I will do all that I please." When we first encounter that passage,
our minds may go to hurricanes, tsunamis, or earthshaking geo-
political events. It's true, God does know those things, and he
knew them before he ever formed the world. But don't miss this:
God's words also apply to you.

He knows your life, your history, and your future, too—
right down to the tiniest detail. God knows what is still to come
in your life, and he declares to you that his purpose for you will
stand.

*Lord, thank you for your divine purpose in my life. Help me to remember
that you're with me even in the lowest of times. Amen.*

Build a Good House

A house is built by wisdom and becomes strong through
good sense. Through knowledge its rooms are filled
with all sorts of precious riches and valuables.

—PROVERBS 24:3–4 NLT

Our homes are built not by sticks and stones, but by our wisdom and knowledge. As we seek God for good sense, he supplies it, then augments our homes with riches and valuables.

What kinds of riches and valuables? Great relationships. A home that feels like a haven from the onslaught of the world. A place where kindness reigns. A house where people feel loved, listened to, and validated. A place of warmth and joy.

How do we have homes like that? By opening the front door and letting God in, allowing him to rearrange our angry attitudes, our unforgiveness, and our temper. Oddly, we're often kinder to strangers than we are to the people in our immediate families. Yet God desires that our homes exemplify him—places of pardon and rest.

Think about your home right now. Is it a place you want to be? Why or why not? If Jesus stepped through the front door, what would he find? Take a moment now to ask him to rearrange your heart so that your home reflects him.

Jesus, build my house. Give me wisdom and strength. Help me to be kind and compassionate within these walls. Forgive me for my angry outbursts and unkindness. I need more of you in my home. Amen.

Shaken and Stirred

Cast your burden upon the LORD and He will sustain
you; He will never allow the righteous to be shaken.

—PSALM 55:22 NASB

The psalmist encourages us to take what burdens us and throw
it onto God's shoulders. In the sheer act of doing that, God will
sustain us, give us strength. But there are times in our lives where
we feel shaken and stirred. Our foundations quake. And we are
so overwhelmed, we can't even think about casting our burdens
on God.

Why? Because this is a preoccupying life. And we have a very
real enemy, Satan, who wants to distract us. He would rather we
be so consumed by our issues and the things that burden us that
we become immobile, scared, and ineffective. He knows that
if we slow down enough to give our burdens to God, we'll be
changed.

It's an act of spiritual warfare to cast our burdens on God. It's
not weakness. It's acknowledging the truth that, in ourselves, we
can't handle our lives. God, who created us, deserves to orchestrate everything about us. He loves it when we relinquish control
to him.

May it be that we take moments every day to stop, slow
down, then cast our burdens on God.

*Jesus, I don't want to be preoccupied with myself or my worries. I want
to cast them on you. Please take my life today and be the owner and CEO
of my life. Amen.*

Rely on God

Then Moses raised his arm and struck the rock twice
with his staff. Water gushed out, and the community
and their livestock drank. But the LORD said to Moses
and Aaron, "Because you did not trust in me enough to
honor me as holy in the sight of the Israelites, you will
not bring this community into the land I give them."

—NUMBERS 20:11–12 NIV

Prior to this passage, God told Moses something very specific.
He instructed Moses to speak to the rock, and the result would
be water gushing. He did not say hit the rock. The last time the
Israelites needed water, Moses struck the rock.

Instead of hearing God's voice and heeding it, Moses opted
to do what worked in the past. He didn't speak. He struck. And
God rebuked him, so much so that Moses was not permitted to
enter into the promised land.

It doesn't seem like a big deal, right? So he struck instead of
spoke. But the principle is this: We're not to trust a method more
than we listen to our Master. We're not to deify what worked in
the past, make it a holy tradition in our eyes, then worship it.

No, God calls all of us to listen to him. To believe him. To do
things that may look counterintuitive. Why? Because he is God
and we are not. He knows things we don't know. He is after our
obedience and growth. And over it all, he is all about his glory. If
speaking to a rock brings him more glory, then so be it.

Lord, I don't always understand why you ask me to do things. Especially
things that seem odd or don't match what you did in the past. Help me to
follow you no matter what. I leave the consequences in your hands. And
I choose to love your glory, not mine. Amen.

Our Unchanging God

Whatever is good and perfect comes down to us from
God our Father, who created all the lights in the
heavens. He never changes or casts a shifting shadow.

—JAMES 1:17 NLT

God is reliable. He is not capricious, changing his mind on a whim. He never, ever changes. That should prove to be great comfort for us in this change-happy world.

As the Internet speeds out of control and our Facebook obligations increase, we are constantly trying to adjust to change. Truth is, we're tired, aren't we? We're weary of learning new technology, of meeting new demands we didn't have three years ago.

And yet God doesn't change.

If we have kids, they never stay two years old, precocious, and hilarious. No, they dare to grow into teenagers, taking our car keys, driving us batty. Then they have the audacity to leave home, leaving us with a quiet nest.

And yet God doesn't change.

If we're married, our husbands may go through job loss, or have an identity crisis, or become different men. We struggle to adjust as our relationship morphs, we change, and we find new equilibrium.

And yet God doesn't change.

God is the one perfect constant in our fluctuating lives. It's reason to praise him right now in this moment.

Jesus, thank you for being consistent and never, ever changing. My life feels chaotic sometimes, and things and people change all the time. I'm getting whiplash from it all. So I rest in you. Hold me and help me to weather all the change. Amen.

Day of Reflection

For no one can lay any foundation other than
the one already laid, which is Jesus Christ.

—I CORINTHIANS 3:11 NIV

THE SOLID ROCK

My hope is built on nothing less
than Jesus' blood and righteousness.
I dare not trust the sweetest frame,
but wholly lean on Jesus' name.

When darkness seems to hide His face,
I rest on His unchanging grace.
In every high and stormy gale,
My anchor holds within the veil.

On Christ the solid Rock I stand,
all other ground is sinking sand.
All other ground is sinking sand.

—EDWARD MOTE, 1834

Your space—a poem, prayer, thoughts . . .

Seeking God for Solutions

> In the thirty-ninth year of his reign Asa was diseased
> in his feet, and his disease became severe. Yet
> even in his disease he did not seek the LORD, but
> sought help from physicians. And Asa slept with his
> fathers, dying in the forty-first year of his reign.
>
> —2 CHRONICLES 16:12–13 ESV

King Asa started his journey well. He tore down the high places in Israel and was known as a godly king. But at the end of his life, physical ailments became so unbearable that he shifted his allegiance from God to doctors.

It's certainly not wrong to go to the doctor for your ailments. The intention of this passage isn't to steer us away from medical care, but it is to show us that our trust must always be in God. We must first seek help from him. He is our provision and strength.

When we panic, whether from pain or awful circumstances, we tend to try to fix things without God. We run to deal with the problem, forgetting that God knows our needs and sees us where we panic. In everything, even in panic, we must seek God.

The result of Asa's turn was death. He didn't end well, though he started beautifully. We have the same set of circumstances before us. Pain can either cripple us to be embittered against God, not seeking his help, or it can fling us into his capable arms. Which will you choose?

Jesus, I want to seek you. I don't want to run after solutions as much as I chase after you and your ways. I want to finish this life well, not giving into panic. Help me today to keep you in mind. I hope in you. Amen.

Living by Our Own Fires

Who among you fears the LORD and obeys his servant?
If you are walking in darkness, without a ray of light,
trust in the LORD and rely on your God. But watch out,
you who live in your own light and warm yourselves
by your own fires. This is the reward you will receive
from me: You will soon fall down in great torment.

—ISAIAH 50:10–11 NLT

If you were to look back on your week, what would you see? Have you joyfully given your hand to Jesus and asked him to help you navigate life? Have you found God's strength in your weakness? Have you coasted? Have you forgotten God's nearness?

Isaiah warns us not to live by our own fires. What does that mean? Living in the light of our own campfires is living solely in our strength, existing by our wits and wherewithal. It means trying to figure out how to solve problems big and small with our own resources.

Left to ourselves and our own devices, though, we will ultimately live frustrated if we light our own fires and try to warm ourselves there. Eventually the flame we've worked so hard to stoke will falter and die. Only God's light, his holy fire, can sustain us for the long journey. Only his guidance will be what's best for us.

God does his greatest work when we recognize the futility of lighting our own fires, when we recognize that our work is small and his is the only work that lasts.

Jesus, forgive me for living by the light of my own wits. I don't want to spend my life lighting my own fires. Please be the fire within me today. I rest in your warmth. Amen.

Look Up

I lift up my eyes to the mountains—where does
my help come from? My help comes from the
LORD, the Maker of heaven and earth.

—PSALM 121:1–2 NIV

We look in many other places for help when we're facing a difficult situation. We may turn to friends. Or we might try to find a job to help make ends meet. Or we might make several lists to get our tasks done in a timely manner. Or we might call the service department. There are many ways to seek help.

Because we live in a culture of convenience, it's our first instinct to find a solution to our problem. Sick? Buy some medicine. Afraid? Text a friend. Alone? Have a party.

None of these ways of finding help are wrong. They're logical. But God wants us to shift our perspective from always solving our own problems, to bringing those same problems to him. He is our help. He wants us to lift up our eyes, hearts, and minds to him when life careens in crazy places.

God who made everything—yes, even the electronic matter in your smartphone—is best equipped to help you thrive right now. He knows you deeply and understands your needs better than you do. Lift up your eyes today. Your help comes from God.

Jesus, forgive me for forgetting to run to you first. I want to reorient the way I think and act so that I constantly talk to you for my needs. I love you and appreciate everything you do. Amen.

Running Life's Marathon

Therefore, since we are surrounded by so great a cloud
of witnesses, let us also lay aside every weight, and sin
which clings so closely, and let us run with endurance the
race that is set before us, looking to Jesus, the founder
and perfecter of our faith, who for the joy that was set
before him endured the cross, despising the shame, and is
seated at the right hand of the throne of God. Consider
him who endured from sinners such hostility against
himself, so that you may not grow weary or fainthearted.

—HEBREWS 12:1–3 ESV

The author of Hebrews issues an important charge to us in these
verses. He asks us to let go of what holds us back, fix our eyes
directly in front of us, and run the marathon he has mapped out
for us.

He gives Jesus as the prime example of this kind of faith. He
endured the torture of the cross because he could see beyond it,
where he would sit at God's right hand, having set free humanity.
He endured the ultimate pain of every single sinner on earth. If
he, who was fully God yet fully human, could endure that kind
of wrath, he knows how to help us endure whatever we face in
our lives.

God places a race before us. He wants us to run it. He longs
for us to look beyond our current circumstances to see into eternity where we will be rewarded for our heart toward him. In
light of that time of great reward, we run with joy and endurance.
And in that running, he promises to grow our faith.

*Jesus, I know you have a marathon mapped out before me. Help me to
start running, remembering that nothing I do for you is in vain. Help me
to joyfully run even when enduring is hard. I need your strength. Amen.*

When God Snaps the Whip

Blessed is the man whom God corrects; so do
not despise the discipline of the Almighty.

—JOB 5:17 NIV

There are times that God "snaps the whip." Actually, Scripture
says it this way: "While we were children, our parents did what
seemed best to them. But God is doing what is best for us, training us to live God's holy best. At the time, discipline isn't much
fun. It always feels like it's going against the grain. Later, of
course, it pays off handsomely, for it's the well trained who find
themselves mature in their relationship with God" (Hebrews
12:10–11 MSG).

God's loving design is to guide us onto a higher path. It's
always for our good. Guidance that's dispensed for our better-
ment gives us a sense of security. It helps us not to resist what
God is doing in our lives, and it reassures us that our difficulties
have not launched us outside of his care, even when we feel we've
fallen headlong into muddled circumstances.

*Lord, help us to trust your discipline to accomplish holy purposes.
Reassure us again that it is never your intent to hurt us but to help us.
Amen.*

Your Destiny Is in God's Hands

So he will do to me whatever he has
planned. He controls my destiny.

—JOB 23:14 NLT

In this busy world, we can sometimes go an entire day without thinking about God's sovereign control over the universe. We forget that he holds our present and our future in his hands. As Job reminds us, God controls our destinies.

As much as we might like to buck up and make things happen, ultimately it is God who is at work. Sure, we are responsible for listening to him and obeying his voice. We are not called to lethargy. But we must also live with a holy anticipation of what he may do each moment.

Look back over your last year. Think about what you tried to make happen. Then grab a piece of paper and list the things that God did out of the blue that surprised you. How did he help you in your career? What relational surprises did he send your way? How did he creatively provide for you and your family?

Sometimes all we need to do is look back and see the hand of God doing unexpected things to remind us of his beautiful control.

Jesus, I want to remember today that you control my destiny, that you are always working behind the curtain of my life. In light of that, help me to place my hope squarely on your shoulders. Keep me open to your work. And most of all, I want to be expectant of what you will do today. Amen.

Day of Reflection

The eternal God is your refuge, and underneath
are the everlasting arms. He will drive out your
enemies before you, saying, "Destroy them!"

—DEUTERONOMY 33:27

LEANING ON THE EVERLASTING ARMS

What a fellowship, what a joy divine,
Leaning on the everlasting arms!
What a blessedness, what a peace is mine,
Leaning on the everlasting arms!
Leaning, leaning, safe and secure from all alarms;
Leaning, leaning, leaning on the everlasting arms.

—ELISHA A. HOFFMAN, 1887

Your space—a poem, prayer, thoughts . . .

Exulting in Surprising Things

And not only this, but we also exult in our tribulations,
knowing that tribulation brings about perseverance;
and perseverance, proven character; and proven
character, hope; and hope does not disappoint, because
the love of God has been poured out within our hearts
through the Holy Spirit who was given to us.

—ROMANS 5:3–5 NASB

The apostle Paul exults in—elevates—tribulations. His counter-intuitive response to severe trials confounds us. Because how the world deals with pain is to push it as far away as possible. Other religions try to minimize pain. Some pretend it doesn't exist. But it does. All you have to do is read the news to know that.

So what's a disciple to do? Paul says we find joy in our trials because we know that instead of avoiding them, we can walk through them and actually grow as a result. If we allow God to work, those deep trials can perfect parts of us that no self-improvement plan could touch. Trials broaden our hearts.

So if we exult in tribulation, the end results are character and hope. With hope being in short supply these days, it's important that we not discount how valuable it is.

May it be that we see tribulations as a sacred doorway to growth and hope—growth because Jesus can do miracles in us when we submit to him, hope because in the midst of the trial we see more clearly what Jesus is up to. He will prevail.

Jesus, help me to elevate tribulations, even though that seems impossible.
I want to bend into you to let you create better character in me. I want
to more deeply understand your hope for me even as I walk through fire.
Amen.

Your Record Cleared

Yes, what joy for those whose record the LORD has cleared
of guilt, whose lives are lived in complete honesty!

—PSALM 32:2 NLT

Sometimes we forget the astonishing news that Christ has cleared us of guilt. Our record of wrongs piled high to the cosmos has been leveled by his sacrifice on the cross. Completely wiped out. When God forgives, the psalmist implies, he does it for good.

Do you live in light of that radical forgiveness? Or do you keep rehashing old sins, taking them as bully clubs and beating yourself up with them? Are you living in the land of regret so much that you've forgotten God has cleared your record?

To live in light of a record cleared means to live with deep, abiding gratitude. It means acknowledging that we are guilty of sin but Christ's sacrifice is greater still. It means we walk humbly. And it means that we forgive others.

Consider this illustration. Picture someone's sins against you in a small pile between you. Even if it's relatively towering, it cannot compare to the mountain of sin between you and God. If God can fully forgive you of the mountain, then surely, by his strength, you can forgive the molehill.

Jesus, help me live in light of your mountain of forgiveness today. Let it sink way down deep into my soul. I don't want to live in the land of regret. Instead I want to be grateful and thankful. And I want to extend that same forgiveness to those who have hurt me. Amen.

Productivity

> Our people must learn to devote themselves to doing
> what is good, in order that they may provide for
> daily necessities and not live unproductive lives.
> —TITUS 3:14 NIV 1984

What does it look like to devote ourselves to doing good? Hard work, no matter what the form, refines us and helps us to live productive, industrious lives. And when we work, we help provide for the people in our lives.

The opposite of productivity is slothfulness. Not that it's wrong to rest—God has specifically ordained that we take off from work once a week—but if we give in to lethargy and stop working, we can fall prey to sin. Simply put, when we're bored, we tend to get into trouble.

If your best friend gave you honest feedback about your life, would she say you're too productive? Not enough? Just right? How do you feel about your current level of work? Are you stressed out? Tired? Bored? Unmotivated? Satisfied?

Paul instructs us to devote ourselves to doing good by working well and providing for our families, however that may look. It's a discipline. But the reward is provision and peace. And when we look back on our lives, will we be thankful for the times we spent in front of a TV show? What things will we be most grateful for, in terms of our productivity?

Jesus, help me to figure out what it is you want me to do in terms of doing good. I want to be productive for you. Help me to find the right balance between work and rest. Open up new avenues of service, Jesus, so I can better serve you and the people you love. Amen.

Your Story

I am the Alpha and the Omega, the first and
the last, the beginning and the end.

—REVELATION 22:13 NASB

God began everything. And he finishes everything. He is the capital letter at the beginning of a sentence and its period too. Our lives are like sentences strung together, woven into an amazing story of God's redemption.

How did God start you on your faith journey? Can you look back on your life and see the hand of God and how he wooed you toward trust in him? What were the circumstances of your birth? How can you see God's protection and initiation in your life as a child? A young adult? An adult?

You are right now living in the story arc. Every day has the potential to be a risky adventure. God is writing your story as you live it, and the question you can ask yourself as you live it is, *Am I living a big story?*

Just as God initiated you in the womb, enticed you toward the faith journey, and walks with you in your story right now, he also will be with you as your story ends. How do you want to be remembered? What will your legacy be? What will people say after you've gone ahead to heaven? Thinking on these things will help you to live the best story now for our Alpha and Omega God.

Jesus, thank you that you are writing my story even as I read this. Help me to live the adventure. I want to remember the times you changed my story's direction and brought redemption to my life. And, oh, how I want to finish my story well. Amen.

Content in All Circumstances

But godliness with contentment is great gain.
—1 TIMOTHY 6:6 NIV

On a human level, being content with our circumstances and having no desire to change them can at times be incomprehensible—simply beyond our understanding. For example, how a pig can be content to snort around in garbage and wallow in the mud? That is incomprehensible to some. Why? Because we are not pigs. Pigs, however, were meant to find contentment in that environment. Then how can a human being be content to live in a filthy environment with rodents scurrying around everywhere? That's equally incomprehensible to us. Why? Because it's not our idea of contentedness.

Yet, as incomprehensible as that is, the apostle Paul lived in a jail cell with rodents scurrying round everywhere and said he was content. His statement reminds us again that contentedness is an inside job; it comes as the pig lives out the destiny for which it was created, and it comes to you and me as we share Paul's trust in God's timing and sovereignty. Contentment is a state of being that is characterized by not wanting more than we have. A contented person is basically satisfied with life's circumstances.

On a spiritual level, we, like the apostle Paul, can be content with life knowing we have a transformed soul and God has sovereignly ordained our circumstances. Because we trust God, we can be content to leave it all to him.

Lord, help me to remember to be content in all my circumstances. Thank you that I can leave it all to you. Amen.

Training for the Race

I press on to reach the end of the race and
receive the heavenly prize for which God,
through Christ Jesus, is calling us.

—PHILIPPIANS 3:14 NLT

Endurance running takes a lot of training. You build up your
ability to run farther and smarter with each mile logged. If you
started a marathon at a sprint—unless you're a world-class
athlete—you'd peter out and never finish.

Our spiritual life is a marathon—a slow, deliberate run over
many, many miles. It's hard to prepare for a marathon, so God
sends us the best trainers available: twins named Problems and
Trials. Though no one would run out and select those coaches,
they're the best at helping us develop endurance.

Once we've learned to embrace Problems and Trials as
teachers, Paul promises us even better qualities. Our character
strengthens. Our hope muscle develops. Our capacity to understand the love of God grows.

It's never easy to let Problems teach us the beauty of endur-
ance. Nor is it naturally instinctive to invite Trials into our lives.
And yet, if we open our hearts to both for the sake of growth,
God makes us a distance runner, with a greater capacity for him.

*Jesus, forgive me for sprinting and stopping. I want to run this marathon
called following you. To be honest, I don't really like Problems or Trials,
so teach me to see them as valuable coaches. Amen.*

Day of Reflection

Jesus said to her, "I am the resurrection and the life. The one who believes in me will live, even though they die."

—JOHN 11:25 NIV

WHEN THE ROLL IS CALLED UP YONDER

When the trumpet of the Lord shall sound,
and time shall be no more
And the morning breaks eternal bright and fair.
When the saints on earth shall gather
over on the other shore,
And the roll is called up yonder I'll be there.

On that bright and cloudless morning
when the dead in Christ shall rise,
And the glory of His resurrection share;
When the chosen ones shall gather
to their home beyond the skies,
And the roll is called up yonder I'll be there.

—JAMES M. BLACK, 1893

Your space—a poem, prayer, thoughts . . .

Jesus Clothes

Clothe yourself with the presence of the Lord
Jesus Christ. And don't let yourself think
about ways to indulge your evil desires.

—ROMANS 13:14 NLT

When we put on our Jesus clothes, we won't think about ways
to sin. Why? Because we clothe ourselves with his presence, and
when we're close to Jesus, sin feels icky. We can't wear holiness
and darkness simultaneously. It would be like pouring mud over a
sequined gown. The two don't mix, and it makes for a dirty mess.

Many of us try to conquer sin on our own. We create elabo-
rate campaigns to stop sinning, rewarding ourselves for good
behavior and punishing ourselves when we fail. We avoid places
where sin is enticing—a good thing.

We forget that the best remedy for sin is being near Jesus
Christ, for actually climbing into Jesus clothes, spending all our
energy becoming fascinated by him. When we fascinate ourselves with Jesus, we no longer have time to be tempted. Sin feels
ridiculous in light of knowing how amazing Jesus is.

Our Christianity is proactive, yes, but it's not a campaign.
We proactively chase after Jesus. In doing so, sin fades. But if
we try to avoid sin, and make avoiding it our purpose, its power
grows. It's better to enamor ourselves with Jesus.

*Jesus, I want to wear your clothes today. I want to experience your pres-
ence in my life so much so that sin seems strange and unappealing. Help
me fall in love with you afresh even now. Amen.*

Heavenly Citizens

But we are citizens of heaven, where the Lord
Jesus Christ lives. And we are eagerly waiting for
him to return as our Savior. He will take our weak
mortal bodies and change them into glorious bodies
like his own, using the same power with which
he will bring everything under his control.

—PHILIPPIANS 3:20–21 NLT

We may be citizens of a country that has its own rulers and laws, but if we call ourselves Christ followers, we are citizens of an imperishable country: heaven. This is the place Jesus lives right now. He breathes and moves and laughs and sings there. He is alive in that realm. He waits there until it is time for him to return to us here on earth.

Someday these bodies we have will be gloriously transformed by Christ's power. No longer will we be beset with aches and pains and fading beauty. We won't be tormented by arthritis or diabetes or cancer. In our new bodies, created for eternity, we will not die.

This is cause for great rejoicing. To endure well on this earth means to live in light of what will be. We fix our eyes on Jesus, alive in heaven, and await his glorious appearing. We long for our new bodies, fit for heaven. And when we live in that great expectation, the pains of this world fade in importance.

In the new heavens and the new earth, after Jesus' return, his rule will be complete. He will be the perfect leader, the spotless lamb, the God who sacrificed everything so we could join him there.

Jesus, help me fix my eyes on you and what you will do in the future. When my body creaks and ages, I want to think about my new body and the ways I will live in your new kingdom. Amen.

The Art of Supplication

Listen to the supplication of Your servant and of Your
people Israel, when they pray toward this place; hear
in heaven Your dwelling place; hear and forgive.

—1 KINGS 8:30 NASB

To supplicate means to beg, entreat, or ask humbly for something. The word connotes humility, of a servant asking a king for a favor.

God asks us to come before him as humble servants, knowing that we cannot solve our own problems, nor can we better our lot without his divine intervention. We must come to God believing that he can and will supply our needs, and we pray to him with great expectation of his deliverance.

The Israelites prayed this way in this particular instance. They faced Jerusalem, the place of the temple, and asked God to change their lot. They asked him to hear from heaven and forgive them.

We now have the temple of God within ourselves. The Holy Spirit rests within us. He quickly hears our needs and pleas. As we ask for help and forgiveness, we can be assured of his presence. May it be that when we approach God, we supplicate, humbly asking him to move in our lives.

Jesus, teach me the art of supplication. I know I can't do this life without your help. Thank you that you empower me through the Holy Spirit within me. Thank you that you aren't far off. Thank you that you hear and forgive. Amen.

A Table Prepared for *You*

You prepare a table before me in the presence of my
enemies; You have anointed my head with oil; my
cup overflows. Surely goodness and lovingkindness
will follow me all the days of my life, and I will
dwell in the house of the LORD forever.

—PSALM 23:5–6 NASB

This commonplace verse sometimes gets overlooked. We hear it
read at funerals, nod at its beauty, but forget its power.

When you walk through a period where you have enemies in
your life, the promise of the first part of this verse is that God pre-
pares everything you need in the midst of your enemies' taunts.
When life feels unfair and you feel overlooked, God cooks up a
banquet for you, a feast.

As a result, you can actually live a very fulfilled life even when
folks slander you or turn their backs on you. It's counterintuitive,
but true. God will become your everything as your relationships
sour. He fills you up where others have taken.

That is why we can find joy even through trial. If we press
into God and lean into his strength, he promises to be the refuge we need. He becomes the feast in our famine. Why? Because
his house is not like earthly houses. When our souls spend time
there, we find love and goodness in ample supply.

*Jesus, thank you that you set the table for me and provide a feast when
I feel deprived and hurting. I choose to dwell in your house when life is
hard. Please fill me up with the feast of your presence. I need your lovingkindness and goodness. Overflow my life today. Amen.*

Making Jesus First

There is only one thing worth being concerned about. Mary has discovered it, and it will not be taken away from her.

—LUKE 10:42 NLT

Jesus' words to Martha in that verse resonate down the centuries to point out the most essential priority any of us should have, even today. We imagine him smiling and shaking his head a little as he looks into her eyes with wisdom and love. Some translations have him saying, "My dear Martha" or "Martha, dear Martha." The Lord's answer to Martha clearly identifies what our number one priority is supposed to be. His words give us the perspective we need in order to understand what's really important: Jesus is the most valuable "possession" we can ever have—because he gives us the hope we need to survive the loss of everything else.

Making Jesus our first priority makes it easier to categorize the rest of our lives. When we filter everything through our focus on him, we see our blessings as gifts and our hardships as challenges that draw us closer to his sustaining love and strength. And the best thing is, once we've found Jesus we can never lose him. We find him by confessing our sins to him, asking him to forgive us, and then believing what he says is true. Doing so sweeps us over the edge of the divine into the Savior's arms, where he promises to hold us for all eternity.

Lord, I want you to be first in my life. I want to filter everything through my focus on you. Thank you for loving me even when I fail to put you first. Amen.

Face to Face

Inside the Tent of Meeting, the LORD would speak
to Moses face to face, as one speaks to a friend.
Afterward Moses would return to the camp, but the
young man who assisted him, Joshua son of Nun,
would remain behind in the Tent of Meeting.

—EXODUS 33:11 NLT

God desires an intimate friendship with us. When he connected with Moses, the Scripture says they spoke as if they were deep, close friends. In this detached, electronic world we live in, face-to-face communication grows rare. We seldom have coffee with a friend, without all the while updating our Facebook status or tweeting about our days. We've become a world of friendly strangers.

But God doesn't want that kind of surface intimacy with us. He wants to spend quality time with us.

How do we develop that kind of Moses-to-God friendship? We share everything. We listen. We whisper—or shout—prayers throughout the day, in continual conversation with God. We share our foibles and heartaches. We praise God when we're thankful. We entrust our joy to him. We listen to his voice in the words of our friends. We learn contentment. We grow up.

Moses spent years with God. He developed a long, persevering friendship. And over the course of your lifetime, you have the same opportunity. God is the best friend you'll ever know. He is worth your time, your treasure, your attention.

God, I want to speak with you face to face, as Moses did. But sometimes
the worries of this life take over and I forget about you. Today I choose
to focus on how great you are. I love you and want to be your close, close
friend. Amen.

Day of Reflection

"Look, he is coming with the clouds,"
and "every eye will see him."
—REVELATION 1:7 NIV

FACE TO FACE

Face to face with Christ, my Savior,
Face to face what will it be
When with rapture I behold Him,
Jesus Christ who died for me?

Face to face I shall behold Him,
Far beyond the starry sky;
Face to face in all His glory,
I shall see Him by and by!

—CARRIE E. BRECK, 1898

Your space—a poem, prayer, thoughts . . .

The In Crowd

But now in Christ Jesus you who once were far off
have been brought near by the blood of Christ.

—EPHESIANS 2:13 ESV

Ever feel like you're not a part of the cool crowd? Junior high
might come to mind. Or high school. Or maybe even college. You
may recall a time in elementary school when the girls wouldn't
invite you to their parties or let you skip rope with them on the
playground.

Even as women today, we have felt the sting of rejection, of
being on the outside looking in. But in God's upside-down economy, we do not have to feel that way. Although there was a long
period of time when humanity was on the outside looking in,
separated from God and certainly not a part of his crowd, God
made a solution by sending his Son to earth.

Not only did Jesus walk the same dusty earth we walk today
so he could empathize with us, he also experienced rejection and
ostracism. He understands keenly what it means to be separated
from others. And in that excruciating cry on the cross where he
experienced God the Father's wrath, he understood more than
anyone how painful being left out can be.

By his blood, thank God, he brought us near to him. He
included us. He welcomed us. Our lives should reflect a holy joy
because we're no longer outcasts, but friends.

*Jesus, thank you for experiencing rejection on every possible level. I know
you understand what it feels like to be on the outside looking in. Thank
you for bringing me near to you because of your sacrifice. Amen.*

Evil Will Cease

Then I heard a loud voice in heaven say: "Now have
come the salvation and the power and the kingdom
of our God, and the authority of his Messiah. For
the accuser of our brothers and sisters, who accuses
them before our God day and night, has been hurled
down. They triumphed over him by the blood of the
Lamb and by the word of their testimony; they did not
love their lives so much as to shrink from death."

—REVELATION 12:10–11 NIV

The Scripture promises that at the end of this age the accuser of
Christians will be hurled down into the lake of fire. Our great
enemy who wants to steal, kill, and destroy will suddenly be
no more. He will be punished for eternity for every single awful
thing he instigated in your life and in every person's life who
ever lived.

This should bring a huge dose of hope to you. Evil will someday cease. God triumphs. We will prevail because of him.

In the meantime, the verse says, we will overcome right now
by two things: the blood of the Lamb and the word of our testimony. Because of Jesus' righteous act on the cross, his shedding
of blood, we no longer need to live as accused people. We are fully
made right before God because of Jesus' blood. And as we share
this amazing truth with the world—sharing our testimony—we
continue to remind Satan that his time on this earth is almost up.

*Jesus, I want to holler about your amazing blood and the redemption you
brought for me. Help me to share that story today. And thank you that,
one day, all evil will be dealt with in a just and perfect way. Amen.*

Only Through Him

Finally, all of you should be of one mind. Sympathize with
each other. Love each other as brothers and sisters. Be
tenderhearted, and keep a humble attitude. Don't repay
evil for evil. Don't retaliate with insults when people
insult you. Instead, pay them back with a blessing.

—1 PETER 3:8–9 NLT

These verses in Peter are pretty overwhelming, with lots of instruction and encouragement. We are to be unified, sympathetic,
loving, tenderhearted, and humble. We're not to be retaliatory or
insulting. Not easy to do, particularly when folks are mean to us.

Yet through the Holy Spirit we can be all these things—and
avoid the bad things. Why? Because the Spirit enabled Jesus to
forgive people who spat on him, to love Judas Iscariot, to wash
his disciples' feet, and to be silent before his accusers.

In our own strength we'd rather retaliate when someone
sneers an insult our way. We'd rather divide friends who are
feuding and take sides. We'd rather take the credit for what we've
done. We'd rather see justice served on our enemy. We'd rather
be served.

Jesus didn't leave us as orphans when he left the earth. He
gave us the beautiful gift of his Spirit to help us obey this verse in
Technicolor. Yes, without him it's impossible. But with his presence within us, it's possible.

*Jesus, I want to exemplify those verses in 1 Peter 3. But I tend to want
my own way. Help me instead rely on the Holy Spirit within me to be the
kind of woman who loves, forgives, unifies, and blesses. Amen.*

Never Give Up

But how much of that kind of persistent faith will the
Son of Man find on the earth when he returns?
—LUKE 18:8 MSG

Jesus told a story showing that it was necessary to pray consistently and never quit. He said, "There was once a judge in some city who never gave God a thought and cared nothing for people. A widow in that city kept after him: 'My rights are being violated. Protect me!' He never gave her the time of day. But after this went on and on he said to himself, 'I care nothing what God thinks, even less what people think. But because this widow won't quit badgering me, I'd better do something and see that she gets justice—otherwise I'm going to end up beaten black-and-blue by her pounding.'" Then the Master said, "Do you hear what that judge, corrupt as he is, is saying? So what makes you think God won't step in and work justice for his chosen people, who continue to cry out for help? Won't he stick up for them? I assure you, he will. He will not drag his feet. But how much of that kind of persistent faith will the Son of Man find on the earth when he returns?" (Luke 18:1–8 MSG)

The question Jesus asked those who were listening is very relevant for us: how much of that kind of persistent faith will he find when he returns again? It is easy to get discouraged when we don't receive an answer to our prayers or see any sign at all of change. But Jesus says, "Don't give up. If an old, cranky, godless judge will eventually answer just because he wants to get back to sleep, how much more will God, our loving Father, give you what you ask?"

Lord, thank you for always hearing my prayers. Help me to remember
that you're listening even when I don't notice the signs of change. Amen.

Truth Brings Freedom

Jesus said, "If you hold to my teaching, you are
really my disciples. Then you will know the
truth, and the truth will set you free."

—JOHN 8:31–32 NIV

Why does truth set us free? Because living a lie requires an inordinate amount of energy to maintain.

Think back to a time you kept a secret. Perhaps you couldn't share about a sin that bothered you. Or maybe a family member kept an unwritten rule with you that you could not share things that might damage the reputation of your family.

Once the cat was let out of the bag of secrets, so to speak, did you feel free? Of course when our sin comes out, there may be a blush of shame initially, but eventually it is much more freeing to live in light of the truth than hiding behind an all-is-well mask.

Jesus came to set us free. He doesn't want us to live in shame, heaping guilt upon ourselves. He doesn't want us to be quiet about what we struggle with. He also doesn't want us to carry our relational burdens alone.

Entrust your secrets to him, then ask him to make you brave enough to tell the truth to a trusted, godly friend. In letting go of your secret, you will find infectious, life-giving freedom.

Jesus, I want to be free. But I also don't like telling my secrets. Could you please be a tender listener as I share them now? Help me to come clean and experience the freedom that comes from telling the truth. Set me free, by your strength. Amen.

Free!

For freedom Christ has set us free; stand firm therefore,
and do not submit again to a yoke of slavery.

—GALATIANS 5:1 ESV

Slavery is working without wages, forced to do something you probably don't want to do for the sake of someone else's self-ishness. Before we were Christians, Satan—the epitome of self-absorption—held us under slavery. He enslaved us to do things we really didn't want to do, for the sake of our own imprisonment.

In short, we were slaves to sin. We couldn't do anything but sin. And our freedom seemed far off. But Jesus Christ has set us free. The moment he uttered his final words on the cross, then resurrected to beautiful life three days later, he broke the chains that Satan had us shackled to.

We are free. Right now. In this holy moment. We no longer need to sin. We no longer have to submit ourselves to Satan's mandates. Jesus took our chains and threw them away.

But some of us forget. We walk around enslaved, thinking we have to live under tyranny. We forget that Jesus set us free. We follow rules, hoping they will save us. We try-try-try to impress God by our own cleverness and wit, but we fail. When we try to earn God's favor, we're enslaved.

Your chains have fallen from your wrists. You've been set free. Live in light of that with joy and thankfulness.

Jesus, thank you for setting me free from sin and Satan's tyranny. I don't want to return to that. Help me to live as a free woman, wholly loved by you. Amen.

Day of Reflection

No one is like you, LORD; you are great,
and your name is mighty in power.
—JEREMIAH 10:6

THERE IS POWER IN THE BLOOD

Would you be free from your burden of sin?
There's pow'r in the blood, pow'r in the blood;
Would you o'er evil a victory win?
There's wonderful power in the blood.

There is pow'r, pow'r, wonder working pow'r
In the blood of the Lamb
There is pow'r, pow'r, wonder working pow'r
In the precious blood of the Lamb.

—LEWIS E. JONES, 1899

Your space—a poem, prayer, thoughts . . .

You Can't Take It with You

Naked a man comes from his mother's womb,
and as he comes, so he departs. He takes nothing
from his labor that he can carry in his hand.

—ECCLESIASTES 5:15 NIV 1984

When children cry their way into the world, they wear their birthday suits. And when we breathe our last breath, we don't take our clothes or shoes to heaven with us. What is the author of Ecclesiastes implying in this verse?

Simply put: you can't take it with you. No matter what your bottom line is, the top line remains—you will die. Rich and poor, oppressor and oppressed, famous and small—all will take a first and last breath.

Because of that, our focus shouldn't be accumulating a bunch of stuff. Nor should it be building our own fame so we feel better about ourselves. Our eternal focus should be heaven—the rewards there that relate to our kingdom building here.

Where is your treasure? Is it your home, your wardrobe, your car? Or does your wealth consist of the people God has surrounded you with? Or your communication with God on a daily basis? These latter two are eternal. The more you invest in those, the less you'll regret when you look back on your life.

Jesus, I don't want to live for clothes or stuff or prestige. I want to live for what matters, what counts in eternity. Refresh my vision for loving others and adoring you. Amen.

Your Best Friend

"I am with you," says the LORD of hosts.
—HAGGAI 2:4

Humanly we feel close to the person who knows us, loves us, and does not judge us. We feel close to the one with whom we can really let our hair down. We're lucky when we have a close earthly friend with whom we can share all our thoughts.

But there's no luck involved in having a divine Friend who offers this kind of solace and understanding. It's God! And he has promised to be with us and love us forever. We don't have to pretend to believe Romans 8:28 at a time when it is totally unbelievable. God knows the moment when that is too great a stretch. If we tell him, we don't create a distance between us. We don't have to be a phony spiritual person, afraid to admit the need to cry out with David, "I'm going down to the pit; I'm a person without strength" (paraphrase of Psalm 88:4). We can be our honest selves with God.

So how do we come to God? Just as we are.

God, show me to approach you just as I am. Help me to remember that you have given yourself up for me and you accept me fully, not because of my own righteousness, but because of yours. Amen.

No More Lightbulbs!

And the city has no need of sun or moon to shine on it, for the glory of God gives it light, and its lamp is the Lamb.

—REVELATION 21:23 ESV

Imagine never needing to turn on another lamp. Imagine never forcing your eyes to adjust to a dark room. Imagine no more night. When the new heavens and the new earth dawn and Jesus establishes his kingdom forever, the Scripture promises us that the things we've relied on for light will no longer be necessary.

The moon? No need, because the night will be vanquished.

The sun? No need, because Jesus will emanate all the light we'll ever need.

It's hard to wrap our minds around a person being light greater than the sun, but it will be true. Even when Jesus walked the earth, he alluded to this by stating that he was the light of the world. (See John 8:12.)

Jesus will be the greater sun because he is the greatest Son that ever lived. When life feels dark, and it's hard to adjust to its dimness, remember that one day Jesus will shed light into every dark recess of this world, including your heart. The beauty of this realization is that you can, right now, ask Jesus to shine inside.

Jesus, I am walking through dark times and I need your light. Help me live in light of the truth that someday you'll brighten this planet with yourself. But right now, I need more of you, more of your light within me. Amen.

A Gratitude List

Let the word of Christ dwell in you richly as you
teach and admonish one another with all wisdom,
and as you sing psalms, hymns and spiritual
songs with gratitude in your hearts to God.

—COLOSSIANS 3:16 NIV

One of the most crucial attitudes we can develop is one of gratitude. A grateful attitude in itself introduces an elevation of mood. When I see my circumstances through the lens of a grateful mind-set instead of the "I'm not getting what I want" mind-set, I feel better; I even have the potential to be happy in spite of circumstances.

Telling you to develop an attitude of gratitude may be so familiar that you simply respond, "Yeah, yeah. I've heard that before." But sometimes we all need to hear it again. Keeping a "gratitude list" may sound corny, but it redirects your mind and lifts your mood. Write a list of everything for which you are grateful: the big stuff and the little stuff. Hopefully your list goes on and on. If it does, you will enlarge your happiness potential.

Here's an example of some things that might be on your gratitude list: the side door no longer sticks, I located more of my favorite hard-to-find vanilla loose-leaf tea, birds are singing again, the new water filter makes the water taste better, my lamp throws light perfectly on my book. And at the top of this list is the greatest source of gratitude: Jesus loves me.

Lord, thank you for all the times you have provided for me and my loved ones. Help me to remember to always show my gratitude toward you. Amen.

Things Above

Set your mind on things above, not on things on the earth.
—COLOSSIANS 3:2

In the hustle bustle of daily life, we forget to think about eternity or our destination after death. We live as if death doesn't exist, and when it rears its dark head, we try to ignore the reality of its finality.

If we forget to think in light of heaven and the reward Jesus has for us there, we'll fill our lives with our own selfish pursuits. Life becomes all about us, our dreams, our plans. But if we live with an eternal perspective, we'll begin to see the shadow of things to come. We'll see this life as fading away. We'll view time as precious and utterly important. We'll long to seize the day for the sake of Jesus.

The truth? Jesus promises us right now that he is preparing an amazing place for us. He's been at work on the new heaven and the new earth over millennia, and it will be far above our imagination. It will be the place of no more sorrows, no more tears, no more heartache.

He will be the illumination of that place. He will radiate warmth. And he will reward us for what we've dared to trust him for on this earth. What are you living for in light of eternity? For the fading light that is today, or the everlasting light that is Jesus?

Jesus, help me remember right now that heaven is a reality. I want to live in light of that great truth. Help me see today through eternity's eyes. I want my life to count not just for this life, but the one to come. Amen.

The Eternal Prize

All athletes are disciplined in their training. They
do it to win a prize that will fade away, but we
do it for an eternal prize. So I run with purpose
in every step. I am not just shadowboxing.

—1 CORINTHIANS 9:25–26 NLT

Paul uses the metaphor of an athlete and training here to help us remember that our lives don't just happen to us. No, we are responsible to train ourselves with a specific goal in mind.

Consider a triathlete. If she trains by running and biking, but neglects swimming, she will tank on the swim. All three sports must be practiced and perfected before she competes. In the same way, our lives are the training ground for eternity. We must become students of heaven to arrive there in triumph.

What do we need to remember about heaven and our eternal prize? We will be rewarded there for the way we live our lives before others, how we love God, and how many seeds we plant in the lives of those who need Jesus.

Our training here, then, is a daily exercise in living a consistent, authentic life, throwing our hands and hearts heavenward in abandoned worship, and actively seeking out opportunities to share Jesus. None of this kind of training is in vain. God will reward it.

Jesus, help me to remember my life is not shadowboxing, training for nothing. Keep that eternal prize ever before me so I can live a joyful, hope-filled, disciplined life today. Amen.

Day of Reflection

I will give you the keys of the kingdom of heaven, and
whatever you bind on earth will be bound in heaven, and
whatever you loose on earth will be loosed in heaven.

—MATTHEW 16:19

WHEN WE ALL GET TO HEAVEN

Sing the wondrous love of Jesus,
sing His mercy and His grace;
In the mansions bright and blessed,
He'll prepare for us a place.

Onward to the prize before us!
Soon His beauty we'll behold;
Soon the pearly gates will open,
we shall tread the streets of gold.

When we all get to Heaven,
what a day of rejoicing that will be!
When we all see Jesus, we'll sing and shout the victory.

—ELIZA E. HEWITT, 1898

Your space—a poem, prayer, thoughts . . .

You Can't Buy Love

Place me like a seal over your heart, like a seal on
your arm. For love is as strong as death, its jealousy
as enduring as the grave. Love flashes like fire, the
brightest kind of flame. Many waters cannot quench
love, nor can rivers drown it. If a man tried to buy love
with all his wealth, his offer would be utterly scorned.

—SONG OF SOLOMON 8:6–7 NLT

Love is the most powerful force in this world. People die for it.
Folks give their lives to be loved. Others, in despair, hurt themselves when they don't have it. Often we look to others to fill us
up with love.

But human love, as amazing as it is, cannot fully fill us.
Of course, if God directs human love our way, we should bask
in thankfulness. But more than that, we must settle our hearts
before him, satisfying ourselves in his irreplaceable love.

God's love never ends. It always forgives. It pardons us when
we're unlovely. It cheers for the best in us. It is eternal, as God is.
He designed it so that we would be restless and seeking until we
find ourselves wrapped in his love.

People will hurt you. Others will disappoint. Some won't
meet your expectations. All of us are sinners, and all of us will
hurt each other. But God's love never fails to fill us completely
up, as a stream overflows its banks.

*Jesus, thank you for the people in my life who I love dearly. Thank you
for the family and friends who love me. But more than that, thank you
for your precious, irreplaceable love. I need it. It's water to me in this
desert life. Amen.*

God Is Mindful of *You*!

When I look at your heavens, the work of your
fingers, the moon and the stars, which you have
set in place, what is man that you are mindful of
him, and the son of man that you care for him?

—PSALM 8:3–4 ESV

Picture God breathing the universe into existence. Imagine
him setting moons, suns, and stars in their proper places. Think
about his ability to create dirt, whales, horses, birds, children,
skies, souls from nothing. He is that powerful.

And yet we serve a mindful God. He takes note of us and
cares for us like a doting Father. He sees our weakness, understands our fears, and is available to us when we're hurting. He
who flung the stars into galaxies concerns himself with us.

Because of that, we need not fear. We no longer have to
wonder if he knows about our issues of the day. He does. He is
omnipresent, a big word that simply means God is everywhere.
And he who holds the universe in his hands can heal what bothers us.

Rest there today knowing that our great God is mindful of
you. He is available, as close as your breath, as near as your next
thought. What a humbling thought that the God of everything
we see sees us.

*Jesus, thank you that you are mindful of me. I can't understand it because
compared to the cosmos, I'm so very small. Thank you for loving me so
specifically. Amen.*

Addicted to Money?

Don't love money; be satisfied with what you have. For God has said, "I will never fail you. I will never abandon you."

—Hebrews 13:5 nlt

All our fretting about money has its root in our theology, or how we view God. If we believe that God is not powerful, that he is not a good provider, we will fix our eyes on money and believe it to be the solution to all our problems.

But money is a terrible drug because its addictiveness is overwhelming. The more you get, the more you want and the more you believe you need. If we love it—think about it, dream about it, fret about it, wake up worrying about it—we reveal that our hearts don't truly trust God.

In this verse, God promises something beautiful. He won't fail us. He won't abandon us. If you struggle today with money issues, choose to repeat those sentences again. Even though you can't see through the next money obstacle, God will remain faithful to you.

Even if you lose everything, God's care for you is constant. It may not look like God has taken care of you, but remember that he takes the long view in mind. He longs for your holiness, so he will use even the most painful circumstances in your life to teach you patience and obedience and contentment.

Jesus, help me to learn the lesson that money isn't everything. That you are everything. I want to trust you right now, believing that you won't fail me or abandon my family. Amen.

Time for a Heart Exam

I know, my God, that you examine our hearts and
rejoice when you find integrity there. You know I have
done all this with good motives, and I have watched
your people offer their gifts willingly and joyously.

—1 CHRONICLES 29:17 NLT

This verse reminds us that God knows every aspect of our hearts. He examines them closely and actively searches for integrity. Integrity simply means acting the same way on the outside as you believe on the inside. Your godly convictions match your outside actions.

And when we have integrity, we have good motives. We want what is best for others. We're not always about doing things for show or to gain something from others. And we act rightly even when no one is looking because we value our reputations before a holy God.

In the last part of this verse, we see folks giving gifts willingly and joyously. When we walk lives of integrity with pure motives, we can't help but give to others and to God willingly and with exuberance.

May it be that we live this verse today, in the integrity of our hearts, with good motives, and hearts bent toward giving with joy.

Jesus, I do want this verse to be true of me. Help me to see where I'm not walking in integrity. Shine your light on my motives. And enable me to give to others and to you with a willing, happy heart. Amen.

The Splendor of His Creations

God saw all that he had made, and it was very good.

—GENESIS 1:31 NIV

We live in a broken world in which many things are askew; so it's no wonder we forget all the lovely things God has written his signature on, starting with the heavens and the earth. How sad for us when we are caught in the tension of our routine and miss the splendor of his creations. Perhaps because children live so close to the earth, they often are the messengers that remind us of a frog's throaty croak or a cricket's high-pitched chirp or a katydid's tattletale song. Kids are the ones who affirm the dandelion's beauty, a stick's usefulness, and a pebble's colors. When was the last time you stared into the dazzling pattern of the stars? Or gathered a fistful of lilies of the valley or crammed a jar full of hydrangeas or arranged a vase of peonies? When did you sit at the water's edge and lean in to hear its song? Has it been too long since you sifted sand through your toes or traced the lines on a beautiful shell that you discovered? Who was the last child you introduced to a tadpole? Or helped to catch a turtle? Creation is bursting with discoveries. A billowing cloud, a sun pattern on a patch of pumpkins, or a bulging garden all comfort us. The Lord knew we would need these undeniable reminders of his presence on earth.

Lord, thank you for all the beauty we have on earth. Help me to remember to appreciate it and not take it for granted. Amen.

God's Very Own

For the LORD will not forsake his people, for
his great name's sake, because it has pleased the
LORD to make you a people for himself.

—1 SAMUEL 12:22 ESV

God's name is great. It reveals his character and reputation. For the sake of who he is, he has chosen—joyfully!—to make you a person just for himself. He created you to be in a dynamic, life-changing relationship with him.

What prevents you from understanding this? Why is it hard to believe that God wants a relationship with you? Perhaps because you know yourself so well. You are well aware of your flaws, sins, and tendencies. You look at yourself in the mirror, and instead of seeing an image-bearer of God's beauty, you count flaws.

Surely God can't want to hang out with you, right?

Wrong.

God discerns every part of you. He understands you better than you know yourself. Even so, even with all the information about your frailty, he still wants to connect deeply with you. Why? Because he created you. He fashioned you with a him-shaped hole in your heart that only he can fill.

That should thrill your heart today. God loves you. He is *for* you. He created you for himself and for his glory. Because of that, there are hope and joy and life ahead.

Jesus, thank you that you created me to be in relationship with you. It's sometimes hard to imagine why. I know all my issues and faults so well, yet you know them more, died for every sin, and still want to pursue my heart. Thank you. Amen.

Day of Reflection

Are not two sparrows sold for a penny? Yet not one of them will fall to the ground outside your Father's care.
—MATTHEW 10:29 NIV

HIS EYE IS ON THE SPARROW

Why should I feel discouraged?
Why should the shadows come?
Why should my heart be lonely
and long for heaven and home
When Jesus is my portion? My constant friend is He;
His eye is on the sparrow, and I know He watches me;

Whenever I am tempted, whenever clouds arise,
When song gives place to sighing,
when hope within me dies,
I draw the closer to Him; from care He sets me free;
His eye is on the sparrow, and I know He watches me;

—CIVILLA D. MARTIN, 1905

Your space—a poem, prayer, thoughts . . .

What's Next, Papa?

This resurrection life you received from God is not a
timid, grave-tending life. It's adventurously expectant,
greeting God with a childlike "What's next, Papa?"
God's Spirit touches our spirits and confirms who we
really are. We know who he is, and we know who we
are: Father and children. And we know we are going to
get what's coming to us—an unbelievable inheritance!
We go through exactly what Christ goes through. If
we go through the hard times with him, then we're
certainly going to go through the good times with him!

—ROMANS 8:15–17 MSG

We are God's beloved children, wildly loved by him. Because
of that we can live in great anticipation of what he will do next
in our lives. We can have an intimate relationship with him, the
kind a daddy has with his daughter.

No longer are we weighed down with regrets and sin. No,
we are living an adventure with Jesus, fascinated not by our own
power, but by his. No matter what happens, because we have this
adoring Father, we will never walk alone. He will be with us in
the good times and bad, ever present, always available.

Take this truth to heart. God is your Daddy. He bounces you
on his lap. He smiles over you. He watches you from heaven with
delight and joy. He is not disappointed in you, but proud of you.
When he sees you, he sees the perfection of his Son.

What a beautiful walk we have with Jesus!

*Jesus, help me to always ask, "What's next, Papa?" in my life. I want to
live in anticipation of what you will do, realizing you'll never, ever leave
me. Amen.*

God Gives Us Skills

I have given special skill to all the gifted craftsmen so they
can make all the things I have commanded you to make.

—EXODUS 31:6 NLT

When we create things, we demonstrate the beauty of God's creativity. After all, he created everything and his creativity knows no boundaries. In this passage, we see that God specifically empowered craftsmen to make what he commanded them to make. Their ability depended solely on the skills God imparted to them.

So when you create something, remember that God gave you the power to create in the first place. This also means that he gives us the ability to mother the children he's given us, to do the jobs he's provided, to sing the songs he's put on our hearts. And it's all for his glory.

The beauty in this is that God equips us to do even what seems impossible. The craftsmen in the Old Testament had probably never created what God asked them to create. Yet he gave them supernatural ability and insight to do so.

Next time you sense God calling you to do something that seems outside of your ability, rejoice! Because this is just an indication that he will empower you to do what he asks. And when you look back on his ability to pull you through, remember to praise him.

Jesus, thank you for reminding me that everything comes from you—even my creativity. When I'm scared to move forward in something you've called me to do, remind me how you empowered the craftsmen to do their work. I trust in you, Jesus. Amen.

Tell the Whole Wide World

Give thanks to the LORD, call on his name; make known
among the nations what he has done, and proclaim that
his name is exalted. Sing to the LORD, for he has done
glorious things; let this be known to all the world.

—ISAIAH 12:4–5 NIV 1984

We thank God privately. We may tell our families and friends of
the great things he has done. But God wants us to expand the way
we praise him. His heart is for the whole wide world. His plan
from the beginning was to bring everyone close to him.

He blessed the nation of Israel so that they could be a blessing
to the world. God's intention was that they'd become a beacon of
his light to a needy and sin-darkened world. Problem was, they
misconstrued this blessing and hoarded it to themselves. They
forgot the whole wide world.

God's great redemptive plan moves on, and we have the
privilege to be a part of it. He blesses us so that we can bless the
world. He sheds his light on our hearts so that we can shine his
light to others. May we not forget that he gives to us so that we
can extend him to others.

In this day with the Internet reaching around the world, we
have a unique opportunity to proclaim God's greatness everywhere. May it be that we shine his light in the darkest corners of
the whole wide world.

*Jesus, thank you that you've placed me in this time period where it's easier
to proclaim you to the whole world. Help me to share your amazing feats
with everyone you put me in contact with. Amen.*

More Than Conquerors

No, in all these things we are more than
conquerors through him who loved us.

—ROMANS 8:37

Suffering, pain, hardship, and tragedy all have a tendency to lie to us. In the darkness they whisper to our tortured souls, "Where is your God now?" When those doubts and lies creep into your head, how do you answer them?

Paul meant that even when people do oppose us, even when they do manage to starve us, strip us, savage us, and slay us, yet we remain "more than conquerors" through him who loved us. It doesn't "feel" like that, but it is true nonetheless.

In times of great sorrow or trial, it isn't productive to deny or ignore your feelings. But don't hand them the steering wheel either! Instead, remember what Paul says here. None of us are "conquerors" on our own, let alone "more than" conquerors. What does it mean to be "more than" a conqueror? Well, conquerors win battles and sometimes wars. They take over someone else's territory . . . for a time. And that's the best they can do. To be "more than a conqueror" means that you do more than win temporal battles, wars, or territory. What you win, you win forever; and if you are connected to Christ, you win everything, quite literally. Not just isolated battles or solitary wars or bits of territory—for a little while—but the whole shebang, for eternity. And over the whole thing is Christ's love. The fierce, unchanging, passionate love of Jesus.

Paul looks forward in this beautiful passage, and so must we. It makes sense in no other way. And so we wait for its full and final fulfillment.

Lord, thank you for your abundant love that allows me to be more than
a conqueror through you. I will always look to you during my suffering.
Amen.

Our Big God

He parted the heavens and came down;
dark clouds were under his feet.

—PSALM 18:9 NIV 1984

God has power over the cosmos. He can part the heavens. He can withstand darkness. He can rescue even the most impossible situation or person. He is big that way.

We run into stress when we forget this simple truth. When things in our lives loom large, God shrinks in our minds. When people's opinions of us seem bigger than God's opinion in terms of importance, we "smallify" God. When our money troubles seem impossible, we forget how God makes much possible.

God is the God who parts the heavens. And not only that, he has the desire and ability to rescue us, to find us in the darkness and save us. In light of that, let's determine to have a big view of God.

A big view of God—a lesser view of people.

A big view of God—a smaller view of our problems.

A big view of God—a diminished view of obstacles.

A big view of God—a miniscule view of relational stress.

The truth? God is bigger than everything, and we can trust him.

Jesus, help me remember how very big you are. I don't want to "smallify" you. When my problems seem big, help me remember you are bigger still. Amen.

God Owns It All

Yours, O LORD, is the greatness, the power, the glory,
the victory, and the majesty. Everything in the heavens
and on earth is yours, O LORD, and this is your kingdom.
We adore you as the one who is over all things.

—1 CHRONICLES 29:11 NLT

Sometimes when life crashes in and our worries multiply, we forget that God is ultimately the CEO of everything. This world is his kingdom. He rules all. To use a big word, this means God is sovereign. In other words, he's the King.

His desire for us is to recognize that. To be so enamored with him and his capability that we let go of our own incapability. His is the power that transforms our hearts. His is the glory that makes the earth orbit the sun. His sacrificial act on the cross assures us of victorious living. And when we hike up a mountain, we remember his majesty.

Every single thing you see is God's. The chair you're sitting in. The birdsongs outside your window. The skin covering your body. The ability to think. The grass in front of your house. The friend you have coffee with. All this is a gift from our amazing God for you to enjoy, and all these point to his power and creativity.

The last sentence of the verse challenges us to a response: "We adore you as the one who is over all things." Take some time today to truly adore God for his outrageous ability.

Jesus, I forget sometimes that you made every single thing I see, taste, touch, hear, and smell. Thank you. I choose to adore you because of your power and creativity. Amen.

Day of Reflection

For the world is Mine, and all its fullness.

—PSALM 50:12

THIS IS MY FATHER'S WORLD

This is my Father's world, and to my list'ning ears,
All nature sings and round me rings
the music of the spheres.
This is my Father's world; I rest me in the thought
Of rocks and trees, of skies and seas;
His hand the wonders wrought.

This is my Father's world, o let me ne'er forget
That though the wrong seems oft so strong,
God is the Ruler yet.
This is my Father's world; the battle is not done;
Jesus, who died, shall be satisfied,
and earth and heav'n be one.

—MALTHIE D. BABCOCK, 1901

Your space—a poem, prayer, thoughts . . .

Nothing Is Too Hard

Ah, Lord GOD! It is you who have made the heavens
and the earth by your great power and by your
outstretched arm! Nothing is too hard for you.
—JEREMIAH 32:17 ESV

A lot of things overwhelm us. A way-too-busy schedule. Money
that doesn't stretch to the end of the month. Relational conflict
that doesn't ever seem to resolve. A wayward child. A to-do list
that keeps growing. And yet, nothing is too hard for God. Not.
One. Thing.

According to Jeremiah, he created the sky and earth all
through his power. He stretched out his arm and formed the
earth from nothing. He said the word and breathed trees, dirt,
birds, mountains, oceans, and even us into existence.

That is the kind of God we can entrust our lives to. That kind
of big, huge, unimaginable God. He is the God who resurrected
his Son, who, through that act, gave us beautiful access to him. He
rescued and saved us from our sin by all that power and might.

This week you will face trials. Small ones. Big ones. Silly,
buzzing ones. You'll have the opportunity to feel small in rela-
tion to them, or to see them through the lens of God's greatness.
The next time something overwhelms you, simply say this out
loud as a prayer and a reminder: "God, thank you that nothing is
too hard for you. Not. One. Thing."

By reminding yourself of God's bigness compared to the
problems you face, you'll find your ability to cope with them
increase. And as you learn to place your burdens and worries in
God's care, you'll have more peace and joy.

*Jesus, help me to remember this week that not one thing is too hard for
you. Sometimes I make my problems bigger than you. Forgive me for
that. Amen.*

Desert Streams

Then the eyes of the blind shall be opened, and the ears of
the deaf shall be unstopped. Then the lame shall leap like
a deer, and the tongue of the dumb sing. For waters shall
burst forth in the wilderness, and streams in the desert.

—Isaiah 35:5–6

Sometimes we come to the end of our situations or the end of our strength and feel as if our lives become wilderness. Sometimes everything we do feels parched and dried up. Instead of experiencing abundance and living water, we walk thirsty. And life seems impossible.

All the things listed in this scripture are near impossibilities. Blind people don't see. Deaf people can't hear. Lame folks can't leap. Dumb people cannot sing. Wildernesses and deserts don't produce streams. But God can change impossibilities. After all, he created people and wilderness and health and streams.

Where are you feeling overwhelmed right now? What is impossible in your life? Remember that God is bigger still. Keep in mind the capability of God to open eyes and mouths, to unshackle lame legs and to loose tongues, to abundantly supply water to a desert land. That's how great God is.

Our job is to remember his greatness and rest where we are, trusting in that greatness. He may not answer our pleas in the moment, but he does listen to them, and he will respond in his perfect timing.

Jesus, I feel like I'm in a desert right now and I could use a refreshing stream in my life. Parts of me feel lame, and sometimes I'm blind to what is good in life. Open my eyes. Unleash my mouth. Help me to walk when I'm weak. And water me today. Amen.

The Pursuit of Happy

> But may the righteous be glad and rejoice before
> God; may they be happy and joyful.
>
> —PSALM 68:3

Let's talk about the word *happy*. There are thousands of books on happiness, and most start their discussion with the question "What is it?" Almost all find happiness difficult to define. Why? Because everyone experiences happiness differently.

We know happiness is a feeling based on an experience; that experience may make one person happy but not another. We also know the feeling of being happy is a relatively brief elevation of mood that for one may be slurping ice cream while for another it's organizing a closet.

So is it possible to be content and also happy? Of course it is, but happy moments come along as additions to the state of contentedness. While he was imprisoned, Paul experienced moments of happiness when he received a supportive and loving letter from the outside. Being happy was a bonus to the contentedness he already felt. So, can a happy person be content? Actually, no—at least not without some groundwork. A person experiencing the feeling of being happy without the grounding of contentment is only going to continue living a craving-for-more existence.

If you have no foundation of contentment, you will blow around the universe in search of more happy feelings. That's the wrong order. You must first find contentment; then you can enjoy the happy moments that come and go throughout a lifetime.

Lord, thank you that I can be both happy and content with my circumstances. Help me to remember that even in rough waters, happiness is just around the corner if I will put my hope in you. Amen.

Singing Salvation

We'll fill the air with salvation songs.

—PSALM 9:14 MSG

God has given us much to sing about. Salvation means rescue from peril. It means he has delivered us from the kingdom of darkness into the kingdom of light. He has taken what was broken and rebuilt us into something whole. He has changed us from sinners in need of grace to victors who walk in freedom.

That's plenty to sing about. We sing not simply to improve our perspective or even praise God. We sing to proclaim how great God is for the rest of the world's sake. We sing to declare his ability to those who stumble in darkness.

Every single day we have a choice to sing. We can either focus on our pain, grumbling our way through the hours. Or we can look upward, remember the radical redemption God has wrought in our lives, and sing with everything inside us.

This is good news, our salvation! We must not hoard our song to ourselves, but be brave enough to sing it for others. They also need to experience the joy of God's salvation. The time is short, and many are walking without hope.

Sing your song today.

Jesus, help me to sing for my sake, to proclaim how good you are. And help me to remember to sing to you, to worship you for your amazing salvation. Help me not to forget to sing outwardly, toward the world that so desperately needs you. Amen.

Hope for a Longing and Hungry Soul

For he satisfies the longing soul, and the
hungry soul he fills with good things.

—PSALM 107:9 ESV

To satisfy means to gratify a genuine need, to get rid of a debt, to free from doubt or question. God wants to fill every part of us, relieving us, helping us find our satisfaction in him alone. He has rid us of the debt of sin that we couldn't deal with on our own. He walks alongside us when we walk on the road of doubt.

What's beautiful about this verse is the word *longing*. For those of us who long for God and his presence, the satisfaction he brings becomes all the sweeter. When we know our souls are empty without God, that's when we go to him to fill us with his good things.

When was the last time you longed for God? That you ached to be near him? If that's been a struggle for you, simply ask him to put the longing there. Ask him to help you realize your deep need for him, that you'll grasp how empty you are without him.

Even if you're angry with him for not doing things the way you'd like him to, or you're confused about the way he works, be assured. He loves to answer our longing prayers.

Jesus, I want to be in the place where I'm longing for you, where I realize I'm empty without you. Forgive me for finding satisfaction outside of you. I may not always understand what you're doing, but today I choose to trust you. Amen.

When God Is Your Song

Behold, God is my salvation; I will trust, and will
not be afraid; for the LORD GOD is my strength
and my song, and he has become my salvation.

—ISAIAH 12:2 ESV

What does it mean here that God becomes our song? Why would Isaiah use music as a metaphor for strength and salvation and trust? Because so much of us is connected to the music we listen to. We identify ourselves often by our particular playlists, our tastes, and even our dislikes.

So when God becomes our song, he becomes everything we are. When we sing to him, whether it be in the car or the shower or under our breath when we're facing a crisis, we engage our souls with him.

When was the last time you sang to God? Just you with him as the audience? If you could have songwriting capabilities, what would the song say? How would you praise God for what he's done? What would you sing about his attributes? Would there be dark notes where you walked through valleys? High notes when victory came? Would your song be a symphony? A pop song? Rap?

No matter what the song, the implication is clear. God wants us to give our souls, the very best parts of ourselves, to him. If we sing our surrender, all the better.

Jesus, help me to sing to you, for you, and about you. Please help me to understand the link between my soul, music, and you. And may it be that my playlists, as well as the way I live my life, reflect you. Amen.

Day of Reflection

And those the LORD has rescued will
return. They will enter Zion with singing;
everlasting joy will crown their heads.

—ISAIAH 35:10

HE KEEPS ME SINGING

There's within my heart a melody.
Jesus whispers sweet and low:
"Fear not. I am with thee; peace be still,"
In all of life's ebb and flow.

Soon He's coming back to welcome me
far beyond the starry sky.
I shall wing my flight to worlds unknown;
I shall reign with Him on high.
Jesus, Jesus, Jesus, sweetest name I know,
Fills my every longing, keeps me singing as I go.

—LUTHER B. BRIDGERS, 1910

Your space—a poem, prayer, thoughts . . .

Be Good, Teach Good

Older women likewise are to be reverent in their behavior,
not malicious gossips nor enslaved to much wine, teaching
what is good, so that they may encourage the young women
to love their husbands, to love their children, to be sensible,
pure, workers at home, kind, being subject to their own
husbands, so that the word of God will not be dishonored.

—TITUS 2:3–4 NASB

In order to teach others how to follow Jesus, we must first be the person we want those folks to become. Everything flows from our hearts; so if we're bitter and gossipy, we'll tend to reproduce that in others. If we are full of Jesus and joy and love, we'll produce that as we teach.

What would this world look like if we not only went to Jesus to refine our character but also took the time to actively encourage others to do so? The model here is living life well, then actively coming alongside others in order to train them. We must messy our hands in the lives of those younger than us to help them love Jesus well in their generation.

Many women today cannot see themselves as mentors. They know themselves well enough to be acquainted with their shortcomings. If all of us shrunk away from mentoring younger women, though, there would be no mentors. Jesus isn't calling us to be perfect, just dedicated. To be able to go to him when we've sinned. To be humble and teachable ourselves.

With hearts like that, he will greatly use us to reach the next generation, to disciple them beautifully.

Jesus, show me women in my life right now whom I can mentor. Please help me move beyond my own insecurity to walk alongside someone who needs a mentor. Amen.

We Are His Body

The body is a unit, though it is made up of many parts;
and though all its parts are many, they form one body.
So it is with Christ. For we were all baptized by one
Spirit into one body—whether Jews or Greeks, slave or
free—and we were all given the one Spirit to drink.

—1 CORINTHIANS 12:12–13 NIV 1984

The body is an interesting metaphor for the church. God could've used a variety of words to describe it: a company, a farm, a plantation. But he used the body. Why? One reason is hinted at here.

Because the body is organic, it depends on every part of it to live. A body needs skin. It needs a heart. A liver is extremely important. The pituitary glands are vital. And when all the parts work together, you have life.

In a similar way, we are his body. We may be a kneecap or a spleen, but nothing diminishes our part. Every single part is important. Working behind the scenes is just as valuable as being an internationally known speaker. In God's economy, according to these verses, we are all level, whether we're "important" or not.

We all have the same Spirit. We all depend on each other. No matter how God has placed you in his body, revel in the fact that he did and do what he has called you to do to the very best of your ability.

Jesus, thank you for your body, the church. Sometimes it's difficult to get along with everyone in the church, but I am realizing just how important each person is. Thank you that in your eyes everyone is equal. Amen.

November 6

We Are Yeast

Again he asked, "What shall I compare the
kingdom of God to? It is like yeast that a woman
took and mixed into about sixty pounds of flour
until it worked all through the dough."

—LUKE 13:20–21 NIV

The woman in these verses worked with sixty pounds of flour—
that's a lot of flour. It would take a lot of kneading to work yeast
through that amount of dough. The result of her labor would be
leavened bread—bread that had the capacity to rise and double
in shape.

Jesus equates the kingdom of God to yeast, the leavening
agent in most of the bread we eat. It permeates and produces an
expansion. The question becomes, how can we be like yeast?
How can we further God's kingdom?

Just as yeast needs to be kneaded in, so we need to be worked
into this world by our Master. We must be willing to be broken
and stretched so that our effectiveness spreads. We have to be
excited about reaching the rest of the dough—those folks we may
not normally associate with. And we have to have a larger view of
our faith, the kind of faith that believes God for expansion.

Being yeast not only makes for an expansive kingdom, but it
also creates an end product: bread. Jesus said he was the Bread of
Life. (See John 6:35.) When we are yeast, Jesus is what we offer to
others, the kind of bread that ultimately fills and satisfies.

*Jesus, help me to be yeast today, to be willing to be kneaded so that your
needy world can have more of you, the Bread of Life. Amen.*

Remaining Faithful

As for me, my life has already been poured out as
an offering to God. The time of my death is near. I
have fought the good fight, I have finished the race,
and I have remained faithful. And now the prize
awaits me—the crown of righteousness, which the
Lord, the righteous Judge, will give me on the day of
his return. And the prize is not just for me but for
all who eagerly look forward to his appearing.

—2 Timothy 4:6–8 NLT

When we start new things, we often start with joy and vigor,
ready to tackle the problem with everything in us. And when we
met Jesus, we most likely started that journey with a similar joy.
But Paul here doesn't speak of beginnings; he speaks of finishing.

It's not hard to initiate, but it's harder to finish well. To
persevere. Our walk with God is not a quarter-mile horse race,
it's a hundred-mile endurance race. We have to pace ourselves.
We also have to remember that folks remember the last part of
our lives first when they mourn our passing. So finishing well is
utterly important.

How do we remain faithful throughout our Christian lives?
Like a long distance runner, we train. We learn to say no to the
things that will prevent our success. We are coached. We run
with friends. We persevere through blisters and naysayers.

In other words, we must train ourselves when trials come,
realizing that trials make us better fit to run. We say no to the sins
that entangle us. We ask others for help and guidance. We find
friends who will encourage us to keep running. And we ask for
God's strength when pain comes.

*Jesus, I want to finish well. I want to run an enduring race. Please send
me coaches and fellow runners on this journey. And please be my hope
and strength. Amen.*

Know Your Enemy

*For we are not fighting against flesh-and-blood
enemies, but against evil rulers and authorities of the
unseen world, against mighty powers in this dark
world, and against evil spirits in the heavenly places.*

—EPHESIANS 6:12 NLT

When evil comes our way in the form of slander, gossip, harsh
words, belittling, betrayal, or any other relational heartache, our
tendency is to look squarely into the eyes of the person hurting
us, leveling all the blame there.

But Paul offers a different perspective. We are not fighting
against people, though it may seem like it at times. We actually
engage in an all-out war with dark spiritual forces. We have a very
real enemy: Satan. His desire is to destroy us, and he'll use any
means he can to trip us up. Not surprisingly, he uses people and
situations to bring the most damage.

So what are we to do when folks are mean? First, place your
eyes on Jesus. He is the victor, and he will ultimately doom Satan
to the lake of fire. He vanquished Satan when he died on the cross,
then rose again. He is able to help you walk through this battle.

Second, place your hatred on the right enemy. Your enemy is
not the person hurting you. It's the spiritual forces of this world.
Pray that the friend who hurts you will have her eyes opened to
that reality. Choose to forgive so that you won't allow Satan a
foothold into your life—oh, how he loves to enter through the
doorway of bitterness.

*Jesus, help me to discern the battle raging all around me. I don't want to
only look at other people as the source of my pain. Thank you that you
are bigger than Satan and his awful activities. You are my hope, and I
love you. Amen.*

The Cost of Worship

But the king said to Araunah, "No, but I will buy it from you for a price. I will not offer burnt offerings to the LORD my God that cost me nothing." So David bought the threshing floor and the oxen for fifty shekels of silver.

—2 SAMUEL 24:24 ESV

In this passage, King David is offered a piece of land so he can make offerings to God. It seems like a great deal! Araunah is giving him the ultimate discount: free. But David's response is perplexing. He believes that when he gives his offerings to God, they must cost him something. So he offers to buy the land.

In our workaday world, we try to avoid pain at any cost. We take the easy way out, the path of least resistance. If something is hard or tries us, we tend to shrink back. And yet David made a deliberate choice to sacrifice when he didn't have to. He loved God so much that he longed to love him in such a way that it cost him cold hard shekels.

This is a great example in terms of loosely holding our money, but it goes much deeper to the heart. Our relationship with God is the most beautiful, costly thing we possess on this earth. It's valuable. The question is: will we choose to view it that way? Are we happy to sacrifice for the sake of God's smile? What are we willing to give up to demonstrate our allegiance to him?

God may not be asking you to buy property or give everything away. Or he might be. But he calls us all to hold everything in our lives loosely so that it's easy for us to worship him no matter what the cost.

Jesus, help me to understand the nature of worship, that it should cost me something. I know you paid the price for my salvation and I can't earn it, but I do want to be like David, willing to to show you afresh just how grateful I am. Amen.

Day of Reflection

Take up your positions; stand firm and see the deliverance
the LORD will give you . . . Do not be afraid; do not
be discouraged . . . the LORD will be with you.

—2 CHRONICLES 20:17 NIV

ONWARD CHRISTIAN SOLDIERS

Onward, Christian soldiers marching as to war,
with the cross of Jesus going on before!
Christ the royal Master, leads against the foe;
forward into battle see his banners go!

At the sign of triumph, Satan's host doth flee;
on then Christian soldiers, on to victory!
Hell's foundations quiver at the shouts of praise;
brothers lift your voices, loud your anthems raise!

Onward, Christian soldiers marching as to war,
With the cross of Jesus going on before!

—SABINE BARING-GOULD, 1865

Your space—a poem, prayer, thoughts . . .

Putting Love into Action

*I always thank my God when I pray for you, Philemon,
because I keep hearing about your faith in the Lord
Jesus and your love for all of God's people. And I am
praying that you will put into action the generosity that
comes from your faith as you understand and experience
all the good things we have in Christ. Your love has
given me much joy and comfort, my brother, for your
kindness has often refreshed the hearts of God's people.*

—PHILEMON 1:4–7 NLT

Paul prays this prayer for Philemon, his friend. Philemon's name actually means "loving," which demonstrates that Philemon lives up to his name because he has great love for all God's people. Paul hopes Philemon will put that love into action through generosity.

It's easy to think of ourselves as generous, but not always to live it out, to put it into action. To feel pity for someone is entirely different from buying her a lunch, or going the extra mile to provide for her. Our faith must be more than pity; it must involve holy action as a result of our empathy.

The last part of this verse shows us how we can be generous—through kindness. Paul commends Philemon's kindness to the folks he's surrounded with, God's people. His kindness refreshed others.

Often we are kinder to outsiders than we are to the people closest to us. May it be that we can put our love into generous action like Philemon and choose kindness for the members of our families, pouring out encouragement. What would our homes look like if we refreshed the hearts of the folks we lived with?

*Jesus, I want to be like Philemon, full of love and generosity. I want to
act on my empathy. And I truly want to be kind, starting at home. Please
help me to become a refreshment to others. Amen.*

Temper, Temper

Everyone must be quick to hear, slow to speak,
and slow to anger; for the anger of man does
not achieve the righteousness of God.

—JAMES 1:19–20 NASB

We see Jesus hanging out with people who had vastly different lifestyles than those considered "holy" in his day. Tax collectors and sinners flocked to him. Children ran to his irresistibility. He was not afraid of their opinions. He always spoke the truth, but seasoned it with grace. He reserved his harshest, most pointed words for those who appeared religious but were hypocritical, but he kept an invitational stance to the masses.

Do we represent the irresistibility of Jesus when we talk to people who differ from us? Would Jesus yell at someone who differed in her political opinion? Would he lash out? Would he scream?

Consider this wisdom from the Proverbs: "An arrogant man stirs up strife, but he who trusts in the LORD will prosper" (28:25 NASB).

"A fool always loses his temper, but a wise man holds it back" (29:11 NASB).

We are more like Jesus when we hold back our tempers, when we choose not to stir up strife for the sake of proving our "correctness." Our job is to represent Jesus, how he talked, how he acted, how he loved.

How well do you love those who differ from you?

Dear Jesus, help me be so settled in your love for me that very little threatens me or pushes me toward anger. I want to be gentle, quick to listen. Help me not be threatened by others' opinions. In the heat of disagreement, give me your perspective and help me love those who differ. Amen.

Our Hiking Partner

> When I thought, "My foot slips," your steadfast
> love, O LORD, held me up. When the cares of my
> heart are many, your consolations cheer my soul.
> —PSALM 94:18–19 ESV

Climbing mountains isn't for the faint of heart, especially if the climb is difficult and the pathway is either hard to navigate or it's slick from rain. We have to be careful to place our feet on solid ground with each step, and often keep the end goal—the summit—in mind as we hike.

But as in life, sometimes our feet slip and we fall. When we do, it always goes better if we have a partner nearby who can offer his or her hand and lift us back up, or prevent us from falling off the precipice in the first place.

God holds us up even after our feet slip. When we tumble, God's love grabs us, lifts us up, and helps us to move on. Not only does God help us on our journeys toward each day's summit, but the psalmist also says God consoles us when our hearts are burdened by too much stress.

What prevents you today from reaching for God's hand after you slip? What holds you back from taking a moment right now to lay before God all your cares and worries? He is available. He will help. He will listen. And, thankfully, he will rescue and console you.

Jesus, I don't much like it when my feet slip. But they do. Thanks for being there for me when I fall. Help me to share my whole heart with you today, every worry, every care, everything that weighs me down. I need you. I hope in you. Amen.

Praise and Cursing

With the tongue we praise our Lord and Father,
and with it we curse men, who have been made in
God's likeness. Out of the same mouth come praise
and cursing. My brothers, this should not be.

—JAMES 3:9–10 NIV 1984

In the context of these verses, James uses the image of a fountain spurting both fresh water and saltwater—an impossibility. Yet, it is possible for us to say mean things about others one moment, then praise another person in the next. James's obvious statement is, "This should not be."

Because we're all created by God and bear his image, we deserve dignity. Sometimes it's easier to insist on that for ourselves, but when someone slights us, we forget. We justify ourselves in our gossip because of the offense of the other, forgetting that gossiping is yet another offense. May it not be that when we're sinned against, we add to it by sinning ourselves.

How do we get out of the habit of tearing others down? If you have a group of friends who primarily talk about others, choose to be brave and either find a new circle of friends, or kindly bow out. "I would rather not talk about someone in a negative light," is all you would need to say.

But deeper than that, we are also responsible for our thought life toward others. We may not say things out loud, but we think awful thoughts. Jesus wants to revolutionize even our thoughts.

Jesus, forgive me for talking ill about someone else. Help me to remember to bow out of those kinds of conversations. And please look inside my heart and clean up my motivations and mean thoughts toward others. I need your help to do that, Lord. Amen.

Covering Up

> Whoever goes about slandering reveals secrets, but he
> who is trustworthy in spirit keeps a thing covered.
>
> —PROVERBS 11:13 ESV

Slander is saying something mean or untrue about people with the intent to harm them or their reputations. Slanderers love to know people's secrets so they can broadcast—or tweet!—them to the world. They are untrustworthy and the damage they create is devastating.

On the contrary, a trustworthy friend covers up a friend's sin. Not that they don't talk to their friends about hard things, or bring up a problem. But when they have the choice to humiliate their friend because of the secret they know, they choose the holy act of silence.

We are most like God when we cover over others' sins. Isn't that what Jesus did for us on the cross? He removed our sins as far as the east is from the west. He doesn't hold them over us. He doesn't shame us or ridicule us publicly.

To be a trustworthy person is to keep secrets, to love well, and do unto others as we'd love to be treated. Would you like your friends to tell your secrets?

Jesus, help me keep my mouth shut when I'm tempted to share a friend's struggle or sin. I don't want to be untrustworthy. Help me remember to treat my friends the same way I'd like to be treated—with kindness and forgiveness. Amen.

What's First Love Like?

But I have this against you, that you have left your first love.
—REVELATION 2:4 NASB

Think back on your first love. What happened? How did you react around him? Did your heart palpitate when he came near? Did you stop eating? Did one simple phone call send you reeling with joy? How much of your mind was occupied with thoughts of him? And how much time did the two of you spend together?

God wants to be our first love. He desires a hope-filled, interactive relationship where we thrill to hear his voice. He's not looking for infatuation or a junior high crush that wavers every three days. He desires first-love status in our lives.

Remember the traits of your first romance. You spent deliberate time together. You asked great questions and talked a lot. You were comfortable just hanging out. You were affectionate with each other, and you started to complete each other's sentences. Your aim was to please your boyfriend, to find out what he loved and bless him accordingly.

It's the same with God. We need to take deliberate time with him. We need to spend time in prayer, asking God questions and being quiet enough to listen back. We need some unstructured time with God, maybe taking a walk or listening to worship music. We need to learn affection for the Almighty, which translates into our gratitude for who he is and what he does. We need to know his Word so well that we recall it during difficult, trying times.

And lastly, we need to find out what pleases God—obedience— and bless him accordingly.

Jesus, life has pelted me lately and I've forgotten about you. Please forgive me. I love you and I want to do the things that bless you today. Amen.

Day of Reflection

So then, just as you received Christ Jesus as
Lord, continue to live your lives in Him.

—COLOSSIANS 2:6 NIV

O FOR A CLOSER WALK WITH GOD

O for a closer walk with God,
A calm and heavenly frame,
A light to shine up
On the road that leads me to the Lamb!

So shall my walk be close with God,
Calm and serene my frame;
So purer light shall mark the road
That leads me to the Lamb.

—WILLIAM COWPER, 1772

Your space—a poem, prayer, thoughts . . .

Wise Silence

He who restrains his words has knowledge, and
he who has a cool spirit is a man of understanding.
Even a fool, when he keeps silent, is considered wise;
when he closes his lips, he is considered prudent.

—PROVERBS 17:27–28 NASB

We tend to like to chatter our way out of painful situations, to defend our cause, to make people understand what we're thinking and why we do things. This is particularly heightened during contentious times when folks argue back and forth.

But this proverb reminds us of the simplicity of silence. In order to appear wise, we only need to shut our mouths. Two things happen when we do that. One: we, by an act of our will, are choosing to entrust our reputation to God. Two: because we are silent, we are forced to listen to the other person.

What would it look like in your home this year if you nurtured a peaceful spirit, if you were known by your friends and family as someone who had great understanding and wisdom? How would your relationships improve if you made a deliberate choice to be silent?

Look back over your week. Take note of the times you talked a lot. What happened? What would've been different had you zipped your lips? May it be that we learn the joy of quietness, letting go of our need to verbally retaliate.

Jesus, when you were accused, you stood silent. Help me to learn how to do that. I don't want to defend myself; it's tiring. Instead, help me to be quiet this week, to truly listen to the people in my life. Amen.

Exclamation!

How amazing are the deeds of the LORD! All who
delight in him should ponder them. Everything he
does reveals his glory and majesty. His righteousness
never fails. He causes us to remember his wonderful
works. How gracious and merciful is our LORD!

—PSALM 111:2–4 NLT

The psalmist exclaims these words, as if he cannot help himself
from proclaiming the wonder of God. He nearly bursts at the
seams of his declaration.

It's hard to watch this when we're feeling bowled over,
though. Others' exclamations seem to say our current trials don't
matter. But here's the interesting truth: the psalmist no doubt had
a difficult day when he penned these words. He felt the weight of
his own worry and sin, yet he made a choice to praise God.

We have that same choice. We can either let the pain around
us embitter us and shrink us away from others, or we can lean
into it, find God in the midst of our turmoil, and shout about his
greatness anyway. When we do that, our new attitude becomes
infectious, and our heart feels fuller.

Why? Because we can never explore the depths of God's majesty and get to the end of it. He has an abundant supply of great
deeds, glory, majesty, righteousness, works, grace, and mercy,
according to this verse. When we feel empty, we actually have
more capacity to experience God's fullness.

Jesus, I want to proclaim how great you are, even when I'm weighed down
by life's great circumstances. Thank you that you have everything I need
in abundance. I treasure you right now. Amen.

No Grumbling

Then they despised the pleasant land; they did not
believe in His word, but grumbled in their tents;
they did not listen to the voice of the LORD.

—PSALM 106:24–25 NASB

These verses from Psalms are referring to the freed Israelites.
When they were hounded and bowed down by severe slavery,
God parted the Red Sea and delivered them from the hands of
their enemies in an amazing show of force. He provided water
and food in surprising ways. He led them forward on a trek
toward abundance.

But they despised what God provided. They chose not to
believe the beauty of the promised land. Instead, they com-
plained and grumbled. Their eyes only saw lack, not plenty.
Because of their skewed perspective, they could no longer see the
pleasantness of the place where they were.

In short, they didn't bloom where God planted them. Instead
of exploring the beauty around them and finding joy in simple
things, they retreated to their tents and whined.

We do that sometimes, don't we? God provides amazing
things, people, and places for us. Because our perspective is
skewed, we take our eyes off all that cool stuff and focus them on
our lack. We retreat from the blessings and prefer the darkness of
our own attitudes.

*Jesus, please free me from my pessimism. I don't want to forget this amaz-
ing place you've put me. I want to be thankful right here. Please prevent
me from retreating from your blessings into my grumbling tent. Amen.*

Give to Those Who Can't Give Back

And He also went on to say to the one who had invited Him,
"When you give a luncheon or a dinner, do not invite your
friends or your brothers or your relatives or rich neighbors,
otherwise they may also invite you in return and that will
be your repayment. But when you give a reception, invite
the poor, the crippled, the lame, the blind, and you will be
blessed, since they do not have the means to repay you; for
you will be repaid at the resurrection of the righteous."

—Luke 14:12–14 nasb

The principle behind Jesus' pointed words is this: as believers,
we should give without thought to receiving anything back.
When you invite rich folk or friends or neighbors over—which is
fine to do—even if you don't expect a return invitation, they still
have the capability to give back to you.

But if you invite people who absolutely can't issue an invitation, Jesus says you'll be blessed. Your pay will come much, much
later on the other side of life.

This doesn't mean we should never invite reciprocal guests.
Instead it means we're to live our lives with eyes wide open to
the needs of the world. We should take great delight in blessing
people who can't repay because it's kingdom work, and Jesus
smiles down upon it.

When we love those who can't love back, or give to those
who can't give back, we are following in Jesus' footsteps. After
all, he gave everything to us, and we have no way to repay him.

*Jesus, open my eyes today to people who need to be loved and blessed. I
want to be extravagant in helping others. Amen.*

Plow Up the Hard Ground

Plant the good seeds of righteousness, and you will
harvest a crop of love. Plow up the hard ground of
your hearts, for now is the time to seek the LORD, that
he may come and shower righteousness upon you.

—HOSEA 10:12 NLT

There is good in your future.

Stop for a moment and read that sentence again.

God's outrageous intention is to come close to you and shower his righteousness upon you, to help you harvest a crop of love. Seem too good to be true? It's not.

But there is a condition to that blessing according to Hosea. A hard heart blocks us from experiencing God's presence. God uses the metaphor of fallow ground, of hard-packed clay, to rouse our attention. Why? Because you can't grow a thing in hard ground. Nor can you grow in righteousness if your heart is hard.

So what to do? To harvest a crop of love, we must sow seeds of righteousness in plowed, ready ground. To have a heart that's ready for that kind of crop, we have to be broken. Our clods of self-righteousness, bitterness, and pride must be pulverized and broken to pieces. All that takes is willingness.

Are you willing to have God break up the hardness of your heart?

Dear Jesus, I want you to bless me with love and righteousness, but my heart sometimes grows hard. I give you permission to plow, to break up the parts of me that are resistant to you. I don't want to be hard-hearted and bitter. I need you. Amen.

The Gift

Peter replied, "Repent and be baptized, every one of you,
in the name of Jesus Christ for the forgiveness of your
sins. And you will receive the gift of the Holy Spirit.
The promise is for you and your children and for all who
are far off—for all whom the Lord our God will call."

—ACTS 2:38–39 NIV

Think back on the best gift you've ever received. It might be a
pony or a piano or a letter of encouragement. What the gift represented to you is what made it meaningful.

Perhaps you pined for a pony for years, and your parents
scraped money together to buy one to demonstrate their love. Or
a friend sold something valuable to buy you a piano so you could
pursue a musical career. Or a favorite relative took the time to write
a note, putting pen to paper, to show you how valuable you are.

Every gift represents love.

The gift of the Holy Spirit is God's gift, representing his passion for you. Because he knew we couldn't live the Christian life
on our own, he gave himself to us—his comfort, his amazing
resources, his compassion.

How can we live in light of that gift? How have you lived in
light of the amazing gifts folks have given you? It boils down to
gratitude. While life may not be what you envisioned it and your
dreams may not seem to be coming true, you can always, always
be grateful for the gift of the Holy Spirit. Thank God for that
today.

*Jesus, your gift of the Holy Spirit to walk with me every single day amazes
me. Help me to be a person of gratitude, thankful for your gift. Thank
you that I don't have to walk alone, that the Holy Spirit is my constant
inner companion. Amen.*

Day of Reflection

Praise be to the God and Father of our Lord
Jesus Christ, who has blessed us in the heavenly
realms with every spiritual blessing in Christ.

—EPHESIANS 1:3 NIV

PRAISE GOD, FROM WHOM ALL BLESSINGS FLOW

Praise God from whom all blessings flow.
Praise Him all creatures here below.
Praise Him above ye heav'nly host.
Praise Father, Son, and Holy Ghost.
Amen.

—THOMAS KEN, 1674

Your space—a poem, prayer, thoughts . . .

Speaking Truth with Grace

*These are the things that you shall do: Speak
the truth to one another; render in your gates
judgments that are true and make for peace.*

—ZECHARIAH 8:16 ESV

Speaking truth to each other is freeing and difficult. It's a discipline and a godly practice. Because we love our friends and family, we owe it to them to be honest, though it's not always intuitive to do so.

We are hiders, often. We'd rather present the pretty parts of ourselves than delve into our worries and stresses. Even harder is when we see someone else's stress and worries and feel urged by the Holy Spirit to address them.

We need only look at Jesus who always spoke with an enticing combination of grace and truth—all in perfect balance. When we err on the side of too much grace, overlooking sin, we enable our friends to sin and don't love them well. When we err on the side of truth without kindness, we become harsh and judgmental, not seeing the person we confront as an image bearer of Christ, but as a person with problems to be solved.

Our love must be both grace and truth—grace to pardon our friends' sins, truth to kindly address them as a fellow struggler. We offer that which we experience—and we've received grace and truth aplenty from Jesus Christ.

Jesus, I want to speak the truth to my friends and family, but please temper what I say with huge shovelfuls of grace. I know I stumble too. Help me to become someone who loves truth, however presented. Above all, I want to grow, and I want to see my friends grow too. Amen.

Lessons from a Pup

In the same way your Father in heaven is not willing
that any of these little ones should be lost.
—Matthew 18:14 NIV 1984

On April 27, 2011, a devastating storm swept through Alabama, reducing the city of Tuscaloosa to rubble. In the midst of the tragedy, reports trickled out of some amazing, even miraculous rescues.

One story in particular tugged at people's heartstrings, the tale of a little girl who refused to stop looking for her dog, Mason, a two-year-old terrier mix. On the day of the tornado, Mason got sucked out of the family garage and disappeared into the whirlwind. The twister reduced the family's home to rubble, but part of the porch remained standing. Day after day, family members returned to the devastated site in case their little dog had somehow, against all odds, survived the storm and found his way home.

Can you imagine their joy and surprise when a full three weeks after the storm hit they found Mason sitting on what remained of the front steps? No one knows how far he had to crawl on his two broken legs just to get there. Mason suffered from severe dehydration and had dropped to half his normal weight. But he was alive! When he saw his family at last, this poor, miserable, terrible-looking little dog eagerly wagged his tail and hobbled toward them.

It seems to me that we could learn a thing or two from this precious puppy. He felt no shame or embarrassment about his condition. He didn't try to run or hide or clean himself up to make himself more presentable. He knew he was lost. He knew he needed help. And so he dragged himself home, straight into the arms of the ones who loved him.

Lord, help me remember that I can come as I am to you. Thank you that I can rest in your arms. Amen.

Living in the Light

Then the LORD said to Moses, "Lift your hand toward
heaven, and the land of Egypt will be covered with a
darkness so thick you can feel it." So Moses lifted his
hand to the sky, and a deep darkness covered the entire
land of Egypt for three days. During all that time the
people could not see each other, and no one moved. But
there was light as usual where the people of Israel lived.

—EXODUS 10:21–23 NLT

In the same way that the Israelites experienced light when the
Egyptians stumbled in the darkness, God's light helps us navigate
our lives when darkness surrounds us.

Have you ever watched someone who didn't know Christ deal
with tragedy? Ever wonder how she made it through? Of course,
our response should be to support those who walk through dark
times, particularly if they don't have the light of Christ. But in the
midst of that, their wandering can also serve as a gentle reminder
that we never walk alone.

When loved ones die, or our dreams seem far away, or we face
financial stress, we can be assured that God sheds his light even in
the darkest of situations. Because the Holy Spirit lives brilliantly
inside us, we are never alone. Never once.

Let's remember the truth that even when life swirls out of
control, we always, always have light. That God is available to us
who feel overwhelmed. That he has favor on his children, and he
shows that favor by shedding light on us.

*Jesus, help me to bask in your light today. I truly don't know how non-
believing people walk through their troubles. Help me to love them well, to
show them the light I've come to appreciate in you. And would you shine on
me today? I could use some warm, affirming light. Amen.*

Humpty Dumpty and Choices

> I place before you Life and Death,
> Blessing and Curse. Choose life.
> —DEUTERONOMY 30:19 MSG

Remember the nursery rhyme describing ol' Humpty Dumpty sitting on the wall? He's up there teetering this way and that. Finally he falls, and look what happens.

But what if he'd fallen on the other side of the wall? Maybe there would have been wise and helpful people waiting there—not all the king's horses and all the king's men but folks who actually knew how to help him put his life back together again.

Think of it as Mr. Dumpty having a choice; that's what an edge is sometimes, a choice. We teeter on that edge, looking on either side of the wall. Neither landing site looks comfortable; there are rocks and sharp points to be endured. But sometimes, if you look a little farther in this imaginary scene, you can make a better choice by checking out the first responders waiting to pick up the pieces. On one side, maybe you can see a hearse surrounded by a coroner's crew, or maybe a trash truck is waiting to haul you off to the landfill. "Off to the dump with you, Mr. Dumpty!"

On the other side you see a team of rescuers. Look: that's an ambulance waiting, with its motor running. And what's that painted on the top of the ambulance? Why, of course! It's a big red cross.

Lord, thank you that I always have choices in life. Help me to make the right ones. Amen.

Unforced Rhythms of Grace

Are you tired? Worn out? Burned out on religion? Come
to me. Get away with me and you'll recover your life. I'll
show you how to take a real rest. Walk with me and work
with me—watch how I do it. Learn the unforced rhythms of
grace. I won't lay anything heavy or ill-fitting on you. Keep
company with me and you'll learn to live freely and lightly.

—MATTHEW 11:28–30 MSG

Ask yourselves the questions at the beginning of this verse. Are
you tired? Worn out? Burned out on religion? If so, Jesus promises to help you recover your life.

The life of the Christian isn't a treadmill constantly stuck
on high with an incline. It's a walk, and not only that, it's a walk
with Jesus holding our hands. He leads us toward rest and peace.
Because he walked this earth and understands the complexities
of being human, he empathizes with our fatigue and restlessness.

Jesus' invitation is to simply take his hand, to be humble
enough to allow him to lead. When we try to be clever and live
the Christian life on our own terms, we burn out. But if we turn
instead to Jesus, he promises he will teach us the art of living
freely and lightly.

What holds you back today from learning the unforced
rhythms of grace with Jesus? Your schedule? Your control?
Others' expectations? Just life itself? Make the choice today to
walk slowly alongside Jesus. And he will give you rest.

*Jesus, forgive me for trying to figure out the Christian life on my own.
I'm burned out and tired. I need your help. I need your rest. I choose right
now to take your hand. Bring grace and peace and rest and hope into my
life right now. Amen.*

Christ's Sacrifice

I do not treat the grace of God as meaningless.
For if keeping the law could make us right with
God, then there was no need for Christ to die.

—GALATIANS 2:21 NLT

In our day-to-day lives, we sometimes forget that we cannot earn our way to heaven. We strive and worry, hoping that our good behavior will catch God's notice. When we live this way, we don't remember grace. It is Jesus' pure unmerited grace that saves us.

Not our keeping a long list of laws. Not our doing everything right. Not as a result of our beauty or fame or wealth or intelligence. Nothing we can do can make us right with God. Only Jesus' sacrifice on the cross ushers us into God's presence.

When we live self-sufficient lives, we treat God's grace as meaningless. We act as if the sacrifice Jesus made was for nothing because we have found all sufficiency in ourselves.

Those who truly recognize God's grace grasp how much they need Jesus' death on the cross. They realize they cannot live his life in their own strength. They understand that only through the power of the Holy Spirit can they accomplish anything in the kingdom of God.

Jesus, your grace is not meaningless. Help me live in such a way that shows the world just how much meaning it has. I don't want to live in my own strength, apart from you. No, I need you every single moment today. Amen.

Day of Reflection

In him we have redemption through his
blood, the forgiveness of sins, in accordance
with the riches of God's grace.

—EPHESIANS 1:7 NIV

AMAZING GRACE

Amazing grace! How sweet the sound!
That saved a wretch like me!
I once was lost, but now am found;
Was blind but now I see.

When we've been there ten thousand years,
Bright shining as the sun,
We've no less days to sing God's praise
Than when we first begun.

—JOHN NEWTON, 1779

Your space—a poem, prayer, thoughts . . .

Scripture Brings Hope

For whatever was written in former days was written for
our instruction, that through endurance and through the
encouragement of the Scriptures we might have hope.

—ROMANS 15:4 ESV

The Jewish people had their Scriptures, the Torah. They read the
Torah to understand the mind of God, to know what he wanted
from them. They memorized portions of it so they could be good
followers. They committed his laws to memory in hopes of pleasing God.

The apostle Paul says that those Scriptures confirmed that
use—that they were used for our instruction, to bring us encouragement. But he adds one more word: *hope*.

In the past, it was hard to know if God had favor on you.
You would work and work. Sometimes you would sin, then have
to bring an offering to atone for that sin. Because the one offering never was enough—it covered one sin—you had a constant
reminder of your sin and your broken fellowship with God.

But Jesus inaugurated a new era, what he called the New
Covenant. This covenant wasn't based on what we could bring
to the table—nothing—but what God could bring—everything.
Because Jesus became the one perfect sacrifice for our sins, we
now have true hope. All the Scriptures point to him. He fulfilled
the law. And now we can live with utter hope, knowing that his
payment was truly enough.

*Jesus, thank you for hope. Thanks that I don't have to run around trying
to earn your love. Help me see the Scriptures as pointing to you and what
you did on the cross for me and everyone else. Amen.*

The Word

In the beginning was the Word, and the Word was
with God, and the Word was God. He was with God
in the beginning. Through him all things were made;
without him nothing was made that has been made.

—JOHN 1:1–3 NIV

With a word, God created the heavens and the earth. The word was his breath, his intelligence, and it captured his power. The ultimate manifestation of his word, though, was and is Jesus. Jesus as God's dearly loved Son represented everything about God the Father—his breath, intelligence, and power.

In this passage we see both the Father and the Son in creation. Both were there. Both created. Both initiated life. And the Scripture says that Jesus was life and the light of all of us, which means that everything that has breath has originated from him.

What a big, enormous, amazing God we serve, who not only created this world and us, but who also gives us light and life. When life feels dark and overwhelming, remember Jesus, the Word of God, creating and bringing life. Surely he will comfort us. Truly he will give us light when we can't see past our hands. He is there.

Jesus, thank you for creating this world, for bringing life to all people.
What an amazing God you are. Remind me that when this world feels
dark, you are brighter still. I need to experience your light today, sweet
Word of God. Amen.

The Secret of Contentment: Jesus

I have learned to be content, whatever the circumstances
may be. I know now how to live when things are difficult
and I know how to live when things are prosperous. In
general and in particular I have learned the secret of
facing either poverty or plenty. I am ready for anything
through the strength of the one who lives within me.

—PHILIPPIANS 4:11–13 PHILLIPS

Paul mentions here that contentment is something that is learned.
It's not easily grasped, nor is it granted outright. We must work at
it, learning its secrets. Contentment is simply being satisfied with
what you have, whether that's in material things, traits, charisma,
friends, relationships, family, business success, or anything else.

We run into problems when we're not content. When we
have everything we need but we feel bad about that, we're not
content. When we're lacking and we complain about that lack,
we're not content.

But walking alongside Jesus means we "learn the secret of
facing either poverty or plenty." No matter where we find ourselves, we know that because of Jesus, we can face anything.
That's the secret of contentment: Jesus.

How content are you today? Are you grateful for what you
have? Are you dissatisfied with where you are in your career? Are
you suffering from want? Or do you have everything you need,
yet feel guilty for it? Either way, we can learn contentment.

*Jesus, I want to learn the secret of contentment through holding fast to
you. No matter what may come my way, thank you that you will never
leave me and you'll provide the strength I need. I am content in you.
Amen.*

Asking Questions

To You they cried out and were delivered;
In You they trusted and were not disappointed.
—PSALM 22:5 NASB

When Jesus' disciples told him that John the Baptist had been beheaded, Jesus got into a boat and went off by himself. Many believe that in those moments his heart broke for John—just as it does for us when life does not turn out as we expected and God does not answer our prayers as we thought he would.

But Jesus said, "Blessed is he [or she] who is not offended because of Me" (Luke 7:23). Jesus blessed John for his belief. And he will bless us as well. We just have to continue in faith. This doesn't mean we won't at times question ourselves and God. And that's okay. I think John's life tells us that asking questions is all right; it is a mark of trust and relationship. When John's disciples told Jesus what John was asking, Jesus was not offended. And he will not be offended by our questions either. So wherever you are today, know that you can ask the hard questions. The "why?" questions. And the "who-what-when-and-where?" questions too. Remember, though, that in the end the only answer that matters is that, yes, Jesus is the One! Sometimes our Father does not give us the answer we want, but he always gives us his Son. If we can remember that—if we can keep loving him even when our hearts are uncertain or broken—we will be blessed.

Lord, thank you for always being available for my questions. Please help me to remember that you'll always provide the right answer. Amen.

Light-Life

What came into existence was Life, and the Life
was Light to live by. The Life-Light blazed out of
the darkness; the darkness couldn't put it out.

—JOHN 1:4–5 MSG

When it's dark, we tend to fear. We can't see in front of us, beside us, or behind us. And we can't see an attack from the darkened shadows. Fears that assail us at night seem silly in the morning.

Before Jesus burst onto the landscape of this world, the Scripture says we lived in darkness, afraid. We groveled in the night, unsure where we walked. Thankfully, life no longer has to be shrouded in black. Jesus came to this earth as light personified, shedding light on our sin, yet also shedding his blood to take care of that sin.

His sacrifice initially looked like a victory for the dark forces of this world. Satan must've cackled an evil laugh when Jesus' light went out, when he breathed his last sacred breath. The darkness, in that moment, won. The earth seemed to feel the bleakness because it turned dark in the middle of the afternoon.

And yet! Light came! The resurrection shed holy light over every single thing on earth. Jesus' light has become for us the greatest pathway to peace with God. The darkness no longer has a hold on us because we are women of light.

Jesus, thank you that you conquered darkness, not only in my life but also for the entire world. Because of that, I choose not to be afraid. Thank you for being my light! Amen.

Worried?

And don't be concerned about what to eat and
what to drink. Don't worry about such things.
These things dominate the thoughts of unbelievers
all over the world, but your Father already knows
your needs. Seek the Kingdom of God above all
else, and he will give you everything you need.

—LUKE 12:29–31 NLT

Sometimes we can skip over verses we've read over and over again and forget their meaning or impact, but when we read them in a different translation, our eyes open to new or deeper meaning. Such is the case with this Luke passage.

How many of us let the worries of this life dominate our thoughts? And yet Jesus says this is the typical behavior of non-believers. When we obsess over our bottom line, what we owe, what we have or don't have, we act like a person who doesn't know Jesus.

The remedy isn't simply choosing not to fret. It's not grabbing our bootstraps and making ourselves not worry. No, Jesus says it's shifting our eyes from what we see here on earth to what we can't see—the kingdom of God. When we become preoccupied with Jesus and what he wants for our lives, we no longer worry, and he promises to supply our needs.

How much life have we wasted worrying over things God already holds in his hands? Today is the day to let go of all you're holding on to and reorient your heart toward the Father who already knows your needs.

Jesus, forgive me for worrying about every little—and big!—thing. Instead, I choose to focus on you and your kingdom today. Help me to rest there, trusting you for what I need. Amen.

Day of Reflection

Before you know it, his justice will triumph;
the mere sound of his name will signal hope,
even among far-off unbelievers.

—MATTHEW 12:21 MSG

JESUS, THE VERY THOUGHT OF THEE

Jesus, the very thought of Thee
With sweetness fills my breast
But sweeter far Thy face to see
And in Thy presence rest

No voice can sing, no heart can frame,
Nor can the mem'ry find
A sweeter sound than Thy blessed name,
O Savior of mankind.

—ATTRIBUTED TO BERNARD OF CLAIRVAUX,
TWELFTH CENTURY

Your space—a poem, prayer, thoughts . . .

Faith Walk

We live by faith, not by sight.
—2 CORINTHIANS 5:7 NIV

It's always easy to walk by faith if we know exactly what will happen in the future. If we all were prophets, able to discern what would happen around the next bend, our faith would be thin and there would be no need to trust. All the mystery would disappear.

But in this world, we don't walk around prophetically. We walk blind. We simply can't see how we'll pay the bills next month. We can't perceive how that broken relationship can be mended. We can't know that our marriage will improve. In the mystery of the future, God simply asks us to have faith.

What does it mean to walk by faith and not by sight? It means that we take our focus off the bigness of our problems, choose to hand them over to God, and trust that he sees us and will take care of us in the best way he sees fit. It means we don't panic when what we see makes no sense.

Walking by faith, however, doesn't mean we're foolish. It means we take note of our situation, acknowledge it, then entrust it to the One who sees and knows everything.

God won't show us the bend in the road, but he will hold our hand in the journey as we walk with him, trusting by faith that he will accomplish his sovereign plan.

Jesus, when I look around at my life and the circumstances surrounding it, sometimes I want to panic. I can't see my way out. But right now I choose to hand everything that bothers me to you. I choose to trust you, to have faith that you will do what will most benefit my soul in the long run. Amen.

Forgive That Friend

*If you forgive those who sin against you,
your heavenly Father will forgive you.*

—MATTHEW 6:14 NLT

We become blocked in our Christian lives when we fail to forgive, or choose to let our hearts become bitter against a friend who has hurt us. The Scripture is clear. God forgives those who forgive. He doesn't ask us to do something he hasn't already performed on our behalf.

When we choose to hold a grudge, we put ourselves in the place of God, becoming judge and jury for another's sin. We think that if we withhold forgiveness, we will punish that person for not meeting our expectations. But really, we're punishing ourselves. When we give in to a bitter heart, we cannot love God or others.

Choose freedom. What does your unforgiveness do for you? Does it have any benefit? How does it imprison you?

What that friend did was wrong. True. But it is not unforgiveable. Their sin against you is small in comparison to your sin between you and a holy God. If God can pardon that gargantuan pile of sin, why not pardon that one sin? You'll be set free to love your friend, and you'll experience a deep kinship with Jesus. Remember, you're more like Jesus when you forgive.

Jesus, I don't want to forgive my friend, but I know you've forgiven me so much that I must also extend that grace. I choose right now to let go of my need to punish. My heart is getting smaller the more I try to judge. I want a bigger heart—a heart like yours. Amen.

Sharing Burdens

Dear brothers and sisters, if another believer is overcome by some sin, you who are godly should gently and humbly help that person back onto the right path. And be careful not to fall into the same temptation yourself. Share each other's burdens, and in this way obey the law of Christ.

—GALATIANS 6:1–2 NLT

We share each other's burdens when we help our friends who are entangled by sin. Our job in doing so is a great responsibility, involving gentleness and humbleness. When God shows us our friend's struggle, he often shows us our own sin.

When we confront, we first look to ourselves, asking God to search us, to see if we have the same bents in ourselves. We also trust God to cleanse us of any sin that separates us from a clear relationship with him. Then and only then can we humbly approach our friend as a fellow struggler.

We can fall prey to the same sin our friend deals with if we don't examine ourselves, or if we become fascinated by that sin. Or if we say to ourselves, "I will never do that awful thing." When we assert our ability, it's often after that we fall. Pride, as the Scripture says many times, comes before our downfall.

When you love others, love involves getting deeply involved in people's lives. This means shouldering burdens, bringing food to sick folks, and loving well in hard times. It also means being willing to confront in a loving way. We share burdens by bearing even our friends' sins alongside them.

Jesus, show me if you want me to bring a friend's sin to light. That's not easy for me, and I really don't want to. But if you are asking me to do it, I pray you would ready me. Show me my own sin so I can repent and come alongside my friend with a humble heart. Amen.

God, Wisdom Giver

God answered Solomon, "Because this was in your heart, and you have not asked for possessions, wealth, honor, or the life of those who hate you, and have not even asked for long life, but have asked for wisdom and knowledge for yourself that you may govern my people over whom I have made you king, wisdom and knowledge are granted to you. I will also give you riches, possessions, and honor, such as none of the kings had who were before you, and none after you shall have the like."

—2 CHRONICLES 1:11–12 ESV

God loves it when we ask for wisdom. He is the source of wisdom. By wisdom he established this earth. And when Jesus walked the earth, he was wisdom personified.

God honored Solomon for asking for wisdom. He could've asked for fame or riches or an easy life. He must've been tempted to seek military might or supreme rulership. He could've begged for attention or worth or health. Instead, he asked humbly for wisdom.

God's response? God granted him more wisdom than any other man. And he added more to his request.

When was the last time you implored God for wisdom? Maybe you're in the middle of a situation now where you truly don't know what to do. Maybe you have a friend in desperate need of guidance and you don't know what to say. Go to God. Ask him. He is the smartest, most intelligent being in the universe. And he loves giving out wisdom to his daughters.

Jesus, I need wisdom in every area of my life. I can't make decisions using my own wisdom. No, I need yours. Please help me be still enough to hear your voice, to discern what to do next. Thank you for being so wise. Amen.

Reconciliation

All this is from God, who reconciled us to himself through
Christ and gave us the ministry of reconciliation: that
God was reconciling the world to himself in Christ,
not counting people's sins against them. And he has
committed to us the message of reconciliation.

—2 CORINTHIANS 5:18–19 NIV

The first part of this verse encompasses so much. All this is from
God. Everything you see, breathe, touch, feel comes from God.
Your life is a gift from him to you. The people in your life are part
of his plan.

And his plan is this: *reconciliation*. The word means to establish a close relationship between two parties, to settle or resolve,
to make consistent, to become compatible.

God sent Jesus to reconcile us to himself, so we could have
a close relationship. He settled and resolved any differences by
his sheer act of love on the cross. In the act of reconciliation, we
become consistent with his character, and we start a compatible
relationship with God.

Not only that, he asks us to be agents of reconciliation. We
are to share our own stories of redemption so others can walk
with God as we do. We are to tell how God made us—who used
to be God's enemies—his friends. In our shaking hands with
God, we offer our hands to a world that desperately needs his
forgiveness.

*Jesus, help me become an ambassador of reconciliation. Thanks for rec-
onciling me through your amazing act of courage on the cross. Thank you
that I can live as a forgiven woman of God. Help me tell my story so that
others will long for your forgiveness. Amen.*

Rest and Rejuvenate

And He said to them, "Come aside by yourselves to a
deserted place and rest a while." For there were many
coming and going, and they did not even have time to eat.

—MARK 6:31

Jesus had deep compassion on his disciples, most likely because
he also experienced the same schedule they did. Wherever he
placed his feet, flocks of people clamored. They wanted something from him, and he gave everything away.

When we have lives where we give, give, give without break
or rest, we start to live margin-less lives. And when we live without margin, our relationships suffer. We stop being kind. We snap
at the people we love the most. We view interruption not as a person needing our love, but as a nuisance bothering our agenda.

When we get to that crazy place, Jesus utters these words to
us. Come aside. Find a quiet place. Rest awhile. For the sake of
your loved ones, take time to rest. Rejuvenate for your own sanity, and so you can be kind to those who populate your life.

Rest is not sin. In fact, it's utterly necessary to having an
engaged, abundant life. What prevents you from stopping today?

*Jesus, I'm just so tired. I snap at my family when I should be cherishing
each of them with joy. Please help me learn how to slow down and find
time to rejuvenate. Please reorient my heart toward rest. Amen.*

Day of Reflection

Therefore the Lord Himself will give you a
sign: Behold, the virgin shall conceive and bear
a Son, and shall call His name Immanuel.

—ISAIAH 7:14

SILENT NIGHT

Silent night, holy night, All is calm, all is bright.
Round yon virgin mother and child;
Holy infant, so tender and mild,
Sleep in heavenly peace; Sleep in heavenly peace.

Silent night, holy night, Son of God, love's pure light.
Radiant beams from Thy holy face,
With the dawn of redeeming grace.
Jesus, Lord, at Thy birth; Jesus, Lord, at Thy birth.

—JOSEPH MOHR, 1818

Your space—a poem, prayer, thoughts . . .

It's All About Him

> Your old life is dead. Your new life, which is your
> real life—even though invisible to spectators—is with
> Christ in God. He is your life. When Christ (your
> real life, remember) shows up again on this earth,
> you'll show up, too—the real you, the glorious you.
> Meanwhile, be content with obscurity, like Christ.
>
> —COLOSSIANS 3:3–4 MSG

We live in a world of fame mongers, of folks who chase after recognition and power. We wrongly think that if many people know about us or like us, we'll be filled up. But only Jesus fills us.

He rewards us when we put fame in its proper place: at his feet. He alone is the famous one, and if we happen to receive any recognition, our goal should be to further God's fame because of it. Our fame is only to make him famous.

Knowing God's fame and being passionate for it makes it easier for us to live in obscurity, to be faithful in the little things. In that secret place, we realize the beauty of God's perfect site. He sees us there.

Our true life isn't lived before others. Our true life is lived ardently before God, in quiet places, in small obedience, in thankless tasks. Jesus becomes our life in those small spaces. He rewards us with his overflowing presence. He gives us life. And no matter how obscure we may feel, it just won't matter. We'll have deep joy because he provided the joy in the first place.

Jesus, thank you that you are my life, my real life. I don't want to chase after my own silly fame. I want to make you famous—not that you need my help! I want to be content in the life of obscurity, living for your favor and smile alone. Amen.

Jesus: The Water of Life

The Spirit and the bride say, "Come." Let anyone who
hears this say, "Come." Let anyone who is thirsty come. Let
anyone who desires drink freely from the water of life.

—REVELATION 22:17 NLT

Jesus said these words to John when John had his vision on the Isle of Patmos. Jesus longs for us to long for his coming. He wants our cries to be, "Come Lord Jesus." He looks for disciples who thirst after him.

The end of the world will eventually dawn. Jesus will come back and establish his kingdom. We will finally be free from the tangle of sin and death. Our motives will be blessedly scrubbed clean. We will live more joyfully than we thought possible. Our greatest, most joyful moments on earth will seem like sorrow to us in light of living in eternity with Jesus.

How can we cultivate a life that thirsts for Jesus' return? We learn not to love and cherish the things in this life. We remember that we live for another kingdom, not the one we see and touch. We operate in countercultural ways, realizing that the first will come last and the last first in God's kingdom. We love the overlooked and bless the outcast.

And as we walk this earth in light of Jesus' imminent coming, we hunger. We thirst. We chase after Jesus. We remember that our hardships have meaning, that God counts our tears, that he sees everything we've done for his sake.

Jesus, I want to be a follower who cries, "Come!" I want to thirst for you
in this desert land. Help me to live for the next world, where you reign
and I'll never thirst again. Amen.

God Loves You Completely

The LORD is merciful and gracious, slow to anger and
abounding in steadfast love. He will not always chide,
nor will he keep his anger forever. He does not deal
with us according to our sins, nor repay us according
to our iniquities. For as high as the heavens are above
the earth, so great is his steadfast love toward those
who fear him; as far as the east is from the west, so
far does he remove our transgressions from us.

—PSALM 103:8–12 ESV

Simply reading and rereading these verses and learning to inter-
nalize their truth will revolutionize your life. God is not like us.
He is not easily angered or pestered. He is patient and kind. He is
gracious and forgetful when it comes to our sinful ways.

But sometimes we picture God as an angry man in the sky,
tsk-tsking us every time we make a mistake. We see him with a
scowl, truly disappointed in us. Sometimes we picture him turning his back to us, in a constant act of shunning.

Reread the psalm.

God is not that way.

He is gracious. Full of mercy. Seldom angry. Loving to a fault.
A parent who loves you enough to discipline you, but not too harsh
that you'll give up. A forgiving God. A God who removes our sin.

He is not angry with you. His first thought is not disappointment. It's delight.

*Jesus, I forget that you're not angry with me. Help me to remember that
I am wildly loved by you, that you take delight in me. Thank you for
removing my sins. Thanks for being patient and merciful and loving.
Amen.*

God's Economy

For who is our hope or joy or crown of exultation?
Is it not even you, in the presence of our Lord Jesus
at His coming? For you are our glory and joy.

—1 THESSALONIANS 2:19–20 NASB

When we look at the world, we see what others prize. Often it's stuff—big houses, cool cars, the right look. Or it's more elusive things like fame, power, or control. But that's not how God's economy is measured. God's economy doesn't involve material wealth; it's counted through relationships.

Paul talks passionately to the Thessalonians about what they mean to him. He doesn't need crowns or praises from many. He doesn't need accolades from the sidelines. He simply sees other people and their growth as his glory and joy.

What would our lives look like if we viewed relationships this way? What if we saw people as our greatest accomplishments? When we see life this way, our great pursuit then becomes discipling others, training them to be more like Jesus. Our great reward won't be a championship ring, but a champion believer who has also chosen to duplicate herself in others.

The beauty of discipleship is this great paying-it-forward. As we invest in people, sharing Christ with them and helping them grow deeply, they do the same thing, expanding the kingdom of God in their sphere.

Jesus, I want to see life in terms of relationships. I want the people I love and disciple to become my glory and joy. Please bring new people into my life with whom I can share you. I want to help make disciples so they can make disciples. Amen.

You Are Loved

Thus says the Lord, your Redeemer, and the one
who formed you from the womb, "I, the LORD, am
the maker of all things, stretching out the heavens
by Myself and spreading out the earth all alone."

—ISAIAH 44:24 NASB

When we perform to prove our worth, we see ourselves as commodities rather than people well loved by God. We wrongly assign worth based on our value to produce, to fill holes, to accomplish a to-do list.

It's not true that we must live up to standards or be super cool to earn our earthly keep. We simply must be. To revel in being a creation dearly loved by Jesus, sacrificed for, graced unconditionally.

We are not a product. We do not need to market ourselves to prove our worth to others.

If we view others as things to be had instead of people to be loved, it's no wonder we've lacked grace for ourselves when we didn't perform up to our own standards.

What if we are simply loved? Right now. Right here. For no other reason than we are a creation who breathes, laughs, weeps, rejoices, hollers, loves?

It may take a while to absorb, but consider the sound of these words: *you don't have to justify the space you take up on earth anymore.*

Dear Jesus, help me to rest today, knowing how much you love me just for me, not for my output. Help me to view myself and others not as commodities but as human beings deeply loved by you. Amen.

Jesus: Loving Master

All things are lawful for me, but not all things
are profitable. All things are lawful for me,
but I will not be mastered by anything.

—1 Corinthians 6:12 NASB

We have amazing freedom as Jesus followers. We are no longer enslaved under the law. Jesus set us free to live in light of his joy. What a great life!

But Paul issues a warning to those of us who become free, free, free. While all things are permissible—with the exception of sin—not everything will benefit us. Food is important. We need it to live. But if we love food more than we love Jesus, and it becomes our obsession, it masters us.

Exercise is good. We all need it to live balanced, healthy lives. But if it becomes obsessive, we can make endorphins our god, neglect our families, or worship our bodies.

Fashion is fine. It helps us express our unique style and it covers us from the cold. But if our wardrobe must be always current, cutting-edge, we become mastered by it and the whims of a fickle fashion industry.

Not everything profits. If we live moderate lives, we can live in freedom, not being enslaved to anything or anyone, but free to serve Jesus with our whole, undivided hearts.

Jesus, I don't want to be mastered by anything. If I am, would you please
show me? You are my Master, and I love you with all my heart. Amen.

Day of Reflection

But the angel said to them, "Do not be afraid. I bring you
good news that will cause great joy for all the people."
—LUKE 2:10 NIV

HARK! THE HERALD ANGELS SING

Hark! The herald angels sing,
"Glory to the newborn King;
Peace on Earth and mercy mild,
God and sinners reconciled."

Joyful all ye nations rise,
Join the triumph of the skies;
With angelic hosts proclaim,
"Christ is born in Bethlehem."

—CHARLES WESLEY, 1739

Your space—a poem, prayer, thoughts . . .

Secret Giving Brings Joy

So when you give to the poor, do not sound a trumpet
before you, as the hypocrites do in the synagogues and
in the streets, so that they may be honored by men.
Truly I say to you, they have their reward in full.

—MATTHEW 6:2 NASB

When we trumpet our good works, the sound of our voice is all the reward we'll receive. Jesus speaks often of secret acts. He rewards those quiet moments when we serve someone without recognition. He notices when we send a card to an ailing friend. Though there is no fanfare when we lick the envelope, Jesus stands by, chronicling every faithful act.

Since that is true, let's start a secret revolution of un-trumpeting. Instead of calling attention to what we do for others, actively try to be as secret as possible. Pay someone's toll. Buy a table dinner, then slip away. Send flowers to a friend in need of encouragement. Find ways to give gifts to friends when it isn't their birthday. Seek out ways to bless people. Give anonymously to a mission trip.

The side effect of un-trumpeting is this: joy. When we give like this, Jesus not only notices, which brings joy, but we also feel an effervescent happiness well up inside us that living only for ourselves cannot bring.

Jesus, help me to be a part of an un-trumpeting revolution this week. Show me someone I can quietly bless. I want to be noticed by you alone. Amen.

Jesus, Thirst Quencher

Jesus replied, "Anyone who drinks this water will soon
become thirsty again. But those who drink the water
I give will never be thirsty again. It becomes a fresh,
bubbling spring within them, giving them eternal life."

—JOHN 4:13–14 NLT

Walking in the heat of summer, we sweat and lose fluid. At the
end of the walk, what we really need is a tall glass of cool water. It
satisfies us more than a glass in winter. Without Jesus we are in a
constant state of summer thirst, longing for a drink to truly satisfy us. But we only receive polluted thimblefuls from the world.
Hardly satisfying.

Jesus promises here that he will truly satisfy our thirst, so
much so that our souls will never thirst again. What our souls
need, he provides in overflowing abundance. We will no longer
be satisfied with the world's terrible thimblefuls. We'll have the
real thing.

When we walk a long time with Jesus, life can sometimes sap
our strength. The sun of constant trials can bring us to a spiritual
sweat. In those times, we must remember the well of Jesus, usher-
ing forth truly satisfying drink.

The water that Jesus provides gives us spiritual life. And this
water is his presence, always constant with us. The closer we stay
to the well, the more available his water is when we need it.

*Jesus, I need your water, the kind that slakes my thirst and gives me life.
Forgive me for resorting to polluted thimbles of the world's water. I want
yours instead. Keep me near to you today and fill me up. Amen.*

We're Made for His Glory

I will say to the north and south, "Bring my sons and
daughters back to Israel from the distant corners of the
earth. Bring all who claim me as their God, for I have
made them for my glory. It was I who created them."

—ISAIAH 43:6–7 NLT

This passage conveys God's great heart toward his children. He
will call them from every corner of the earth to be near them.
Isaiah said that God created his people for his glory, which shows
why he is so passionate about them.

God made us for his glory. He created every aspect of us, the
way we look, the way we think, the way we perceive the world. He
knows us intimately. And he created us with his glory in mind.
This means we live on this earth not just to live for ourselves and
do the tasks assigned. We are image-bearers of God, and as we
love him, we show his glory.

This also involves responsibility and privilege. We are responsible to convey God's reputation in the way we live our lives as his
dearly loved children. And we are privileged to receive his attention and affection every day of our lives.

God loves you. Stop there and rest. Let that truth sink way
down deep. He has imparted his amazing glory in you because he
loves you. He chased the corners of the earth in pursuit of you.
He sent his Son to die for you on the cross. He rescued you.

*Jesus, thank you that you made me for your glory. Sometimes that's hard
to understand and wrap my mind around. But I'm trying. Thank you
that I'm your dearly loved child, that you rescued me. I rest there. Amen.*

God, Master Sculptor

But God demonstrates his own love for us in this:
While we were still sinners, Christ died for us.

—ROMANS 5:8 NIV

Imagine taking a gigantic piece of stone, say fourteen feet tall, and chiseling a figure out of it. Now imagine carving not just any figure but one of the most famous images in art, the statue of David. That's what Michelangelo did.

That sounds pretty amazing, wouldn't you say? But even more astounding is that the piece of granite Michelangelo used was riddled with cracks. Not only was the marble full of fissures, but some other sculptor had already tried to use the massive rock, creating a crack that caused a chunk of marble to fall off. Why, that rock had so many cracks that no other artist considered working with it. Talk about a reject!

What did Michelangelo see in that slab of stone that no one else did? After three years of intense labor, the finished work was unveiled. Today art aficionados can see that Michelangelo worked around his material's limitations, shifting David's weight onto his right leg to counter the big crack. Seeing the piece's flaws, he managed to make it into something magnificent.

Like Michelangelo, God is dealing with flawed stone. At times, he encourages us to take a certain position, but we bend our heads in stubborn resistance. Other times, little rivulets of imperfections show up as God works on us. So what does he do? Toss out our rocklike souls? No, he works around our hard heads and stony hearts to make us into something remarkable.

Master Sculptor, I appreciate your willingness to work with me despite my hard head and heart. Help me to be willing to let you have a free hand with my life. Amen.

Stay Close to Jesus

They wandered in the wilderness in a desolate way;
they found no city to dwell in. Hungry and thirsty,
their soul fainted in them. Then they cried out to the
LORD in their trouble, and He delivered them out of
their distresses. And He led them forth by the right
way, that they might go to a city for a dwelling place.

—PSALM 107:4–7

Have you ever been lost? Have you wandered in circles, passing the same landmarks, finally giving in to panic? So have the Israelites. When they wandered, they found their lives in grave danger because they were hungry and thirsty. It was in this distress that they lifted their voices to God who rescued them and led them to safety.

Sometimes we wander and don't realize it. Enticed by worldly renown or riches, we chase after things we think will satisfy, only to find ourselves lost, tired, hungry, and thirsty. In these times of realization, we, too, cry out to God and he rescues us.

But what if we chose to live our lives dependent on God in the first place? What if we sought him every day, asking him to lead us to the places he has for us? What if we always grabbed his hand instead of straying into back alleys?

Jesus is always there, always available to help you along your journey. All that's necessary is constantly crying out to him in prayer, seeking his wisdom and guidance.

Jesus, I don't want to lose my way. And when I have, I thank you so much
that you rescue me and set me on the right path. I want to be a woman
who follows closely to you every day. Help me stay near, Jesus. Amen.

Show Kindness and Mercy Where You Are

The LORD of Heaven's Armies says: Judge fairly,
and show mercy and kindness to one another. Do
not oppress widows, orphans, foreigners, and the
poor. And do not scheme against each other.

—ZECHARIAH 7:9–10 NLT

The minor prophet Zechariah gives simple yet difficult instructions to all of us. He tells us to be a fair, kind, and merciful people, looking out for those less fortunate. He warns us not to plot evil for others.

But it's not so easy to manage. Because of media and the Internet, we can constantly be reminded of the overwhelming needs of this world. In that glut of information, it's easy for us to shut it out, thinking, *I can't possibly help all these people, so why try?*

If we think we have to show mercy to the entire world, we'll stress out. But God is the God of the up close and personal. He will show you people in your own life, through your personal connections, to whom he wants you to show mercy and kindness. He has followers all around the world who have their own circles of influence, and if each of them would simply reach out to their small circle, the world would be a healthier, happier place.

Don't let the big needs of the world prevent you from being kind to the checkout lady at the grocery store. Simply be kind where you are. Show mercy in your home. Reach out as God prompts. In those small acts, you'll find joy.

Jesus, open my eyes to the needs in my circle. Help me to be merciful and kind. Instead of feeling overwhelmed, give me joy when I'm able to meet a need. Amen.

Day of Reflection

The Lord is not slack concerning His promise,
as some count slackness, but is longsuffering
toward us, not willing that any should perish
but that all should come to repentance.

—2 PETER 3:9

COME, THOU FOUNT OF EVERY BLESSING

Come, Thou fount of every blessings,
tune my heart to sing Thy grace.
Streams of mercy, never ceasing, call for songs of loudest praise.
Teach me some melodious sonnet,
sung by flaming tongues above.
Praise the mount! I'm fixed upon it,
mount of God's unchanging love.

Oh, to grace how great a debtor daily I'm constrained to be!
Let thy grace, Lord, like a fetter,
bind my wand'ring heart to Thee:
Prone to wander, Lord, I feel it, prone to leave the God I love.
Here's my heart, Lord, take and seal it,
seal it for Thy courts above.

—ROBERT ROBINSON, 1758

Your space—a poem, prayer, thoughts . . .

A Prayer-Filled Life

> The first thing I want you to do is pray. Pray every
> way you know how, for everyone you know. Pray
> especially for rulers and their governments to
> rule well so we can be quietly about our business
> of living simply, in humble contemplation. This
> is the way our Savior God wants us to live.
>
> —1 TIMOTHY 2:1–3 MSG

God wants us to live prayerful, prayer-filled lives. Prayer is the air we breathe, the communication we utter in our heads throughout our days. What should we pray for? Everything that concerns us. Why should we pray? To have fellowship with God. Who should we pray for? Everyone in our lives, but also the whole world and its governing authorities.

The goal of praying for our leaders is to help us live this kind of life: one of simple, humble contemplation.

With all the fanfare about doing things for Jesus, this scripture is curious. Our doing equals prayer, and our action equals contemplation. These both are internal disciplines, things other people don't see. It's our hidden life that God is after.

God rewards what we do in the hidden places of our lives. He hears us when we pray throughout the day. He comes near when we slow down enough to contemplate him, our lives, the goals we have. Spend some time today asking yourself: Who am I? Who is God? What is my role in this world? Who can I pray for?

Jesus, help me to pray throughout the whole day, particularly for the rulers of my country, despite what I think about their politics. I know that you desire for me to live a humble, contemplative life, but sometimes my world is so loud. Help me slow down enough to quiet myself. Amen.

God Knows You

The LORD is good, a stronghold in the day of
trouble; he knows those who take refuge in him.

—NAHUM 1:7 ESV

This scripture from Nahum gives true encouragement, saying that God knows it when we take refuge in him. In other words, he is mindful.

Others may not know that you are taking refuge in God. Even your family might not understand that you've chosen to believe in the goodness of God when things are swirling out of control. Your closest friend might not "get" your peace from trusting God in this trial.

But God knows.

He knows you. He sees you. He watches over you. He understands your situation better than you do. He carries you when you feel faint. He orchestrates miracles behind your back, weaving a surprising, redemptive plan. He even discerns your motives and the things in your heart you've never verbalized.

This is the God you serve—the refuge, stronghold, giver, enabler. When life takes strange turns and you careen toward despair, remember God is mindful of you.

Jesus, thank you that you are mindful of me, that you know when I take refuge in you. Even if no one understands, you do. I love you for that. Thank you for giving me hope and joy. Amen.

Sources

Clairmont, Patsy. *Stained Glass Hearts*. Nashville: Thomas
    Nelson, 2011.

———. *All Cracked Up*. Nashville: Thomas Nelson, 2009.

Harper, Lisa. *Stumbling into Grace*. Nashville: Thomas Nelson,
    2011.

Meberg, Marilyn. *Constantly Craving*. Nashville: Thomas
    Nelson, 2012.

———. *Tell Me Everything*. Nashville: Thomas Nelson, 2010.

Patty, Sandi. *The Edge of the Divine*. Nashville: Thomas Nelson,
    2010.

Walsh, Sheila. *God Loves Broken People*. Nashville: Thomas
    Nelson, 2012.

———. *Get Off Your Knees and Pray*. Nashville: Thomas Nelson,
    2008.

About the Contributors

An original Women of Faith speaker, Patsy Clairmont's quick wit and depth of biblical knowledge combine in a powerful pint-size package. A recovering agoraphobic with a pronounced funny bone, Patsy speaks to women from all walks of life. She is the author of multiple best-selling books for adults and children. Patsy and her husband live in Tennessee.

Lisa Harper is a gifted communicator whose writing and speaking overflow with colorful, pop-culture references that connect the dots between the Bible era and modern life. For six years Lisa was the national women's ministry director at Focus on the Family, followed by six years as the women's ministry director at a large church. The author of nine books, with a Masters of Theological Studies from Covenant Seminary, Lisa is a featured speaker with Women of Faith.

Marilyn Meberg speaks each year to 350,000 women at the Women of Faith conferences and is the author of several books. Never one to avoid the hard questions of life, Marilyn Meberg shares the wisdom she's gained from two master's degrees and a private counseling practice.

Sandi Patty has amassed more awards than any other female vocalist in contemporary Christian music history. She's been inducted into the Gospel Music Hall of Fame, received thirty-nine Dove Awards, five Grammy Awards, and three RIAA-certified platinum and five gold recordings. But it's Sandi's down-to-earth style that has endeared her to Women of Faith audiences. Sandi is the author of seven books, including *The Edge of the Divine*. Sandi and her family live in Oklahoma City.

Sheila Walsh is a powerful communicator, Bible teacher, and best-selling author with more than four million books sold. A featured speaker with Women of Faith, Sheila has reached more than 3.5 million women by artistically combining honesty, vulnerability, and humor with God's Word. Sheila lives in Texas with her husband and son.

Mary DeMuth is an author and speaker who loves to help people live uncaged, freedom-infused lives. She's the author of fourteen books, including six novels and her critically acclaimed memoir, *Thin Places*. After church planting in Southern France, Mary, her husband, and their three teenagers now live in a suburb of Dallas. Find out more at marydemuth.com.